1996

Jonathan Swift

W9-ABR-667

Jonathan Swift

ESSAYS ON HIS SATIRE
AND OTHER STUDIES BY

·Herbert Davis

A GALAXY BOOK
NEW YORK OXFORD UNIVERSITY PRESS 1964

ACKNOWLEDGEMENTS

The two little volumes of lectures, *Stella* and *The Satire of Jonathan Swift*, which were published by the Macmillan Company in 1942 and 1947 respectively, have long been out of print. I have received lately various suggestions that they might be made available; they are therefore included here with some alterations and omissions.

The Sedgewick Memorial Lecture, "The Augustan Art of Conversation," delivered at the University of British Columbia and printed by the University Press there in 1957, is included here with their permission.

I am much obliged to the University of Toronto Press for their permission to reprint "Swift's View of Poetry," which first appeared in *Studies in English*, collected by Malcolm W. Wallace, in 1931; and to the Columbia University Press, New York, for allowing me to include "The Augustan Conception of History," which appeared in *Reason and the Imagination*, a volume of studies presented to Marjorie Nicolson, edited by J. A. Mazzeo, in 1962.

I am also indebted to the editor of the Virginia Quarterly Review, for permission to reprint "Some Free Thoughts of a Tory Dean," which appeared in 1952; and to the editor of the *Review of English Literature*, for permission to reprint here "Alecto's Whip," which he had included in the special number, devoted to Swift studies, in August, 1962. In this collection, I am also including "Swift and the Pedants," which appeared in the 1942 edition of the *Oriel Review*.

I have always tried to concern myself with what Swift wrote; I have
therefore quoted freely. For the prose works I have used the text of the
Shakespeare Head edition, which I have just finished, published by
Blackwell, 1939-62; for the poems I have used the Clarendon Press edition, edited by Sir Harold Williams in 1937, reprinted 1958; for the
letters I have used *The Correspondence of Jonathan Swift,* published
by G. Bell and Sons, Ltd., and edited by Elrington Ball, 1910-14; for
the letters to Stella, quoted in my lectures of 1942, before Sir Harold
Williams's edition was published, I used the excellent text of Everyman's Library, edited by J. K. Moorhead. Further reference to particular studies will be found in the notes.

Iffley, Oxford   HERBERT DAVIS
March 1963

CONTENTS

Jonathan Swift

INTRODUCTION

It is more than forty years ago since I gave my first lectures on Swift not long after I had become a member of the English Faculty in the University of Leeds. I can remember only that some of Swift's remarks gave me considerable satisfaction, and seemed to have a particular appeal to my audience, a good many of whom had lately returned like myself from active service. We were then happily unaware of the dangers and difficulties of attempting to interpret the meaning of *A Tale of a Tub* or *Gulliver's Travels,* and were ready to delight in the most outrageous things that the satirical rogue had written and to accept them as in accord with what we had come to think of the human situation.

The first of the following essays was printed ten years later, when I had begun to feel that we had not paid enough attention to the poetry in which Swift sometimes seems to throw off all his disguises and speak with great directness, so that we cannot mistake his meaning and intention. And then I became aware of the need for caution in accepting all the works that had come to be included in the course of time in his collected editions; and I began to notice the disturbing variations in the text of different editions. It became evident that the first thing which needed to be done was to provide a more reliable text of his genuine writings and to separate them from a good deal that had been attributed to him by later editors on very insufficient evidence. But I found that this work was already being done. Sir Harold Williams was finishing his edition of Swift's *Poems,* which was published by the Clarendon Press in 1937, and Professor Nichol Smith was at work on the manuscripts of *The Letters of Jonathan Swift to Charles Ford,* which provide us with so much fresh information about the composition of Swift's books and valuable evidence for establishing the canon.

I therefore undertook to prepare an edition of *The Drapier's Letters,* which was published by the Clarendon Press in 1935, and after that continued work on the later Irish political writings, until I was diverted by the proposal that I should undertake an edition of the complete prose works for the Shakespeare Head Press.

The other essays in this volume consist of lectures and studies connected with my work on Swift during the last twenty years.

I do not wish to disguise the fact that much of this is old-fashioned stuff. I fully realize how rash it is for one who has not concerned himself so much with the higher matters of analytical and exegetical interpretation of texts, but has been a mere drudge occupied with the pedantries of editing and textual scholarship, to venture among the critics and dare to offer an opinion about Swift's meaning and intentions. But I could not allow these opinions to be reprinted now in my old age without at least some indication that I have not been unaware of what has been written in recent years, and without some attempt to try and explain why it has not seemed to me to be necessary to modify very much my earlier views of the character of Swift's satire.

This recent criticism is concerned with the wholly admirable and proper business of interpreting the meaning of his work, and of analysing as fully as possible all the technical devices he makes use of for his various purposes. Some of these studies are very enlightening and there can be no doubt that the writings of Swift have never been studied with such care before. Instead of being concerned with the perplexities of his character and temperament there has been a real attempt to understand the range and power and variety of his satire and to discover its meaning. But the immediate result has been that we are now offered interpretations of his works which differ enough to have caused a good deal of argument, and to provide material enough for a Martinus Scriblerus to surround the text of the satires with a learned apparatus of annotations and remarks and explanations, which may seem to be a rather dangerous and questionable method of dealing with one to whom Pope could fittingly dedicate his

Dunciad, since he had himself not infrequently directed his satire against the pedantries of the learned world and "the ignorant, the unnatural, and uncharitable Applications of those who have neither Candor to suppose good Meanings, nor Palate to distinguish true Ones."[1]

It may require some explanation why a writer like Swift, who claimed always to use such language as to be immediately understood by the vulgar, and affected to dislike nothing more than "multiplying unnecessary words or using various expressions" should have succeeded so ill even in his most popular work that its real meaning has only recently been discovered by these academic critics. It is not perhaps surprising that such claims have aroused fierce protest from Ireland and an outcry against this academicism, so improperly and unnecessarily applied to Swift. "The one thing"—says Mr. Donald Davie, of Trinity College, Dublin—

> that really distinguishes the critical pedantry of today is the high price set upon complexity . . . the more complex the work the better. The many works of wit, distinguished for massive simplicity, directness of approach, unaffected lucidity of language are undervalued—or complexity is put upon them.[2]

But no one can go far into the study of Swift's work without discovering that he needs to be read with care; and we may remember that he found it necessary to write an Apology for his *Tale of a Tub* five years after it was first published in order to warn his readers not to forget that the "Author" had been indulging in parody and irony. And in much less difficult works we find him putting on a disguise, or wearing a mask, or borrowing the tricks of a puppet-show; and even in political controversy and in his most direct and bitter attacks upon his personal opponents, he found many opportunities to practise himself in the art of literary parody, imitating in verse or prose modern or classical forms such as best fitted his particular purpose at the moment.

The use of parody provides full scope for the play of wit and humour in adapting for instance Ovid's *Fable of Midas* to certain characteristics of the Duke of Marlborough:

[1] *The Prose Works of Jonathan Swift*, ed. Herbert Davis, 1939-62, I, 2.
[2] Donald Davie, "Academism and Jonathan Swift," *Twentieth Century* (1953), CLIV, 217.

> This Tale inclines the gentle Reader,
> To think upon a certain *Leader,*
> To whom from *Midas* down, descends
> That Virtue in the Fingers Ends:
> What else by *Perquisites* are meant
> By *Pensions, Bribes,* and *three per Cent?*
> By *Places* and *Commissions* sold,
> And turning *Dung* itself to *Gold?*[3]

Cicero's oration against Verres may be turned with a little modification into a perfect indictment of Lord Wharton. The *Windsor Prophesy* can be given the form of one of Merlin's prophecies and printed in Black Letter to look as if it had really appeared in 1530. The Astrologer Partridge can be most effectively exposed by an imitation of his own Almanack exploiting his own method of filling it up with dire prognostications; and the foolish reasoning of the Freethinkers can be most fittingly demonstrated by presenting an "Argument" set down exactly in the manner of the logicians. Mr. Bullitt has demonstrated the value of recognizing the details of Swift's parody of the forms of the "Argument" if we wish fully to understand all the turns of his irony and to recognize the perfection of the structure and the unity of this admirable piece. They said that Swift was not very good at logic when he was at Trinity College, but he seems to have remembered enough to use it for his purpose, when he explains the argument of the free thinker, who, hearing that there was some doubt about the Scriptural foundation for the doctrine of the Trinity—

> By a sudden Deduction of a long *Sorites,* most logically concluded: 'Why, if it be as you say, I may safely whore and drink on, and defy the Parson.'

In analyzing Swift's use here of the technical term and his reference to the "logical conclusion" Mr. Bullitt makes this comment:

> But the example here has also the secondary purpose of dramatizing what Swift thought to be the true logic of free-thinkers, and the form of the 'sudden deduction', the logical proof by which the freethinkers arrive at their immoral conclusion is a sorites expressed as an enthymeme.[4]

[3] *The Poems of Jonathan Swift,* ed. Harold Williams, 1958, p. 157.
[4] John M. Bullitt, *Jonathan Swift and the Anatomy of Satire,* 1953, p. 93.

INTRODUCTION 7

This may seem to clinch the matter, but somehow, by pushing the use of technical terminology one step further, the comment seems to topple us over completely into a world where the atmosphere is too heavy for the quick light flashes of Swift's wit. Mr. Bullitt himself in the course of his attempt at an Anatomy of the satire was the first to realize the danger of relying upon "sheer formal analysis." And at the end he seems to conclude that neither detailed analysis nor the recognition of the rhetorical devices employed necessarily give us help when we most need it to interpret the meaning; and he has to fall back on a remark of George Sherburn's that ultimately we have to rely on the "tone of voice." But that itself is not a very certain guide, since we have discovered that the voice sounds very different to different readers.

This has led to the attempt to try and find something in the work itself, which might give us a safer clue to the true meaning. If we examine the structure of a work, which must be the final result of a conscious design, we should have no difficulty in recognizing the purpose which shaped it, and therefore we might feel some confidence that we could not be wholly mistaken in our understanding of the author's main intentions. "Rhetoric, like architecture, in its satisfaction of several ends, becomes a problem of design." It is this that creates meaning, and therefore the study of this design should provide us with the proper interpretation of meaning. The emphasis on this sense of design leads Mr. Price to say rather darkly:

> What saved Swift from a career of literary mischief . . . was a strong sense of design, a power to turn his wit to rhetorical ends.[5]

Some of Swift's contemporaries thought there was a good deal of "literary mischief" in A Tale of a Tub, and certainly could find in it no signs of any architectural design. But such a brilliant composition, clearly the work of a remarkable genius at the height of his powers, could not have been haphazardly thrown together. Mr. Elliott set himself to demonstrate the unity in the structure of the book by emphasising the importance of the "central fictive character, an ingénu, who egregiously identifies himself with the very abuses Swift is attacking." But he does not become so preoccupied with Swift's persona, as to forget the fact that the author never surrenders his con-

[5] Martin Price, Swift's Rhetorical Art, 1953, p. 43.

trol. He says "There is a fine intelligence here, but it is that of Swift, who, from behind the scenes, pulls the strings of the puppet. . . . he is the prime instrument of Swift's irony, and most skilfully manipulated."[6] Here we are on firm ground, so long as we always recognize that the voice is Swift's and that he is manipulating his puppets. Mr. Elliott is careful to omit the "Apology", as properly not a part of the *Tale* originally, and to accept this as a relatively straightforward defence of the *Tale*. But this does not satisfy Mr. Paulson, who has recently given us a book on the same subject—*Theme and Structure in Swift's Tale of a Tub*. Here Swift's persona is dubbed "the Hack," and all our attention is directed upon him, as though he were indeed a very real and separate person; and we are even led to consider whether the Hack may also have been the author of the *Battle of the Books* and the *Mechanical Operation of the Spirit*. And he concludes very emphatically that

> It is an error to suppose that the 'Author's Apology' is spoken by Swift himself; its 'author' is as much a part of the fiction as the Hack.[7]

He must be a different person from Swift and from the Hack, because he is referred to in the third person (in contrast with the Hack, who always uses the first person). I confess that I find this particular doctrine of a trinity of persons a little confusing, and I would like to make a plea for a less abstract conception of authorship. I do not find it so important to strive to find unity in its theme or structure. It may be better to admit that the *Tale* contains things which Swift must have written down as early as 1696; that he added and corrected during the following seven years, when it was printed in the form we know it in the first edition of 1704; and that the Author's *Apology* was written probably five years later. It was thus written at different times and in different places, and Swift himself must have changed a good deal in the course of those years. I find it safer to remember always the figure of Swift himself, with a paper before him, and his pen in his hand, indulging as explained in the "Author's Apology" in parody and irony and allowing himself to write as though he had himself been in Bedlam, or as though he were himself writing a report as a member of the Royal Society. I would like to quote what seems

[6] *PMLA*, June 1951, LXVI, 441.
[7] Ronald Paulson, *Theme and Structure in Swift's Tale of a Tub*, 1960, p. 163.

to me to be a more cautious view, as put forward in Kathleen Williams's recent book:

> Swift's manipulations are too complicated and too rapidly changing to be easily tabulated, except as part of the indirection which is essential if he is to express several things at once, as he is usually trying to do. . . .
>
> Of all Swift's mouthpieces, the 'supposed author' of *A Tale of a Tub* is one of the least tangible . . . it is not really possible to regard him as a person . . .
>
> We share the true author's creative liberty, not the supposed Author's captivity in chaos.[8]

In any study of the disguises or masks that Swift puts on for his particular purpose, we should do well to remember this—that the reader can and should share the true author's creative liberty. The safest image is I think that of a puppet show, not, as Mr. Bullitt describes it, with the puppets on wires—but the real puppet show, where we watch the actions of the puppets as they are manipulated on the showman's fingers, and hear his voice changing its tones as it impersonates the different characters. Often the impersonation is very simple, and just serves to determine the point of view from which the letter will be written or the project devised; occasionally a detail will be emphasised if it can be turned to account humorously, or to sharpen the irony. In the *Directions to Servants,* for instance, Swift changed his role from that of the Butler to the Footman, who could draw from his own varied experiences and recommend to the others "several wise expedients which he had found useful in some circumstances." No one, who has ever read the *Modest Proposal for preventing the Children of poor people from being a Burthen to their Parents,* is likely to forget that little personal touch added at the end, just to prove his disinterestedness:

> I have no Children, by which I can propose to get a single Penny; the youngest being nine years old, and my wife past Child-bearing.

If we wish to watch Swift at work, disguised for a purpose where there is no possible chance of mistaking his intentions at every moment, I would suggest that we observe that dramatic performance which he put on in Dublin in 1724, representing the fight between

[8] Kathleen Williams, *Jonathan Swift and the Age of Compromise,* 1959, pp. 130 f.

M. B. Drapier of Dublin and William Wood, Hard-wareman, who had acquired a Patent to coin copper for Ireland. It is worth remembering that in the spring of 1724 when this started, he had just about finished the first draft of *Gulliver's Travels,* where he had been trying out a remarkable series of puppet-shows, so that he was in good practice. Here in the *Drapier's Letters* he does not bother to make much use of his disguise at first. He tells us that "he has a pretty good shop of Irish Stuffs and Silks." He is not so much concerned for the threat of Wood's halfpence for himself:

> I can live better than many others; I have some Gold and Silver by me, and a Shop well furnished; and shall be able to make a Shift when many of my Betters are starving.[9]

When he is led in the Third Letter into serious legal arguments, he explains that though he is an illiterate shopkeeper, unskilled in the Law, he has received some assistance from an Eminent Person, but he has probably spoiled it by endeavouring to make it of a piece with his own productions. And then he does a brilliant change of his caste—the draper and Mr. Wood make their little bow and disappear, and up pop two well-known figures, David with his sling and stone and the giant Goliath in all his armour, and the voice of the draper, (or is it the voice of Jonathan?) goes on:

> I was in the Case of *David,* who *could not move in the Armour of* Saul; and therefore I rather chose to attack *with a Sling and a Stone* . . . *this uncircumcised Philistine,* who resembled Goliath in so many circumstances, . . . for *Goliath* had *a Helmet of* BRASS *upon his Head, and he was armed with a Coat of Mail, and the weight of the Coat was Five Thousand Shekles of* BRASS, *and he had Greaves of* BRASS *upon his Legs, and a Target of* BRASS *between his Shoulders.* In short he was like Mr. *Wood,* all over BRASS.

And the voice goes on reminding them that the conditions of the combat are the same; and we are brought back sharply to the present as the Drapier appears again:

> *If he prevail against us, then shall we be his Servants.* But if it happen that I *prevail* over him, I renounce the other Part of the Con-

[9] This and the following examples are from *The Drapier's Letters.* See *Prose,* X, 22, 48, 62, 86, 93, 83.

ditions; he shall never be a *Servant* of Mine; for I do not think him fit
to be trusted in any *honest* Man's Shop.

Here we may observe the creative liberty of the author. The Drapier
is now associated with David the champion of his people, who won
against desperate odds; and who can therefore appear on the next occasion as the challenger of the whole might of England, repudiating
the assumption that Ireland is a dependant Kingdom.

Let whoever think otherwise, I, *M. B. Drapier,* desire to be excepted.
For I declare, next under God, I *depend* only on the King my Sovereign, and on the Laws of my own Country, etc.

And it is entirely like Swift, using his full liberty, when he writes a
fifth letter addressed to Lord Molesworth, one of the leading Whigs in
Ireland, to change the whole character of the Drapier, for this special
purpose. He is no longer the ignorant illiterate fellow of the First
Letter. He gives much more information about himself, and explains
that during his apprenticeship in London and a long residence there
after he had set up for himself, he had developed a habit of writing
and discoursing and

conversing with the writings of liberals like Locke and Molyneux and
other dangerous authors, who talk of *Liberty as a Blessing, to which the
whole Race of Mankind hath an Original Title; whereof nothing but
unlawful Force can divest them.*

He is evidently using his disguise here to reveal as much as possible
of himself; and to make sure that no one could mistake his meaning,
he goes on to speak of the advice he had received from a certain *Dean,*
who had warned him not to trust to the general good will of the
People:

He produced an Instance of a Person as Innocent, as disinterested
and as well meaning as my self; who had written a very seasonable and
inoffensive Treatise, exhorting the People of this Kingdom to wear
their own manufactures.

In the Dublin collected edition of 1735, there are two footnotes, the
first to a certain Dean—viz. "The *Author,* it is supposed, means himself"; the second, to the innocent Writer—viz. "The *Author* means
himself again." In the *Drapier's Letters* there can never be any doubt

what Swift meant, whether he is writing with or without a mask. We might wish, however, that he had been a little more careful to add some few footnotes of this kind to *Gulliver's Travels,* so that there would be a clear indication whenever he is really speaking himself. I might even venture to suggest that there may be a memory of his recent experience among the Houyhnhnms, from whose country he had not long returned, in that reference to the Nag he used to ride about the grounds in the neighbourhood of Molesworth's house at Swords:

> where I fancied myself to feel an Air of *Freedom* breathing round me. . . . But I have lately sold my Nag, and honestly told his greatest Fault, which was that of snuffing up the Air about Brackdenstown; whereby he became such a Lover of *Liberty,* that I could scarce hold him in.

Does this possibly indicate that Swift had already realized that in his idealization of the Houyhnhnms he had got himself into strange company, among liberal thinkers and writers of Utopias? I will leave that question to be answered by the controversialists who are deeply engaged in trying to solve that difficult and important problem, the correct interpretation of the Fourth Book of *Gulliver's Travels.*

What I have been trying to show, in glancing over the *Drapier's Letters* to see how Swift used his disguise as a shopkeeper of Dublin, is this: we observe that he is perfectly free to adjust it to serve the particular purpose of the moment. It may be only a cloak to hide his identity; it may consist in a few properties, like the black and white stuffs, which the Drapier spreads out before his customers, intended therein to identify him completely with Dean Swift, and the printed sheets just back from the press of John Harding. He is always master of his puppets; he makes them function on the fingers of his two hands. He never creates characters like the dramatist, characters who have a life and a voice of their own. He could never have trusted anyone to speak for him. He could be content only to set it down in black and white, to weave a few pieces of the best Irish wool he could get. And it would I think please him to know that still some folks complain that when they put on one of them, "they felt a *Shuddering in their Limbs,* and have thrown it off in a Rage, cursing to Hell the poor *Drapier* who invented it."

In *Gulliver's Travels* Swift imitated Dampier's *Voyages,* and made use of the fact that his readers would be familiar with this kind of tale as well as with imaginary voyages, and therefore was prepared to offer them in the usual fashion some account of the adventurer and narrator, and to let him tell his tale in his own way; and though in choosing this form of narrative, he subjects himself to some necessary limitations, he still, I believe, remained the master of it, preserving his creative freedom to make both the situation, the action and the narrative-comment serve the purpose of his satire. Of course Swift makes use of Gulliver in a very different way in the first book when he is a giant among the pigmies, or in the third where he is rather a sensible and intelligent person among the fantastic inhabitants of the Flying Island. In these books there is not much difference of opinion as to Swift's intention except in minor details. It is clear enough in the First Book that he is satirising the ways of courts and ministers, and has in mind particular events which had occurred during the previous fifteen years from the time when he had himself taken an active part in politics during the last years of Queen Anne's reign. Similarly in the Third Book it has been fully demonstrated that in his satire of scientists and projectors Swift made use of his knowledge of actual experiments which were being undertaken by members of the Royal Society, possibly drawn to his attention by his friend Dr. Arbuthnot.

But in the Second and Fourth Books Gulliver is in a very different position—subject to all sorts of humiliations when he lives among the Giants, which Swift makes use of either just for fun, or for the purposes of his profoundest satire. Gulliver even for a moment becomes a sort of Machiavellian politician, when he proposes to teach the King of Brobdingnag the use of gunpowder—but this is only to allow Swift the opportunity of putting into the mouth of the king that bitter and contemptuous comment on the folly and pride of these odious little vermin crawling on the face of the earth.

Swift used Gulliver with complete freedom for his immediate purpose. He took him on those voyages, created all those situations; and we should be able to hear his voice throughout. I cannot therefore share the view that Gulliver is "a fully rendered, objective, dramatic character, a Shylock or a Lear, who like King Lear, began in simplicity, grows into sophistication, and ends in madness."[10] I don't believe

10 S. H. Monk, "The Pride of Lemuel Gulliver," *Sewanee Review* (Winter 1955), LXII, 56.

that Swift was capable of any such dramatic detachment; I never get away from the sound of his voice, and I always have the image of a Gulliver, whose features have been carefully carved and whose clothing and accoutrements have been all lovingly made by the hands of his creator, who delights to show him to us in all his strange behaviour —just as the King of Brobdingnag used to like to take him into his hands and stroke him gently, while he complimented him upon his admirable panegyrics on behalf of his countrymen. And I cannot feel so sure that when Gulliver found himself again being stroked very gently over his body by that other master in the land of the Houyhnhnms, who was so distressed by this entirely new experience of trying to understand what "lying and false representation" could mean, that here Swift intended us to recognize "so obviously" that we were in a land of Cartesians and Stoics.

I would even go so far as to suggest that we confine our interpretation and limit our enjoyment also, if we are too much concerned to protect the author himself from any extravagant views or from possibly sharing in any of the unbalanced revulsions experienced by the simple traveller—and thus to keep Swift as a sort of perfect calm moderator of unsullied wisdom in this age of compromise.

It was I think first suggested that we need to beware of the mistake of identifying the opinions of Lemuel Gulliver with his creator in an article by John F. Ross, entitled "The Final Comedy of Lemuel Gulliver," which was published in 1941. It is allowed that Gulliver's complete acceptance of the Houyhnhnms involves "a final refusal to accept the nature of mankind." But, "to charge Swift with the same refusal is to ignore the evidence." In the last chapters of the book the foolishness of Gulliver is clearly shown to us in his attitude to the kindly Portuguese captain and in the comedy of his behaviour when he returns to his family. Gulliver's attitude, it is true, is "a kind of misanthropic solution of the problem of evil." But we are intended to see the final joke, the comic dénouement, which takes place in the last chapters of the book. "Swift is not with him, Swift is above him in the realm of comic satire."[11]

This is a brilliant piece of analysis, offering us a very tempting in-

[11] John F. Ross, "The Final Comedy of Lemuel Gulliver," *University of California Publications in English* (1941), Vol. VIII, no. 2, pp. 195-6.

terpretation, which exposes those critics who have so bitterly attacked him for his misanthropy as humorless dullards who have not had the wit to see that Swift is a great comic writer as well as a "corrosive satirist." Of course there is truth in this. But if we were to accept it wholly, it would seem to me to involve the assumption that this master of narrative, this successful controversialist, this great wit and satirist had nevertheless failed in that very work, which brought him his widest fame; since he had evidently not succeeded in making his meaning clear and had been so long and so generally misunderstood.

It has led a number of others in the last twenty years to probe further into the significance of these last chapters and, sometimes forgetting the spirit of comedy which Swift has most certainly given free play there, to come forth with a rather solemn statement of Swift's ultimate meaning. Thus even a scholar, so expert in all matters connected with Swift as Professor Ehrenpreis, could allow himself to make this somewhat unguarded and almost disdainful statement:

> My commentary on the fourth voyage helps to destroy the misconceptions of innumerable scholars and critics who identify the author, through Gulliver, with the values of the houyhnhnms. Swift was himself saying, in the fourth voyage, that anyone who believes in the adequacy of reason without Christianity must see himself as a houyhnhnm and the rest of mankind as yahoos. By innuendo, he argues that the deists and neo-stoics cannot, with any consistency, believe their own doctrine.[12]

A somewhat similar view, which has been even more widely accepted, was put forward by Miss Kathleen Williams in a study which is most persuasively written and often marked by splendid insight, *Jonathan Swift and the Age of Compromise,* 1959:

> Swift is telling us, as always, not to expect too much and not to simplify what is essentially a difficult matter. The proper life for man is not that of Yahoo or of Houyhnhnm, for he has in him something of both, and in the blending of passion and reason, body and mind, something different from these simple, natural creatures is engendered. The Brobdingnagians and Don Pedro are, in a way, a compromise between extremes, and therefore they are indirectly presented, because

[12] I. Ehrenpreis, *The Personality of Jonathan Swift,* 1958, p. 115.

we are to understand that we should not aim too high, as Gulliver does when, in trying to ignore part of his human nature, he becomes less than a human being.[13]

No. I do not believe that Swift had to make all those voyages and go through all those adventures to come gravely back with such a message. He had started out with a good deal of bitter experience, and in going himself to those strange places he had had a good deal of fun, and had made some discoveries which had not left him less sceptical or less out of love with the human race than he had been before. In a letter to his very close friend Charles Ford, who knew more about the progress of the *Travels* than anybody else, Swift reports on Jan. 19, 1724:

> I have left the Country of Horses, and am in the flying Island, where I shall not stay long, and my two last Journyes will be soon over; so that if you come here this Summer you will find me returnd.

He would have returned to Dublin, to his ordinary life there again; but he would have his friends know

> that I hate Yahoos of both Sexes, and that Stella and Madame de Villette are onely tolerable at best, for want of Houyhnhnms.[14]

That was in reply to some remarks of Bolingbroke in a letter to Ford, which he had sent on to Swift. From this letter it is clear that Ford had said something about the adventures that Swift met with during his third voyage—as it then was, and that Bolingbroke had expressed in his reply a certain anxiety about Swift's condition, and about the violence of the mood in which his book was written:

> Every great genius borders upon folly. Her dominions embrace those of Reason on every side; & the two frontiers are so alike, that he who pushes to the extremitys of one, wanders often into the other, & seldom finds his way back. . . .
>   if [Stella] had not fix'd his course, our poor friend would have wander'd from one ideal world to another, and have forgot even the Species he is of. he had been att this very instant perhaps freezing in Saturn, burning in Mercury, or stalking along with a load on his back,

[13] Kathleen Williams, op. cit., pp. 204-5.
[14] *The Letters of Jonathan Swift to Charles Ford,* ed. D. Nichol Smith, 1935, pp. 100-101.

a bell under his chin, a plume on his head, and a fox tail att each ear, in that country which he discover'd not long ago, where Horses and mules are the reasonable Creatures, and men the Beasts of burden.[15]

That is the simplest and most precise way of describing what Swift set himself to do in the Fourth Book of Gulliver's Travels—to create a country where the horses were the rational creatures and the men the irrational beasts. He had in fact, as Professor R. S. Crane has recently shown[16] in the most masterly and convincing fashion, just reversed the statement to be found in all the logic books of his time, the generally accepted axiom—"Homo est animal rationale."

He has demonstrated that this must have been in Swift's mind when he wrote to Pope, after finishing his Travels, that it had been his aim "to vex the world rather than divert it"—to prove the "falsity of that definition *animal rationale,*" and concluded:

But principally I hate and detest that animal called man, although I heartily love John, Peter, Thomas, and so forth.

After searching through all the logic books Professor Crane found that combination of names extremely unusual; but it does occur in Archbishop Marsh's *Institutio logicæ,* which he had prepared for the students of Trinity College, Dublin, and which was in use when Swift entered in 1682.

There is really nothing more to be said. We can see here—and there can be no doubt about it—how the whole conception of the Fourth Book started; and from that beginning we should be able to trace with more confidence what the humorist and the satirist did to make it serve their purpose. We may get a little further guidance if we observe what Swift's closest friends made of it when the book first appeared. For, though it may be maintained that a great book has a life of its own and may come to take on a somewhat different colour and significance for later generations, we may nevertheless learn something of the way in which it was intended to be read from the effect that it had immediately upon its first readers.

What did his friends make of it? What did they say of it after-

[15] Ibid., p. 238.
[16] R. S. Crane, "The Houyhnhnms, the Yahoos, and the History of Ideas," *Reason and the Imagination,* Studies presented to Marjorie Nicholson, ed. J. A. Mazzeo, 1962, pp. 231-53.

wards? Something we might infer perhaps from the tone of Dr. Arbuthnot's compliment, congratulating Swift "that at his age he could write such a merry book"; he would I think have enjoyed that, and would doubtless have known exactly how much irony there was in that remark. Pope said that he had not seen the book until it was printed; and then he gives no indication of any other feelings but his sheer delight in the fun of it, which set him to work on those amusing verses Swift was content to accept as ornaments for his second edition.

I find no sign in the "expostulating, soothing and tenderly complaining epistle of Mary Gulliver, apprehending from his late behaviour some Estrangement of his Affections" that Pope was shocked by the detestable behaviour of Gulliver on his return from his visit to the Houyhnhnms or that he felt him to have become "a ludicrous yet terrible misanthrope," whose judgment of the Houyhnhnms or of his own kind can no longer be taken seriously.[17] Indeed Mary Gulliver is far indeed from questioning his admiration for the Houyhnhnms though she is disturbed by those visits to the sorrel mare—yet she is willing to woo him again by any name he likes:

> If Ducal *Nardac*, *Lilliputian* Peer,
> Or *Glumglum's* humbler Title sooth thy Ear:
> Nay, wou'd kind *Jove* my Organs so dispose,
> To hymn harmonious *Houyhnhnm* thro' the Nose,
> I'd call thee *Houyhnhnm*, that high sounding Name
> Thy Children's Noses all should twang the same.
> So might I find my loving Spouse of course
> Endu'd with all the *Virtues* of a *Horse*.[18]

And certainly in the other lines addressed to Gulliver by one of the enslaved Houyhnhnms now in England, Pope is content to accept Gulliver's view that they embodied the perfection of virtue:

> O happy *Yahoo*, purg'd from human Crimes,
> By thy sweet Sojourn in those virtuous Climes,
> Where reign our Sires! There, to thy Countrey's Shame,
> Reason, you found, and Virtue were the same.
> Their Precepts raz'd the Prejudice of Youth,
> And even a *Yahoo* learn'd the Love of Truth.[19]

[17] Kathleen Williams, op. cit., pp. 200f.
[18] Pope, *Minor Poems* (Twickenham ed.), VI, 279.
[19] Ibid., p. 274.

Of course Pope is merely amusing himself in these verses, which were prompted by his delight in all the details of the imaginative world that Swift had created. But there is nothing in those lines I have quoted to suggest that Pope read the fourth book in the way we are asked to read it by those modern critics who say that we should recognise that Swift did not share or intend his readers to share Gulliver's foolish enthusiasm for the Houyhnhnms.

Nor can I believe that Swift himself had the Deists in mind when he created the virtuous Houyhnhnms, for ten years later he wrote a poem in which he mentions them by name:

> Hobbes, Tindal, and Woolston, and Collins, and Nayler,
> And Muggleton, Toland, and Bradley the taylor,[20]

and compares them to a herd of Yahoos. It may be true that the Houyhnhnms are not intended to represent Swift's "moral ideal for Mankind," but it is in the course of Gulliver's stay among them that Swift comes nearest to giving us his idea of Utopia. For if ever he was so foolish as to allow himself for a brief moment to indulge in Utopian dreams it is in the tenth chapter of the Fourth Book of his travels, where he begins in Rabelaisian fashion to list all the horrors of ordinary human society, which were there unknown:

> I enjoyed perfect Health of Body, and Tranquility of Mind; I did not feel the Treachery or Inconstancy of a Friend, nor the Injuries of a secret or open Enemy. I had no Occasion of bribing, flattering or pimping to procure the Favour of any great Man, or of his Minion. I wanted no Fence against Fraud or Oppression: Here was neither Physician to destroy my Body, nor Lawyer to ruin my Fortune: No Informer to watch my Words and Actions, or forge Accusations against me for Hire: Here were no Gibers, Censurers, Backbiters, Pickpockets, Highwaymen, House-breakers, Attorneys, Bawds, Buffoons, Gamesters, Politicians, Wits, Spleneticks, tedious Talkers, Controvertists, Ravishers, Murderers, Robbers, Virtuoso's; no Leaders or Followers of Party and Faction; no Encouragers to Vice, by Seducement or Examples: No Dungeon, Axes, Gibbets, Whipping-posts, or Pillories; No cheating Shopkeepers or Mechanicks: No Pride, Vanity or Affectation: No Fops, Bullies, Drunkards, strolling Whores, or Poxes: No ranting, lewd, expensive Wives: No stupid, proud Pedants: No importunate, over-bearing, quarrelsome, noisy, roaring, empty, conceited, swearing

[20] *Poems*, p. 815.

Companions: No Scoundrels raised from the Dust upon the Merit of
their Vices; or Nobility thrown into it on account of their Virtues: No
Lords, Fidlers, Judges or Dancing-masters.

And then the loveliness and beauty of those quiet conversations:

Where the greatest *Decency* was observed, without the least Degree of
Ceremony; where no Person spoke without being pleased himself, and
pleasing his Companions: Where there was no Interruption, Tedious-
ness, Heat, or Difference of Sentiments.[21]

Was Gulliver such a fool to hate to return to our world after living in
such a pleasant place? Are we to suppose that Swift did not wish his
readers to surrender to the spell of such a Paradise? But he does not
let us linger, and too soon we have to face with him that dreadful
journey back into the world. And still the author uses every chance to
have his fun, to rail at our pride, to nettle us, as he brings the unhappy
Gulliver back from the last of his voyages. We need to remember that
Swift uses Lemuel Gulliver with the same freedom as he used M. B.
Drapier. He is not writing a play or a novel, with Gulliver as a hero;
he is parodying the books of travels, with Gulliver as the narrator of
the strange adventures that happen to him, sometimes made use of as
a fool, an innocent, in the hands of the gigantic majesty of Brobdingnag, who strokes him gently to soothe his injured pride; sometimes as a mouthpiece for his creator's irony, as in his comment in
Lilliput after he has heard of the articles drawn up against him:

if I had then known the Nature of Princes and Ministers, which I
have since observed in many other Courts, and their Methods of
treating Criminals less obnoxious than myself; I should with great
Alacrity and Readiness have submitted to so *easy* a Punishment.[22]

In the Third book, which came last in the first draft—and one might
have thought that there could not be a better ending than the description of the Struldbruggs—the voice of Swift is clearly heard without
disguise, as in this comment:

I thought this account of the *Struldbruggs* might be some Entertainment to the Reader, because it seems to be a little out of the common

[21] *Prose*, XI, 260, 276.
[22] Ibid., p. 57.

INTRODUCTION

Way; at least, I do not remember to have met the like in any Book of
Travels that hath come to my Hands.[23]

Throughout, as Miss Williams has noticed, Gulliver is

> so tenuous a character that we scarcely feel his presence, and by the
> time Book IV is reached we are well aware that Gulliver, as much as
> anyone else, is being manipulated in the service of his creator's moral
> and satiric intention.[24]

She further points out, very rightly, I think, that in some of the passages of direct satire in Book IV such as the open invective against the
First or Chief Minister, Gulliver has vanished into the brain which
conceived him.

The different interpretations of the way he is manipulated are not
due to the simplicity of those readers who are charged with being
taken in by foolishly thinking that Gulliver's views are always those
of his creator; they are due to something much more difficult and dangerous to dogmatize about, and that is—the different views of the
satiric intention of Swift.

We may also get some indication of Swift's general intentions by
remembering his main concern when he was preparing the text of
Gulliver's Travels for the Dublin edition of his collected works, which
appeared in 1735. He did not worry much about the literal faults,
some of which had been corrected in the second edition; but he was
determined to remove what he calls "the trash" which had been inserted through the timidity of his first publisher, and to restore the
several passages, as he had originally written them, for—he says to
Ford—

> the whole Sting is taken out in severall passages, in order to soften them.
> Thus the Style is debased, the humor quite lost, and the matter
> insipid.[25]

When we examine these passages we find that Swift wished to restore
in all the full force of its invective his attack on lawyers and judges
(and he had a good deal more reason to dislike them than Gulliver

[23] Ibid., p. 199.
[24] Kathleen Williams, op. cit., pp. 196-7.
[25] *Letters of Swift to Ford*, p. 162.

had) his description of a "first" or "chief minister of State" and how
he gets power and preserves himself in power, and "the whole tribe
of informers . . . prosecutors . . . swearers and their subalterns,
marching under his colours." I doubt whether we need to assume that
it was Gulliver who was clever enough to give those examples of the
way in which accused persons were found guilty of a plot, by discovering mysterious meanings in the words and syllables in their papers.
For instance, he remarks so innocently,

> they can decypher a Close-stool to signify a Privy-Council: a Flock of
> Geese, a Senate; a lame Dog, an Invader; the Plague, a standing Army;
> a Buzard, a Minister; the Gout, a High Priest; a Gibbet, a Secretary of
> State; a Chamber pot, a Committee of Grandees; a sieve, a Court Lady;
> a Broom, a Revolution; a Mouse-trap, an Employment; a bottomless
> Pit, the Treasury; a Sink, a C - - t; a Cap and Bells, a Favourite; a
> broken Reed, a Court of Justice; an empty Tun, a General; a running
> Sore, the Administration.[26]

Swift does not even seem to mind that Gulliver rather repeats himself
in the Third and the Fourth books, whenever he has a chance to refer
to a minister of state or a court of justice.

He never tires of hunting down this game. Seven years later in one
of his most familiar poems—*Epistle to a Lady*—he is still at it, protesting

> Wicked Ministers of State
> I can easier scorn than hate:
> And I find it answers right:
> Scorn torments them more than Spight.

He talks about spending his rage in a jest, but admits

> I would hang them if I cou'd:

and finally in a passion he gloats over the thought of lashing them
with a whip of scorpions—

> Then, apply *Alecto*'s Whip
> Till they wriggle, howl, and skip.[27]

[26] *Prose*, XI, 175.
[27] *Poems*, p. 634-5.

I did not foist that image on him. It is Swift himself who more than once refers to Alecto's whip—the worst of the Furies if there could be any difference, whose task it was to punish all sorts of criminals who had escaped their deserts. That is what he is doing when after his attack upon chief ministers in Chapter six he goes on in the following chapter to give a kind of ghastly parody of the performance of the chief minister.

Through all this Swift seems to me to have Gulliver and his master quietly conversing together but they are no more than hand puppets— the head of Gulliver and the head of a horse, mere symbols, and the voice with all its changing tones, and its diabolical laughter:

> I DURST make no Return to this malicious Insinuation, (says G.) which debased human Understanding below the Sagacity of a common *Hound,* who hath Judgment enough to distinguish and follow the Cry of the *ablest Dog in the Pack,* without being ever mistaken.[28]

I think both Gulliver and the reader are having their eyes opened to understand some of the malicious insinuations of Gulliver's Houyhn- hnm master; here is the sting that Swift wanted to be sure was there. We can protest, and protect ourselves by saying that Gulliver is a fool, and Swift wishes us to understand what a fool he is and to draw a moral from the tale; but that is not very different from the Victorians who protected themselves by saying that the author was a mad Yahoo, flinging his curses at humanity.

We need—if we are to read satire with confidence—above all to know whom we are dealing with, and what is his ultimate purpose. We need to recognize Swift not only as Addison spoke of him as "the greatest genius of his age," but as Shaw and as Pope saw him, as among the great satirists of the ages. When someone once wrote to Shaw and asked him why he did not write a book about his great predecessor, he replied on his usual postcard: "I am too busy carrying on Swift's work to have time to write about him." Shaw recognized him as one in the same tradition, at work on the same job, exposing the same follies and absurdities, disturbing the same complacencies. And Pope, when dedicating to him the *Dunciad,* though remember- ing all his various disguises, is mainly concerned to place him beside Rabelais and Cervantes in the European tradition:

[28] *Prose,* XI, 247.

> O Thou! whatever title please thine ear,
> Dean, Drapier, Bickerstaff, or Gulliver!
> Whether thou chuse Cervantes' serious air,
> Or laugh and shake in Rab'lais' easy chair—[29]

You may say of course that Pope intended no more by this superb compliment than to indicate certain characteristics of Swift's genius, certain traits in his parody and irony, certain qualities of imagination which remind us of Rabelais and Cervantes. Or you may say with Coleridge that Pope had little real understanding of the qualities of those great Europeans. Coleridge himself had no doubt that Rabelais was among the great creative minds of the world, Shakespeare, Dante, Cervantes etc. "among the deepest as well as the boldest thinkers of the age" as he called them, and therefore disliked Pope's image of him "laughing in his easy chair." "Never was there a more plausible and seldom I am persuaded a less appropriate line."

Nevertheless I am concerned with the fact that Swift is placed in the line of Rabelais and Cervantes; and that is where I would like to keep him. That is where such different critics of Swift as Lady Mary Wortley Montagu and Voltaire placed him, both as a humorist and as a satirist. If we see him in that company we are perhaps less likely to mistake his intentions or overlook any of the humour in *Gulliver's Travels*. And that is perhaps the essential ingredient, which has given it its place among the books known throughout the world.

This humour "in its perfection" Swift once wrote "is allowed to be much preferable to wit, if it be not rather the most useful and agreeable species of it." Far from being a thing peculiar to the English nation, as Sir William Temple had maintained, Swift found it in many Spanish, Italian and French productions and claims that

> a *Taste* for *Humour* is in some Manner fixed to the very Nature of Man, and generally obvious to the Vulgar, except upon Subjects too refined, and superior to their Understanding. . . .
>
> It is certainly the best Ingredient towards that Kind of Satire, which is most useful, and gives the least Offence; which, instead of lashing, laughs Men out of their Follies, and Vices; . . .
>
> There are two Ends that Men propose in writing Satire; one of them less noble than the other, as regarding nothing further than the private Satisfaction, and Pleasure of the Writer; but without any View to-

[29] Pope, *Dunciad* (Twickenham ed.), V, 270.

wards *personal Malice*: The other is a *Publick Spirit*, prompting Men
of *Genius* and Virtue, to mend the World as far as they are able. And
as both these Ends are innocent, so the latter is highly commendable.[30]

I have quoted at some length from this *Intelligencer* paper of May
1728, written in defence of Gay's *Beggars Opera*, eighteen months
after the appearance of *Gulliver's Travels*; because I think it is a saner
statement of Swift's own intentions than will be found in many of the
books about him. Swift would have expected his readers to recognize
how much Cervantian humour there was in it, how much put in just
for fun. Many instances could be given, but there is one I wish particularly to mention, because it is evident from some of the recent
comments upon it that the humour of it is not apparent to all readers.

In the last chapter of Book II, Swift describes Gulliver's return to
his family:

> When I came to my own House, for which I was forced to enquire,
> one of the Servants opening the Door, I bent down to go in (like a
> Goose under a Gate) for fear of striking my Head. My Wife ran out
> to embrace me, but I stooped lower than her Knees, thinking she
> could otherwise never be able to reach my Mouth. My Daughter
> kneeled to ask me Blessing, but I could not see her till she arose; hav-
> ing been so long used to stand with my Head and Eyes erect to above
> Sixty Foot; and then I went to take her up with one Hand, by the
> Waist.

To excuse such nonsense, he adds as a sort of moral:

> This I mention as an Instance of the great Power of Habit and
> Prejudice.[31]

There is a delicious parallel to this scene at the end of Book IV, which
is often quoted as an example of Swift's horrible and disgusting loath-
ing of humanity. It was intended to be humorous, and could hardly
have been omitted without destroying the balance between these two
parts of the story; it follows inexorably as a result of his enlightenment
after living among the Houyhnhnms, and realizing the beastliness of
the Yahoos:

> As soon as I entered the House, my Wife took me in her Arms and
> kissed me; at which, having not been used to the Touch of that odious

[30] *Prose*, XII, 33, 34.
[31] Ibid., XI, 133.

Animal for so many Years, I fell in a Swoon for almost an Hour. At
the Time I am writing, it is five Years since my last Return to England: During the first Year I could not endure my Wife or Children in
my Presence, the very Smell of them was intolerable; much less could
I suffer them to eat in the same Room. To this Hour they dare not presume to touch my Bread, or drink out of the same Cup; neither was I
ever able to let one of them take me by the Hand.[32]

It is because of its humour, of course, that *Gulliver's Travels* has had
the odd fate to become a popular story-book for children; they are always amused and not a bit horrified by this last episode.

In the passage just quoted from Swift's defence of the *Beggar's
Opera*, he spoke of

> two Ends that men propose in writing satire: and the nobler is that
> prompting men of genius and virtue to mend the world as far as they
> are able.

This purpose is clearly evident in his own work, as it is in the work of
Rabelais and Cervantes. But he is too much of a humorist to allow
himself to be taken in even here,—and when he was preparing a corrected text of *Gulliver's Travels* for the Dublin edition of his *Works*,
1735, he added a letter from Gulliver to Captain Sympson, dated
April 2, 1727, which would have been about six months after the
book had first appeared, in which Gulliver blames himself for his great
want of judgment in giving an account of his adventures, and complains in a manner and tone, in which there is a striking blend of
Rabelaisian eloquence with Cervantian irony, that

> instead of seeing a full Stop put to all Abuses and Corruptions, at least
> in this little Island, as I had Reason to expect: Behold, after above six
> Months' Warning, I cannot learn that my Book hath produced one
> single Effect according to my Intentions: I desired you would let me
> know by a Letter, when Party and Faction were extinguished; Judges
> learned and upright; Pleaders honest and modest, with some Tincture
> of common Sense: and *Smithfield* blazing with Pyramids of Law-Books;
> the young Nobility's Education entirely changed; the Physicians ban-
> ished; the Female *Yahoos* abounding in Virtue, Honour, Truth and
> good Sense; Courts and Levees of great Ministers thoroughly weeded
> and swept; Wit, Merit and Learning rewarded; all Disgracers of the

[32] Ibid., p. 273.

Press in Prose and Verse condemned to eat nothing but their own Cotton, and quench their Thirst in their own Ink. These, and a thousand other Reformations, I firmly counted upon by your Encouragement; as indeed they were plainly deducible from the Precepts delivered in my Book. And, it must be owned, that Seven Months were a sufficient Time to correct every Vice and Folly to which *Yahoos* are subject; if their Natures had been capable of the least Disposition to Virtue or Wisdom.[33]

Even to the last Swift forced himself to see and acknowledge the truth—that his work had not produced the effect he intended. At the end the humorist compels him to recognize that however well he has done it, and however much he may have suffered for his pains, it yet remains to be done again and again in every generation. The words of the inscription for a black marble tablet above his tomb, which he ordered to be "deeply cut and strongly gilded", have been often quoted; but they are more frequently used to remind us of "the fierce indignation tearing at his heart" than to recall the direct appeal, addressed to the traveller who reads them:

Go, and imitate, if you can, one who strove his utmost to champion the liberty of man.[34]

or better as put into verse by Yeats:

Imitate him if you dare,
World-besotted traveller; he
Served human liberty.

He had satirized and laughed at the ways of mankind, to try and amend them, knowing that it was necessary to do the work of Rabelais and Cervantes over again; and knowing likewise that though their works yet remained and continued to be read, it would still be necessary in later generations for others to arise who could carry on their work. And since that day others have indeed come to take over the task; in different countries and in different tongues, from Voltaire to Shaw, and in our own generation, the work has been gaily and triumphantly carried on.

[33] Ibid., p. xxxiv.
[34] Ibid., XIII, 149.

STELLA
A Gentlewoman of the Eighteenth Century

The Alexander Lectures at
the University of Toronto, 1942

CONTENTS

SWIFT AND STELLA

> . . . among them there was one (they say) that was the *Star*, whereby
> his course was only directed.

Let me say at once that I have no secrets to reveal, no theory to put
forward concerning the relationship of Swift and Stella. I have not
discovered any fresh manuscripts of his letters to her, or of hers to
him. I cannot prove that they were or that they were not married; nor
am I much concerned or much impressed by old or recent suggestions
that their parentage was more noble than honest. We know that the
story that Swift was her half-brother is false; and though it cannot be
so easily disproved, the story that he was her uncle is also pure conjecture.

But I must not dismiss so abruptly the latest explanation of the
mystery of Swift and Stella, which was first put forward in a radio
programme by Mr. Denis Johnston in 1938, since he complains that
for three years no one gave him any serious consideration. In June
1941, therefore, he published a brilliant defence of his theory in the
Dublin Historical Record entitled, "The Mysterious Origin of Dean
Swift." The theory then received further attention from the *Times
Literary Supplement,* and the discussion concluded with an answer
from Mr. Harold Williams on November 29, 1941, which leaves little
more to be said.[1] But in a volume which bears the title, *Stella*, it is
perhaps fitting that I should state my own view of a theory which provides such a simple solution of the problem of her relationship with
Swift. For while it would give me the fullest support in my attempt to

[1] Further developed by Denis Johnston in his book *In Search of Swift*, Dublin,
1959.

expose some of the sentimental nonsense that has been written about
them (for instance, the phrase "Only a woman's hair" would lose
some of its poignancy, if it should really mean "Only the hair of my
niece") it would also make nonsense or folly or lying hypocrisy of
some of the letters and poems which in the following pages I have assumed to be the very essence of truth and sincerity.

I am admittedly, therefore, a little biased against Mr. Johnston's
theory from the start, and inclined to look for flaws in his entertaining
presentation of his case.

His conclusions are founded upon a careful examination of documents available in Dublin concerning Swift's family. Some of these
documents had been neglected by Swift's biographers, and Mr. Johnston is able to correct a few minor details by the evidence of the mu-
nicipal records. But Mr. Johnston ignores the fact that already in 1820
William Monck Mason, one of Swift's best biographers, was fully
acquainted with the most important document of all—the Black Book
of the King's Inns, containing information about the appointment of
Swift's father as Steward in 1666, which was printed from the original
documents in Duhigg's *History of the King's Inns, Dublin* (1806).
The only point of interest that Swift's biographers have failed to mention is that among the five signatures authorizing this particular appointment is that of the Master of the Rolls, Sir John Temple. This is
Mr. Johnston's discovery; this is the foundation stone of his whole
edifice. He leads us to it with great excitement:

> So there are other Temples besides Sir William! And some of them
> actually in Dublin! And are they any connection? Yes, indeed! One of
> them—a hale, elderly man of 66—is Master of the Rolls and the owner
> of a fine house situated between Dame Street and the River Liffey. He
> is one of those who has the Stewardship of the Inns in his gift. And,
> moreover, he is Sir William Temple's father!
> Now surely we are on the track of something.[2]

We are indeed. On this fact alone, that the signature of the Master of
the Rolls is among the five of those who granted the Stewardship to
Swift's father, we are asked to believe that, in the light of other suspicious circumstances, there is evidence that Sir John Temple was im-

[2] Denis Johnston, "The Mysterious Origin of Dean Swift," *Dublin Historical
Record* (June 1941), Vol. III, no. 3, p. 93.

properly using his patronage to provide a livelihood for the younger
brother of the Attorney-General of the County of Tipperary, to whom
a year or so earlier he had married his former mistress, Abigail Erick,
of Leicestershire, who became later the mother of Dean Swift. The
scandal that was current in the eighteenth century that Swift was
really the son of Sir William Temple, was so easily disproved that
biographers were put off the scent, until Mr. Johnston caught sight of
Sir John Temple's signature on this incriminating document, and was
able to start a fresh tale on the evidence that at least one member of
the Temple family was living in the same city as the parents of the
Dean in the year before he was born.

The other suspicious circumstances are that Swift's mother was ten
years older than his father, and that at the time of their marriage he
was able to settle upon his wife an annuity of twenty pounds a year
although there is nothing in the record to show that he then possessed
any means of livelihood. Mr. Johnston is content to accept Jane Swift
as a legitimate daughter whose birth and baptism were properly regis-
tered in 1666. But he insists that the biographers are wrong in their
date of the death of the elder Jonathan Swift. The only evidence
we have is that it was before April 15, 1667, when the Benchers of
the King's Inns received from his widow a petition to collect the
dues owing to his estate. Mr. Johnston argues rather unconvincingly
that if we allowed time for such a petition to have been drawn up his
death must have been early in 1667—"March at the very latest, but
more probably January or February." He tries to arouse our suspicions
again in connection with the records of Dean Swift's own birth, which
took place on November 30, 1667. He reminds us that the parish
records contain no entry of his baptism, that there is still controversy
in Dublin as to the exact place where he was born, and that in his
autobiography Swift wrote simply: "He was born in Dublin on St.
Andrew's Day," adding the year afterwards in the margin.

Therefore Mr. Johnston would have us assume that the Dean was
not the posthumous child of Jonathan Swift, but that he was the son
of Sir John Temple, to whom his mistress had returned either during
her husband's last illness or immediately after his death. Mr. Johnston
is cautious enough to admit that a good deal of this is speculation.
"There is no positive evidence left to prove that what I suggest actually took place." But, he goes on, "alone of all the explanations that

have been offered it squares up fully with every fact that we do know, and once one accepts it everything else falls neatly into place."

But there is one fact which Mr. Johnston does not mention, although he has examined the original manuscript of Swift's autobio- graphical fragment with great care and with a good deal of suspicion. It is curious that he does not mention it. It is this, that Swift himself states that Sir William Temple's father—this same Sir John Temple, Master of the Rolls in Ireland—"had been a great friend to the family"; and he states it in such a way as to imply specifically that it was owing to this friendship that he was later on taken into the family of Sir William Temple. I would suggest that it is possible that Sir John Temple may have had other obligations to the Swift family than those assumed by Mr. Johnston, and that the connection was one of which Swift had no reason to be ashamed.

Such a theory, however, would not serve Mr. Johnston's other purpose, which is to prove that he was related through the Temple family to Stella. And here again he can offer only conjecture and gossip—the old story which appeared in the *Gentleman's Magazine* nearly sixty years after Temple's death for which there is also no evidence, that Stella was the daughter of Sir William Temple.

But Mr. Johnston is ambitious. He wishes by one stroke to destroy the mystery of Swift, to solve all the riddles and take away all the strangeness out of the story of his life. If he would devote as much time to the writings of Swift as he has done to the study of his biographers, he would discover that his theory raises as many new difficulties as it seems to solve; or else he would be forced to admit that Swift was a greater monster of hypocrisy and cant than his enemies ever dared to suggest. We need only to remember one or two sentences from the Autobiography.

Of his father he wrote:

> He dyed young, about two years after his marriage: he had some employments and agencyes; his death was much lamented on account of his reputation for integrity, with a tolerable good understanding.[3]

Of the marriage he wrote:

> This marriage was on both sides very indiscreet, for his wife brought her husband little or no fortune, and his death happening so suddenly

[3] *Prose*, V, 191.

before he could make a sufficient establishment for his family: And his son (not then born) hath often been heard to say that he felt the consequences of that marriage not onely through the whole course of his education, but during the greatest part of his life.[4]

It may be said that this is either formal piety or a deliberate attempt to deceive posterity. But it cannot be said that he acted from these motives when, in 1710, on receiving the news of his mother's death, he entered into his private note-book this memorandum, so characteristic and so precise:

On Wednesday, between seven and eight in the evening, May 10, 1710, I received a letter in my chamber at Laracor, (Mr. Percival and John Beaumont being by,) from Mrs. Fenton, dated May 9th, with one enclosed, sent from Mrs. Worrall at Leicester to Mrs. Fenton, giving an account, that my dear mother, Mrs. Abigail Swift, died that morning, Monday, April 24, 1710, about ten o'clock, after a long sickness, being ill all winter, and lame, and extremely ill a month or six weeks before her death. I have now lost my barrier between me and death; God grant I may live to be as well prepared for it, as I confidently believe her to have been! If the way to Heaven be through piety, truth, justice, and charity, she is there.[5]

I do not need to prolong this discussion further. My real answer to Mr. Johnston is given below.

My material is neither gossip nor conjecture. It consists of documents—letters, essays and poems, in which I find certain tones recurring either separately or blended variously together. I shall attempt to distinguish them by labelling them in literary fashion as the tones of satire, of comedy, and of sentiment. They are, I believe, dominant throughout all Swift's work; they are, as it were, the limited range of colours he deliberately chose to work with because he could use them so effectively. But now, in these three lectures, I wish to try and show them to you as they appear in part of his work, when he is writing to Stella, or when he is writing about Stella. I soon discovered, however, that in the process of making literature out of his experience of friendship with Esther Johnson, in all the various studies and sketches that he made of her, Swift does more than set before us an

[4] Ibid., p. 192.
[5] Ibid., p. 196.

individual person who lived a very private life among a small circle of friends in Dublin during the first quarter of the eighteenth century; for he is working at the same time at a larger subject in which he was always intensely interested, a study of the English gentlewoman, and her place in an enlightened and civilized society. I have, therefore, particularly in the first lecture, extended my investigations in order to explain his attitude by showing what views he was protesting against and what views he shared with his own contemporaries.

I shall not attempt to justify my subject in such days as these. I will only say that it is not entirely an escape. I must apologize if I seem to have enlarged it, so that the title has become a symbolic one. I have indeed been tempted to make it a modest appendix to that very thorough study, *The Allegory of Love,* in which Mr. C. S. Lewis traced the development of the romantic conception of woman from the court of love tradition down to its final form in the poetry of Spenser and Sidney. I offer you the sketch of a further study as far as Swift.

SATIRE

To most English readers the name Stella is perhaps first associated with the *Journal to Stella,* which consists of a collection of sixty-five letters mostly written in journal form, addressed by Swift to Rebecca Dingley and Esther Johnson jointly between September 1710 and June 1713. The name Stella, however, is never actually used in these letters, and the title *Journal to Stella* was first supplied by Thomas Sheridan in his edition of Swift's *Works,* 1784, when these letters were for the first time arranged in their proper order and printed consecutively in volumes fourteen and fifteen of that edition.

Swift himself had first used the name Stella in the verses which he had addressed to Esther Johnson on her birthday in March 1719, and he continued to use it in similar compliments until her last birthday in 1727. And after 1722 he also referred to her occasionally as Stella in letters to their close friend the Rev. Thomas Sheridan. The name may have been adopted between them at any time as a poetical alternative to Esther; but when it appeared in a series of poems in honour of their friendship, it could not have been without a particular literary association both for them and for their friends. And it seems not unlikely that Swift and Stella, too, assumed the name in pleasant mockery of Sidney and his Stella, and intended it as a little joke at the expense of all romantic nonsense, particularly romantic love poetry; and this would be all the more satisfactory to them, because paradoxically it could at the same time hide and flaunt the truth that she was "the star whereby his course was only directed."

When he began to write these birthday poems to Stella, he was fifty-one, and she was thirty-seven. They had known each other for almost thirty years, though naturally enough in this exchange of compliments he dates their friendship from the time when he returned to Moor Park to find her a beautiful girl of sixteen, without recalling his first stay there when she was a child of eight.

This is the first of them:

> Stella this Day is thirty four,
> (We won't dispute a Year or more)
> However Stella, be not troubled,
> Although thy Size and Years are doubled,
> Since first I saw Thee at Sixteen
> The brightest Virgin of the Green,
> So little is thy Form declin'd
> Made up so largly in thy Mind.
> Oh, would it please the Gods to split
> Thy Beauty, Size, and Years, and Wit,
> No Age could furnish out a Pair
> Of Nymphs so gracefull, Wise and fair
> With half the Lustre of Your Eyes,
> With half thy Wit, thy Years and Size:
> And then before it grew too late,
> How should I beg of gentle Fate,
> (That either Nymph might have her Swain,)
> To split my Worship too in twain.[1]

There is nothing left in these easy lines of the heavenly star and the knightly worshipper in *Astrophel and Stella*. Here is only an affectionate, intimate raillery such as is possible between old friends in a relationship which has been entirely freed of all romantic distance. There is no room here for the conventions of the tradition of courtly love, or for the ecstasies of passion and the worship of beauty belonging to that world of romance where moved the radiant figures of Sidney and his Stella.

In all the varied moods of the sonnets he addresses to her Sidney's Stella remains a creature of another sphere, a star whose influence, when unfavourable, arouses emotions of jealousy or the anguish of unrequited passion, and when propitious, draws forth protestations of

[1] *Poems*, pp. 721-2.

chivalrous devotion and loyalty. Sometimes in the Songs he puts aside
the courtly convention, and speaks simply but hesitatingly in words of
tenderness and affection; but he never divests himself of the cloak of
humility or rises from his knees while he chants his prayers of suppli-
cation:

> Graunt, o graunt, but speech alas,
> Failes me fearing on to passe,
> Graunt, o me, what am I saying?
> But no fault there is in praying.
>
> Never season was more fit,
> Never roome more apt for it;
> Smiling ayre allowes my reason,
> These birds sing: "Now use the season."
>
> This small wind which so sweete is,
> See how it the leaves doth kisse,
> Ech tree in his best attiring,
> Sense of love to love inspiring.

and her reply:

> Then she spake; her speech was such,
> As not eares but hart did tuch:
> While such wise she love denied,
> As yet love she signified.
>
> 'Astrophil' sayd she, 'my love
> Cease in these effects to prove:
> Now be still, yet still beleeve me,
> Thy griefe more then death would grieve me.
>
> 'If more may be sayd, I say,
> All my blisse in thee I lay;
> If thou love, my love content thee,
> For all love, all faith is meant thee.[2]

For the most part he uses the more formal sonnet with its inevitable
conventions, making it superb and splendid in its magnificent rhetoric
and in its aristocratic and courtly manner:

[2] *The Poems of Sir Philip Sidney*, ed. William A. Ringler, Jr., 1962, pp.
219-20.

> O Joy, too high for my low stile to show:
>> O blisse, fit for a nobler state then me:
>> Envie, put out thine eyes, least thou do see
> What Oceans of delight in me do flow.
> My friend, that oft saw through all maskes my wo,
>> Come, come, and let me powre my selfe on thee;
>> Gone is the winter of my miserie,
> My spring appeares, o see what here doth grow.
>> For *Stella* hath with words where faith doth shine,
> Of her high heart giv'n me the monarchie:
> I, I, o I may say, that she is mine.
> And though she give but thus conditionly
>> This realme of blisse, while vertuous course I take,
>> No kings be crown'd but they some covenants make.[3]

Finally at the end of it all, after the ecstasy and the pain, the hope and the longing, there is no happy ending in a marriage song, but the knight is left prostrate before another altar dedicating himself to a higher service.

> Leave me o Love, which reachest but to dust,
> And thou my mind aspire to higher things:
> Grow rich in that which never taketh rust:
> What ever fades, but fading pleasure brings.
>
> Draw in thy beames, and humble all thy might,
> To that sweet yoke, where lasting freedomes be:
> Which breakes the clowdes and opens forth the light,
> That doth both shine and give us sight to see.
>
> O take fast hold, let that light be thy guide,
> In this small course which birth drawes out to death,
> And thinke how evill becommeth him to slide,
> Who seeketh heav'n, and comes of heav'nly breath.
>> Then farewell world, thy uttermost I see,
>> Eternall Love maintaine thy life in me.[4]

What had happened in the century that lies between Sidney and Swift to Sidney's romantic conception of Stella? It had been attacked in several different ways.

[3] Ibid., p. 200.
[4] Ibid., pp. 161-2.

In the aristocratic tradition Donne and his followers mocked at the idea of Love's constancy:

> . . . Some two or three
> Poore Heretiques in love there bee,
> Which thinke to stablish dangerous constancie.[5]

The theme of love poetry is no longer the pangs and hopes of the wooer, a humble suppliant in the courts of love, but the moods of the experienced lover playfully addressing his mistress: a Julia or a Celia, gay, charming, and quite approachable, takes the place of the heavenly Stella.

> It is not, Celia, in our power
>   To say how long our love will last;
> It may be we within this hour
>   May lose those joys we now do taste:
> The blessèd, that immortal be,
> From change in love are only free.
>
> Then, since we mortal lovers are,
>   Ask not how long our love will last;
> But, while it does, let us take care
>   Each minute be with pleasure passed.
> Were it not madness to deny
>   To live, because we're sure to die?[6]

Moreover, the whole magnificent dream of romance, the faith and religion of love, is terribly vulnerable to laughter. The melancholy lover becomes a stock figure of comedy; his disease is thoroughly anatomized by Robert Burton, or it is laughed out of existence to the tune of one of Banister and Low's *News Airs*:

> When I a lover pale do see
> Ready to faint and sickish be,
> With hollow eyes, and cheeks so thin
> As all his face is nose and chin;
> When such a ghost I see in pain
> Because he is not loved again,

[5] *The Poems of John Donne*, ed. Herbert J. C. Grierson, 1912, I, 13.
[6] Sir George Etherege, 1667. From *Seventeenth Century Lyrics*, ed. Norman Ault, 1928, p. 344.

And pule and faint and sigh and cry,—
Oh, there's your loving fool! say I.

'Tis love with love should be repaid
And equally on both sides laid;
Love is a load a horse would kill
If it do hang on one side still;
But if he needs will be so fond
As rules of reason go beyond,
And love where he's not loved again,
Faith, let him take it for his pain.[7]

And finally in Restoration Comedy we enter a world of intrigue which may be regarded as a perfect parody of the courts of love, in which all the virtues and all the conventions are turned completely topsy-turvy.

But even more important in its general effect on the romantic conception embodied in Sidney's Stella was the Puritan and middle-class literature of love and marriage, with its exclusive emphasis on the relationship between husband and wife. For in this relationship the lady is no longer the queen or the star by whom his course is only directed; she is changed into the dutiful, submissive and obedient wife. It is true that William Gouge in his *Domesticall Duties,* first published in 1622 and reprinted in 1626 and 1634, uses the image of a star, but with a dangerously changed significance.

A wife must be milde, meeke, gentle, obedient, though she be matched with a crooked, perverse, prophane, wicked Husband: thus shall her vertue and grace shine forth the more clearly, even as the Starres shine forth most brightly in the darkest night.

The image is used again differently by Daniel Rogers in his *Matrimoniall Honour,* 1642, but here the man and woman are on equal ground, bred under the same stellar influence, and moved alike by it to recognize their affinity:

Husbands and wives should be as two sweet friends, bred under one constellation, tempered by an influence from heaven, whereof neither can give any great reason, save that mercy and providence first made them so, and then made their match; Saying, see, God hath determined us, out of this vast world, each for other; perhaps many may deserve as

[7] Ibid., p. 399.

well, but yet to me, and for my turne, thou excellest them all, and
God hath made me to thinke so (not for formality sake to say) but because it is so.

But in general the Puritan art of love was the most direct challenge
to the romantic conception of woman, because of the vigorous reitera-
tion of the preachers that the wife must be subject to her husband.
Take these solemn words from William Whately's *Bride-Bush,* 1617:

> Whosoever therefore doth desire or purpose to bee a good wife, or to
> live comfortably, let her set downe this conclusion within her soule:
> Mine husband is my superiour, my better: he hath authoritie and rule
> over me, nature hath given it him, having framed our bodies to ten-
> dernesse, mens to more hardness; God hath given it him, saying to our
> first mother *Evah; Thy desire shall be subject to thine husband, and
> hee shall rule over thee.*[8]

It is not necessary to follow William and Malleville Haller further in
their investigations of *The Puritan Art of Love,* which has provided
me with these instances; if more is needed, we can find it in Milton.

Beginning as a pupil of Spenser, he had not hesitated in his youthful innocence to declare himself a servant of the Muse and of Love;
and his later bitterness is a protest against that romanticism which had
ill prepared him to meet women's wiles. It is all summed up in his
last statement on the subject in *Samson Agonistes:*

> What e're it be, to wisest men and best
> Seeming at first all heavenly under virgin veil,
> Soft, modest, meek, demure,
> Once join'd, the contrary she proves, a thorn
> Intestin, far within defensive arms
> A cleaving mischief, in his way to vertue
> Adverse and turbulent, or by her charms
> Draws him awry enslav'd
> With dotage, and his sense deprav'd
> To folly and shameful deeds which ruin ends.
> What Pilot so expert but needs must wreck
> Embarqu'd with such a Stears-mate at the Helm?
> Favour'd of Heav'n who finds
> One vertuous rarely found,

[8] William and Malleville Haller, "The Puritan Art of Love," *HLQ* (1941-2),
V, 242-52.

That in domestic good combines:
Happy that house! his way to peace is smooth:
But vertue which breaks through all opposition,
And all temptation can remove,
Most shines and most is acceptable above.
    Therefore Gods universal Law
Gave to the man despotic power
Over his female in due awe,
Nor from that right to part an hour,
Smile she or lowre:
So shall he least confusion draw
On his whole life, not sway'd
By female usurpation, nor dismay'd.[9]

There, as strongly put as you could wish to find it, is the full Puritan reply to the romantic view of Stella. And if you protest that I have quoted from a Chorus in a drama, and that in other places Milton has expressed himself differently, let me remind you that in his happiest mood, when he writes his most exquisite lines of tenderness and loving devotion, he reverses the normal procedure of the poetry of love. He gives them to Eve, who sings them in adoration of her lord and master:

> With thee conversing I forget all time,
> All seasons and their change, all please alike[10]

and as she gazes upon Adam

>   with eyes
> Of conjugal attraction, unreprov'd,
> And meek surrender[11]

she solemnly and submissively confesses that from the moment she first espied him fair and tall under a Platan, and yielded to him her hand, she had seen

> How beauty is excell'd by manly grace
> And wisdom, which alone is truly fair.[12]

[9] *Samson Agonistes*, ll. 1034-60.
[10] *Paradise Lost*, Book IV, ll. 639-40.
[11] Ibid., ll. 492-4.
[12] Ibid., ll. 490-91.

Thus the Puritan tradition, wherever in its idealization of marriage it takes over and transforms romantic love, is bound to place the man, the head of the family, the superior, at the centre, and give to the woman the virtues of the courtly lover, the virtues of humility and devotion and constancy. It is almost startling to turn directly from Milton to Swift, remembering Milton's desire to find in marriage the joy of companionship, a remedy for loneliness, for Swift was himself the recipient of so much devotion and constancy, and enjoyed in his friendship with Stella just that very "apt and cheerful conversation" which Milton emphasizes as the one thing essential in a Christian marriage. And if I may digress a moment to take notice of some of Swift's biographers, I would suggest to them that before condemning him and pitying Stella, they might consider a passage from the second chapter of Milton's *Doctrine and Discipline of Divorce*:

> And indeed it is a greater blessing from God, more worthy so excellent a creature as man is, and a higher end to honour and sanctifie the league of marriage, whenas the solace and satisfaction of the mind is regarded and provided for before the sensitive pleasing of the body. And with all generous persons married thus it is, that where the mind and person pleases aptly, there some unaccomplishment of the body's delight may be better born with, than when the mind hangs off in an unclosing disproportion, though the body be as it ought.

In view of the double reaction which we have traced through the seventeenth century against romantic love poetry and the romantic idea of woman, both in court poetry and drama as well as in Puritan and middle-class literature, it may seem that there was little further for Swift to go. But he was neither a disillusioned cynic nor a Puritan divine; and though he seems to take the position now of the one and then of the other, his expression of it in his satire differs from anything in the seventeenth century, at least in its total effect. He uses another method, he employs a different palette from theirs. And as I hope to be able to show, he sets before us in his own inimitable fashion a new view of woman, unromantic but not unpleasing. She is able to take her place in the world on equal terms, a free, intelligent gentlewoman, worthy of man's highest regard and friendship whether within or without the bounds of holy matrimony.

In everything a sceptic, hard, distrustful, refusing the happiness of being well deceived, he must begin here as always by sweeping his mind clear of all preconceptions, emptying it of all dim beliefs, half-truths, passing fancies, that trouble the crystal fountain of the sight, all antic shapes in dreams, kindled while reason sleeps; at whatever risk of worse visitants, he will labour until it is swept, cleaned and garnished. And there, alone, in the light from those bare white walls, he carries out his examination, or makes his dissections of the tissue of life, before writing down his observations.

His method of satire is then often a very unpleasant trick of breaking the vehicle of delusion, and showing us a thing as it appears shrunk in the glass of nature; "an Employment—to quote his own words—neither better nor worse than that of *Unmasking,* which I think, has never been allowed fair Usage, either in the *World* or the *PlayHouse.*"[13] As a young man he had recognized the danger of his bent.

> Now, I take all this to be the last Degree of perverting Nature; one of whose Eternal Laws it is, to put her best Furniture forward. . . . Last Week I saw a Woman *flay'd,* and you will hardly believe, how much it altered her Person for the worse. Yesterday I ordered the Carcass of a *Beau* to be stript in my Presence; when we were all amazed to find so many unsuspected Faults under one Suit of Cloaths: Then I laid open his *Brain,* his *Heart,* and his *Spleen;* But, I plainly perceived at every Operation, that the farther we proceeded, we found the Defects encrease upon us in Number and Bulk.[14]

A love letter to a lady on whom he had bestowed the romantic name Varina, and whom he had earlier addressed in terms of the most extravagant courtship, indicates rather clearly what he is capable of when this rash spirit takes possession of him. It is an attempt to clear up matters between them, by putting before her a few simple questions, which he had always resolved to propose to her with whom he meant to pass his life. After preliminaries with regard to her health, and her ability to manage domestic affairs on a small income, he goes on:

> Have you such an inclination to my person and humour, as to comply with my desires and way of living, and endeavour to make us both as

---

[13] *Prose,* I, 109.
[14] Ibid., pp. 109-10.

happy as you can? Will you be ready to engage in those methods I shall
direct for the improvement of your mind, so as to make us entertaining
company for each other, without being miserable when we are neither
visiting nor visited? Can you bend your love and esteem and indiffer-
ence to others the same way as I do mine? . . .
and whenever you can heartily answer these questions in the affirmative, I shall be blessed to have you in my arms without regarding
whether your person be beautiful or your fortune large. Cleanliness in
the first, and competency in the other, is all I look for.[15]

All beauty and grace and loveliness,

> the blazon of sweet beauty's best,
> Of hand, of foot, of lip, of eye, of brow,[16]

are tossed aside—for cleanliness and health. In all his work, but especially in the pages of the *Journal*, Swift appears almost obsessed with
the effort to preserve bodily health. His tenderest thought and care
for Stella turns again and again into admonitions to walk and to ride,
or to go to Wexford to take the waters there. And this preoccupation
shows itself in its most violent form later in the letters he writes to
her friends and his during her last years of illness.

Nothing disturbs Swift more deeply than the frailties that flesh is
heir to; he can never find anything romantic in the pallor of illness.
After going to see a lady, "just up after lying-in" he writes to Stella
that evening almost with violence: "the ugliest sight I have seen, pale,
dead, old and yellow, for want of her paint. She has turned my stom-
ach. But she will soon be painted, and a beauty again."[17]

And, alas, he was a person of a hard-mouthed imagination, easily
disposed to run away with him, and of a fastidious taste revolted by all
the disguises used to hide deformity and sickness, never able to forget
the wretched devices of nostrums and pills which a degenerate and
disease-ridden society needed to keep it tolerably alive. Likewise all
false arts used to disguise the ravages of sickness and old age, all the
horrors of a rotten carcass that has been painted and restored, provide
material in plenty for his roughest satires. All these details are used

[15] *The Correspondence of Jonathan Swift*, ed. F. Elrington Ball, 1910-14, I,
34-5.
[16] Shakespeare, Sonnet CVI.
[17] *Journal to Stella*, ed. J. K. Moorhead, 1924; Dec. 21, 1711, p. 289.

in the most nauseating fashion in one of the cruder of his poems,
"written for the honour of the Fair Sex," with the innocent title, *A
beautiful young nymph going to bed*.[18] It is a purely Hogarthian
piece, with a moral and a savage gesture of disgust added.

He will never forget or let us forget the corruptions and pains of
mortal flesh. He is impatient at the sound of madrigals, with their
gaiety and freshness of spring—"Corinna's going a maying" and all the
rest of the verses to Corinna that fill the later songbooks. Look
through them, and imagine Swift turning the pages:

> Rise and put on your foliage, and be seen
> To come forth, like the spring-time, fresh and green,
>   And sweet as Flora. Take no care
>   For jewels for your gown or hair.[19]

Or another Corinna of a different sort:

> Corinna is divinely fair,
> Easy her shape and soft her air;
> Of hearts she had the absolute sway
> Before she threw her own away:
> The power now languishes by which she charmed;
> Her beauty sullied, and her eyes disarmed.[20]

But the greatest cant of all to Swift was the Corinna of *The Reformed
Wife*, 1700:

> Corinna with a graceful air
>   Her symptoms does reveal:
> Such charms adorn the sickly fair
>   We scarce can wish her well.
>
> How does the pale complexion please!
>   Faint looks and languid eye!
> New beauties rise with her disease,
>   And when she's sick we die.[21]

I sometimes suspect that Swift was easily bored by the songs and
lyrics of the seventeenth century, which must have been very popular

---

[18] *Poems*, pp. 580-83.
[19] *The Poetical Works of Robert Herrick*, ed. Leonard C. Martin, 1956, p. 68.
[20] *Seventeenth Century Lyrics*, p. 440.
[21] Ibid., p. 462.

during his early days; he knew the tunes very well because he often parodied them in his political squibs. I am not trying to apologize for his verses written for the honour of the fair sex if I suggest that there may be an element in them of mere exasperation at these earlier love lyrics. I shall quote only the first twenty lines; where he has so much detail to draw upon Swift is inclined to run on to an extravagant length of thinly woven octosyllabics.

> *Corinna,* Pride of *Drury-Lane,*
> For whom no Shepherd sighs in vain;
> Never did *Covent Garden* boast
> So bright a batter'd, strolling Toast;
> No drunken Rake to pick her up,
> No Cellar where on Tick to sup;
> Returning at the Midnight Hour;
> Four Stories climbing to her Bow'r;
> Then, seated on a three-legg'd Chair,
> Takes off her artificial Hair:
> Now, picking out a Crystal Eye,
> She wipes it clean, and lays it by.
> Her Eye-Brows from a Mouse's Hyde,
> Stuck on with Art on either Side,
> Pulls off with Care, and first displays 'em,
> Then in a Play-Book smoothly lays 'em.
> Now dextrously her Plumpers draws,
> That serve to fill her hollow Jaws.
> Untwists a Wire; and from her Gums
> A Set of Teeth completely comes.[22]

There is no laughter here, but a serious purpose, a desire to arouse disgust in order that humanity should change its ways. Donne could still make fun of such things, or at least use them as the material for a youthful paradox "that women ought to paint." *"Foulness is Lothsome:* can that be so which helps it? who forbids his beloved to gird in her waste? to mend by shooing her uneven lameness? to burnish her teeth? or to perfume her breath?"[23] Or else he lost sight of them because of his constant awareness of the skeleton beneath the flesh, of the thought of the grinning horror to which she must come paint

[22] *Poems,* p. 581.
[23] *Donne's Poetry and Selected Prose,* ed. John Hayward, 1929, p. 338.

she never so thick. That overpowering sense of human mortality
which pervades so much of the poetry of the seventeenth century,
and that sense of tragedy which, by giving such short shrift to our
loves and hates, can at the same time throw such long shadows before
and after, belong alike to a conception of man's life as transitory, as
carrying only the values of another world than this, values essentially
tragic, and therefore both terrible and beautiful.

Much of Swift's satire seems small against such a background; all
satire, in so far as it is the satire of the moralist and the reformer, is
bound to seem circumscribed, because it must recognize the bounds
of this mortal life, and the possibilities within the framework of our
common nature. This kind of satire might be called Bickerstaffian,
that lighter raillery which Swift brought into fashion and then be-
queathed to Steele to start the *Tatler* on, keeping back something,
however, for his own use both in verse and in prose. In the first volume of *Miscellanies,* which he published in 1711, the earliest composition he included was a trifle called *Verses wrote in a Lady's Ivory
Table Book.*

> Peruse my Leaves thro' ev'ry Part,
> And think thou seest my owners Heart,
> Scrawl'd o'er with Trifles thus, and quite
> As hard, as senseless, and as light:[24]

Then he gives in a dozen lines particular examples in what he calls
beau-spelling of these assorted trivialities, the paints and perfumes
of the heart and of the dressing table, and adds in the same humorous
biting way his moralist's comment:

> Whoe're expects to hold his part
> In such a Book and such a Heart,
> If he be Wealthy and a Fool
> Is in all Points the fittest Tool,
> Of whom it may be justly said,
> He's a Gold Pencil tipt with Lead.[25]

Thirty years later he is still writing in the same vein in a poem called
The Furniture of a Woman's Mind, a title which in its drabness is

[24] *Poems,* p. 60.
[25] Ibid., p. 61.

well adapted to the depressing picture presented in the poem, unre-
lieved by the brightness and brilliance of the effect of Pope's urbane
wit, and the gaiety and play of fancy in that other image, "the toy-
shop of their heart"—

> With varying Vanities, from ev'ry Part,
> They shift the moving Toyshop of their Heart;
> Where Wigs with Wigs, with Sword-Knots Sword-Knots strive,
> Beaus banish Beaus, and Coaches Coaches drive.[26]

This is a sort of mocking dance, with no offence in it. But Swift has
too often the fault of her whom he attacks who

> calls it witty to be rude
> And, placing Raillery in Railing,
> Will tell aloud your greatest Failing;[27]

Or he will protest his innocence, and gravely claim to be full of zeal
for all the female commonweal.

> How cou'd it come into your Mind,
> To pitch on me, of all Mankind,
> Against the Sex to write a Satyre,
> And brand me for a Woman-Hater?
>
> 'Twas you engag'd me first to write,
> Then gave the Subject out of Spite:
> The *Journal of a Modern Dame,*
> Is by my Promise what you claim;
> My Word is past, I must submit,
> And yet perhaps you may be bit.
> I but transcribe, for not a Line
> Of all the Satyre shall be mine.[28]

And this is followed by a complete and detailed account of the lady's
life from noon when she rises, till four o'clock the next morning when
she rises from cards. It is a kind of crude Hudibrastic burlesque of
Pope's *Rape of the Lock* with the same episodes: the awakening, the
tea-table, the cards. I do not know any better way of showing the dif-

[26] *Rape of the Lock,* Canto I, 99-102.
[27] *Poems,* p. 416.
[28] Ibid., p. 445.

ference of tone in Swift's satire than to compare his work with that of
his closest friends and contemporaries. Here is the awakening in
Pope:

> Thrice rung the Bell, the Slipper knock'd the Ground,
> And the press'd Watch return'd a silver Sound.
> *Belinda* still her downy Pillow prest,
> Her Guardian *Sylph* prolong'd the balmy Rest.[29]

And this is Swift:

> The modern Dame is wak'd by Noon,
> Some Authors say not quite so soon,
> Because, though sore against her Will,
> She sat all Night up at *Quadrill*.[30]

And later, I hardly need to quote the lines from Pope:

> And now, unveil'd, the *Toilet* stands display'd,
> Each Silver Vase in mystic Order laid.
> First, rob'd in white, the Nymph intent adores
> With Head uncover'd, the *Cosmetic* Powr's.[31]

But I doubt very much whether you are familiar with these vivid,
plain, and in their way not less convincing lines of Swift:

> She stretches, gapes, unglues her Eyes,
> And asks if it be time to rise;
> Of Head-ach, and the Spleen complains;
> And then to cool her heated Brains,
> Her Night-Gown and her Slippers brought her,
> Takes a large Dram of Citron Water.
> Then to her Glass; and, "*Betty*, pray
> Don't I look frightfully to Day?"[32]

One more comparison where they both describe the afternoon's conversation at the tea-table:

> In various Talk th' instructive hours they past,
> Who gave the *Ball*, or paid the *Visit* last:
> One speaks the Glory of the *British Queen*.

[29] *Rape of the Lock*, I, 17-20.
[30] *Poems*, p. 446.
[31] *Rape of the Lock*, I, 121-4.
[32] *Poems*, p. 446.

> And one describes a charming *Indian Screen;*
> A third interprets Motions, Looks, and Eyes;
> At ev'ry Word a Reputation dies.
> *Snuff,* or the *Fan,* supply each Pause of Chat,
> With singing, laughing, ogling, and all that.[33]

That is lovely and decorous and mischievous. But Swift, I contend, startles us by his horrible verisimilitude; we recognize the scene of a reception at once:

> Now Voices over Voices rise;
> While each to be the loudest vies,
> They contradict, affirm, dispute,
> No single Tongue one Moment mute;
> All mad to speak, and none to hearken,
> They set the very Lap-Dog barking;
> Their Chattering makes a louder Din
> Than Fish-Wives o'er a Cup of Gin:
> Not School-boys at a Barring-out,
> Rais'd ever such incessant Rout:
> The Jumbling Particles of Matter
> In Chaos made not such a Clatter:
> Far less the Rabble roar and rail,
> When drunk with sour Election Ale.

Then, as if following Pope consciously, Swift goes on from the conversation to motions, looks and eyes:

> Nor do they trust their Tongue alone,
> To speak a Language of their own;
> But read a Nod, a Shrug, a Look,
> Far better than a printed Book;
> Convey a Libel in a Frown,
> And wink a Reputation down;
> Or by the tossing of the Fan,
> Describe the Lady and the Man.[34]

Throughout the *Journal to Stella* there is an undertone of good-humored raillery of this sort. He makes fun of her peculiar spelling, carefully collects a number of examples of mistakes in one of her

[33] *Rape of the Lock,* III, 11-18.
[34] *Poems,* p. 450.

letters, jokes about her ignorance of the Bible, notes the absurdity of
so gravely talking to her about politics; and then he tells her to go
back to her card game and laughs at her for making mistakes and
losing money. Stella did not protest against this treatment, but others
among his friends grew tired of this constant ridicule and begged
him sometimes to suspend his paltry burlesque style. Lady Acheson,
for instance, complains that it is too late for her to change her ways;
she has been badly brought up and is now too old to learn. He might
as well therefore try to find something to praise in her, and make
verses about her in the heroic style. His reply is a very simple one
and couched in that tone of innocent simplicity which he was inclined to adopt whatever his particular disguise at the moment,
whether a harmless old gentleman like Bickerstaff, or a simple linen
draper of Dublin, or that honest seaman, Lemuel Gulliver. Among his
intimate friends he posed similarly as a trivial scribbler of easy rhymes,
mere bagatelle to make them smile. And so he answers her:

> For your Sake, as well as mine,
> I the lofty Stile decline.
> I Shou'd make a Figure scurvy,
> And your Head turn Topsy-turvy.
>
> . . . . .
>
> To conclude this long Essay;
> Pardon, if I disobey:
> Nor, against my nat'ral Vein,
> Treat you in Heroick Strain.
> I, as all the Parish knows,
> Hardly can be grave in Prose:
> Still to lash, and lashing Smile,
> Ill befits a lofty Stile.
> From the Planet of my Birth,
> I encounter Vice with Mirth.[35]

Many of Swift's critics have overlooked the large amount of good-
humored raillery to be found in his work, perhaps because they have
given little attention to what he wrote in verse. They have forgotten
that he continued in his later years still to play the role of Bickerstaff.
That was not a youthful frolic which he later grew out of. Throughout his work there is a great variety of tone in his satire from the

[35] Ibid., pp. 637, 634.

lightest jesting and ridicule to a dangerous and bitter irony. What distinguishes him from other satirists is not, as so often supposed, that his mood is fiercer and his rage more violent, but that both in his jesting and in his irony alike he is able to disturb us by his searching judgment on the ways of men and women. Nevertheless I should find Swift much less intriguing if I were not frequently aware in the best of his satire, that is, in his irony, of a larger reference, and a greater validity in his judgments which may have roused resentment against him. He has been accused of sheer hatred of the human race, "of degrading human nature, and of abusing the female sex." That is I believe because his hardmouthed imagination carries him over the boundary line of comedy, and at times leaves us with wry faces. The comedy is strained until it breaks.

For instance, in *Gulliver's Travels* there are certain inevitable patterns the form of the book forces him to repeat. We have already noticed the parallels between the second book, the voyage to the Brobdingnagians, and the fourth book, the voyage to the Houyhnhnms. When he comes home from the land of the giants, we are amused by his difficulties in adjusting himself to things of normal size.

> My Wife ran out to embrace me, but I stooped lower than her Knees, thinking she could otherwise never be able to reach my Mouth. My Daughter kneeled to ask me Blessing, but I could not see her till she arose; . . . I told my Wife, she had been too thrifty; for I found she had starved herself and her Daughter to nothing.[36]

When he returns from his fourth voyage, we expect him to have similar difficulties; we almost anticipate the shock; but the effect upon us shatters the illusion of comedy.

> As soon as I entered the House, my Wife took me in her Arms, and kissed me; at which, having not been used to the touch of that odious Animal for so many Years, I fell into a Swoon for almost an Hour. At the Time I am writing, it is five Years since my last return to *England*: During the first Year I could not endure my Wife or Children in my Presence, the very Smell of them was intolerable; much less could I suffer them to eat in the same Room.[37]

Five years had not removed the effects of his discovery that his family

[36] *Prose*, XI, 133.
[37] Ibid., p. 273.

were really Yahoos, of the same species as the young female who had
rushed upon him and embraced him, when he was one day bathing
in the river, an incident which had proved to his master that Gulliver
himself must be indeed a real Yahoo. And we may well wonder why
he added: "Neither was the Hair of this Brute of a Red Colour,
(Which might have been an Excuse for an Appetite a little irregular)
but black as a Sloe, and her Countenance did not make an Appearance altogether so hideous as the rest of the Kind."[38]

This is the completion of his dissection of human tissue. There is
nothing more left, no possibility of any further deception. He has rid
himself of all romantic nonsense. He has freed himself even of that
last deception of the satirist and the moralist, who expects that his
observations might be for the public good, and produce some reforma-
tion in the Yahoo race.

On this foundation of complete scepticism, just as in matters of
faith and morality he puts his trust in traditional religion, so in matters of human relationship he accepts the discretionary codes and
traditional conventions of civilized society. And in that human comedy with its rules and its forms, Stella has her proper place, and in
the performance of her role gives to the comedy its particular quality
of delight.

[38] Ibid., p. 251.

COMEDY

The stage had been set for comedy a long time before 1700 when Stella was nineteen; and she had been prepared for her part under tutelage which cannot have failed to make her aware of the character of the times and the change in values which had taken place during the preceding generation. She must have seen Swift at work, even if she had not actually helped him, upon the edition of Sir William Temple's *Letters* and *Miscellanea*, which occupied him during the last years of the century, his last years at Moor Park. From these writings, or from Temple's conversation, she must have heard comments on the difference between the times of Charles II and those of Charles I, the changes from a world of romance to a world of comedy, such as those which occur in the following notes designed for an essay on Conversation:

> In King *Charles* the First's Time, all Wit, Love, and Honour, heightened by the Wits of that Time into Romance.
> Lord *Goreing* took the Contrepied, and turned all into Ridicule.
> He was followed by the Duke of *Buckingham,* and that Vein, favoured by King *Charles* the Second, brought it in Vogue.[1]

Now, Temple argues, it is necessary that this fashion for ridicule and raillery should be mingled with good sense and good humour, in order to provide the essential ingredients for that good conversation which is the mark of a really civilized society, in which the human

[1] Sir William Temple, *Works,* 1740, I, 311.

comedy may be played agreeably and gracefully. The qualities to be developed in the coming age, therefore, are good nature, good sense, and good breeding; and it must be remembered that "Humour is more than Wit, Easiness more than Knowledge."

At the same time, in 1700, there happened to be published two other collections containing essays, which had already become very popular, by two noble authors of like temperament: the *Works* of the Seigneur de St. Évremond, translated into English, and the *Miscellanies* of George Savile, Marquis of Halifax. They are also in part concerned with the manners and social standards necessary for men and women who are to take their place in a civilized world, and with the kind of art and literature which belongs there.

The vogue for this kind of book and the preoccupation in England at this time with the development of the art of conversation may perhaps be accounted for by the criticism implied in one of St. Évremond's neatest epigrams:

> The finest Gentlemen in the World, are the *French* that think, and the *English* that speak.[2]

Swift and Congreve, Steele and Addison alike felt it to be their task to teach their countrymen to speak—not to preach or make orations, not to indulge in declamations or incantations, not to soar into romantic poetry, but to converse together agreeably. As St. Évremond had written in his old age,

> Poetry requires a peculiar Genius, that agrees not overmuch with good sense. It is sometimes the Language of Gods; sometimes of Buffoons; rarely that of a Gentleman.
>
> Comic Poets are of all most proper for the Converse of the World: For they make it their Business to draw to the Life what passes in it, and to express the Sentiments and Passions of Men.[3]

That kind of literature which is most like the converse of the world brings him much pleasure; but the highest pleasure, which he knows will ever most sensibly affect him, is the pleasure of conversation itself, especially in a mixed company of civilized men and women, where it is possible to enjoy what he describes as "pleasing and reasonable friendship, that has none of the uneasiness of love."

[2] St. Évremond, *Works*, 1714, II, 81.
[3] Ibid., I, 335-6.

It is a world dominated by the desire for ease and pleasure, not of the grossest but of the nicest sort, where manners and conventions serve as a protection against the play of violent emotions which might disturb the gaiety and peace of its Augustan comedy. It is a world in which we do not expect to find heroic figures; the men are not flowers of chivalry or romantic lovers, they are men of the world and therefore possessed of all the faults and weaknesses of the society they belong to; the women are neither innocent nor guileless, but gifted in varying degree with the wisdom and discretion necessary to make such a society tolerable to them.

If we pick up that other volume I have referred to, containing the *Works* of the Marquis of Halifax, and turn to those charming pages in which he offers *Advice to a Daughter,* we find there the same conception of a world to be accepted and made the best of; we overhear him as it were gently and delicately breaking the news of it to the child who has not yet been allowed to venture forth alone. She must first of all endeavour to forget the great indulgence she has found at home, and that tenderness peculiar to kind parents, which is of another nature from the ways of the world. She is not allowed for a moment to consider the remotest possibility of any romance in love or marriage. His care is entirely to show her how "by a wise and dexterous Conduct to relieve herself from anything that looketh like a Disadvantage in marriage."[4] She is to be prepared for a partner who may be either unfaithful or drunken, or choleric, or ill-humoured, or covetous, or a mere fool or idiot. All these situations are to be handled with good humour, good manners and discretion. In a romantic world such situations will become the stuff of tragedy and will rouse us to indignation or to pity, but in a world of comedy

a *Wife* is to thank God her *Husband* hath *Faults.* Mark the seeming Paradox my Dear, for your own Instruction, it being intended no further. A *Husband* without *Faults* is a dangerous Observer; he hath an Eye so piercing, and seeth every thing so plain, that it is expos'd to his full Censure. And though I will not doubt but that your *Vertue* will disappoint the sharpest Enquiries; yet few Women can bear the having all they say or do *represented* in the clear Glass of an Understanding without *Faults.* Nothing softneth the *Arrogance* of our *Nature,* like a

[4] *Works of George Savile, Marquess of Halifax,* ed. Walter Raleigh, 1912, p. 10.

Mixture of some *Frailties*. It is by them we are best told, that we must
not strike too hard upon others, because we our selves do so often deserve Blows: They pull our Rage by the Sleeve, and whisper Gentleness to us in our Censures, even when they are rightly applied. The
Faults and *Passions* of *Husbands* bring them down to you, and make
them content to live upon less unequal Terms, than Faultless Men
would be willing to stoop to; so haughty is Mankind till humbled by
common Weaknesses and Defects, which in our corrupted State contribute more towards the reconciling us to one another, than all the
Precepts of the *Philosophers* and *Divines*.[5]

Though Halifax struggles bravely to accept for her the world which
she is about to enter, and wishes her to be reconciled to its ways, his
anxiety and tenderness for her cast a shadow over the scene. He promises the sober rewards of discretion and carefulness rather than the
ease and pleasure of a well-ordered and civilized society. He had
something of the character of a "Trimmer" in life as well as in politics; this makes him content with a rather negative attitude, which
allows to woman at best a role of wise passivity.

Swift's method of preparing Stella for the world must have been
very different. He had the courage to train her from the beginning
to take her place in the kind of society into which he hoped to force
his way, where he would be the companion of the leading men and
women of his time in church and state, and in the world of letters.
We can learn something from what he wrote later in 1720 in a *Letter
to a very young Lady on her Marriage*. He is not, like Halifax, concerned to give general advice; he has a more precise situation to deal
with. For the young lady has just been married to a man "of good
education and learning, of an excellent understanding and an exact
taste," combined with "modesty, sweetness of temper, and an unusual
disposition to sobriety and virtue." He writes therefore to convince
her of her good fortune and to urge her not to spoil such an unusual
chance of happiness.

He begins by sweeping away all romantic nonsense:

I hope, you do not still dream of Charms and Raptures; which Marriage ever did, and ever will put a sudden End to. Besides, yours was a
Match of Prudence, and common Good-liking, without any Mixture of

[5] Ibid., p. 12.

that ridiculous Passion which hath no Being, but in Play-Books and Romances.[6]

and gives advice on her general behaviour, which reminds us of the code of behaviour drawn up by Millamant on the eve of her marriage:

> I must likewise warn you strictly against the least Degree of Fondness to your Husband before any Witnesses whatsoever, even before your nearest Relations, or the very Maids of your Chamber. This Proceeding is so extremely odious and disgustful to all who have either good Breeding or good Sense, that they assign two very unamiable Reasons for it; the one is gross Hypocrisy, and the other hath too bad a Name to mention. If there is any Difference to be made, your Husband is the lowest Person in Company, either at home or abroad; and every Gentleman present hath a better Claim to all Marks of Civility and Distinction from you.[7]

This is further developed by a strong recommendation to her to fit herself for conversation in a mixed company, in which Swift saw the only possibility of escape from the dangers on the one hand of dullness and pedantry, and on the other of scandalmongering and detraction.

> I advise that your Company at home should consist of Men rather than Women. To say the Truth, I never yet knew a tolerable Woman to be fond of her own Sex: I confess, when both are mixt and well chosen, and put their best Qualities forward, there may be an Intercourse of Civility and Goodwill; which with the Addition of some Degree of Sense, can make Conversation or any Amusement agreeable.[8]

The comedy of life as Swift and Congreve saw it was not the whole of life, far from it; it was strictly limited—by the exclusion of children and adolescents, and by its unconcern with the work and business of life and with the proper privacy of the individual. But because of these rigid bounds it can offer to men and women, mature and experienced in the way of the world, a complete freedom and a perfect equality in its society. Swift states this view without any qualifications:

[6] *Prose*, IX, 89.
[7] Ibid., p. 86.
[8] Ibid., p. 88.

I am ignorant of any one Quality that is amiable in a Man, which is not equally so in a Woman: I do not except even Modesty, and Gentleness of Nature. Nor do I know one Vice or Folly, which is not equally detestable in both.

And as the same Virtues equally become both Sexes; so there is no Quality whereby Women endeavour to distinguish themselves from Men, for which they are not just so much the worse; except that only of Reservedness; which, however, as you generally manage it, is nothing else but Affectation, or Hypocrisy. For, as you cannot too much discountenance those of our Sex, who presume to take unbecoming Liberties before you; so you ought to be wholly unconstrained in the Company of deserving Men, when you have had sufficient Experience of their Discretion.[9]

You may say that I am nevertheless blurring the clear outline of the world of comedy by speaking of Swift and Congreve together. Swift's little world may seem to you a very drab and sober scene, with too many parsons and squires and schoolmasters about, lacking all the gaiety and sparkle of Congreve's drawing-rooms, and the excitement of extravagant compliments and gallantries. There the dance whirls a little faster:

Lord, what is a Lover, that it can give? Why one makes Lovers as fast as one pleases, and they live as long as one pleases, and they die as soon as one pleases: And then if one pleases one makes more.

Or the counterpart to this:

Think of you! To think of a Whirlwind, tho' 'twere in a Whirlwind, were a Case of more steady Contemplation; a very Tranquility of Mind and Mansion. A Fellow that lives in a Windmill, has not a more whimsical Dwelling than the Heart of a Man that is lodg'd in a Woman.[10]

Swift would undoubtedly have retorted with some scathing remark about play-books and romances, or would have reminded us that in an ideal society, as in heaven, there would be little concern with marrying or giving in marriage. Nevertheless it must be admitted that the comedy in which Swift and Stella take part would have to

[9] Ibid., pp. 92-3.
[10] See *The Way of the World*, II, iv & vi; *Comedies by William Congreve*, ed. Bonamy Dobrée, 1925, pp. 372, 375.

be described as domestic comedy, and the language used is that of very intimate and household speech.

In spite of this, however, Stella appears only in a rather formal way, and in all that Swift has written to her or about her she remains like a character in a comedy, of whose personality we know nothing beyond that which is revealed in the playing of the part set down for her.

This is due of course to the fact that we do not possess any of the letters she wrote, and cannot be sure that the three short poems attributed to her were really her work. We have in her handwriting only some manuscripts of poems and other scraps she had copied out. Finally we have the *Bons Mots* of Stella, a dozen sentences which Swift had remembered from her conversation, but which add nothing to our knowledge of her.

The so-called *Journal to Stella* which we have is only a part of their correspondence. In addition to the sixty-five letters it contains, Swift had written twenty-four letters to her while on his former visit to England, between the spring of 1708, after a winter spent in London together, and June 1709. During that period he notes in his account books nineteen letters received from her, and two more in October and December 1709, when he was away from Dublin at Laracor and at Clogher. Then during the period of the *Journal,* he received forty-one letters from her between September 21, 1710 and June 6, 1713. None of these letters have survived as far as we know; but Swift had carefully noted and numbered each one as it arrived, and after he had answered it, put it away in his orderly fashion. He tells her, for instance, when he is moving out to Chelsea, that he has packed up and sealed her twelve letters, after writing down in his account book the last commissions she had given him to perform. It does not seem to me very likely that these packets of letters will now be found; probably he destroyed them himself before he died.

It is not difficult to put together some of the contents of these letters of hers, by studying closely Swift's detailed replies. He describes how he deals with each one: "I tell you what I do; I lay your letter before me, and take it in order, and answer what is necessary; and so, and so."[11]

[11] *Journal,* April 24, 1711, p. 155.

But there must have been much that required no answer to which we have no clue; and all the facts that we can put together are of less significance than would be a page or two of the original.

A good deal is Dublin gossip about their friends, their state of health and the constantly recurring births and deaths of their children. She reports regularly on their own household accounts and on his affairs in so far as they were not in his agent's hands; for instance, what should be done with the Laracor apples? She enquires about his fires and his nightcaps and his colds, or about the editions of his latest pamphlet. She makes fun of him for mistaking the date of his own birthday, and indulging in his annual lamentations two days too late; and she sends him the verses which his Dublin friends made as a birthday greeting for him, with their good wishes for his health and for his preferment.

But we get perhaps even more vivid impressions of her life with Dingley from the imaginary scenes of domestic comedy which Swift includes in his letters to them, as he pictures them settling down on their arrival to take the waters in Wexford.

> How do you pass your time at Wexford? . . . Tell me all the particulars . . . the place, the company, the diversions, the victuals, the wants, the vexations. Poor Dingley never saw such a place in her life; sent all over the town for a little parsley to a boiled chicken, and it was not to be had: the butter is stark naught, except an old English woman's; and it is such a favour to get a pound from her now and then . . .[12]

and when they get back to Dublin safe again in their own lodgings at St. Mary's—

> And so your friends come to visit you; and Mrs. Walls is much better of her eye; and the dean is just as he used to be; and what does Walls say of London? 'tis a reasoning coxcomb. And goody Stoyte, and Hannah what d'ye call her; no, her name en't Hannah, Catherine I mean; they were so glad to see the ladies again; and Mrs. Manley wanted a companion at ombre.[13]

And there in that quiet corner of Dublin in the midst of the trivialities of this provincial life, Stella's education was continued through these

[12] *Journal*, July 24, 1711, p. 203.
[13] Ibid., August 20, 1711, p. 214.

letters, and their friendship ripened and matured. One may of course read too much as well as too little underneath those repeated jocularities at her bad spelling, her ignorance of the Bible, her laziness, and the absurdity of talking to her about politics. But if we are to believe not only what Swift wrote about her after her death, but what he said again and again in letters to close friends of them both, she continued to play her rather difficult role with discretion, with a good deal of wit and humour, and with remarkable understanding and judgment both in the world of affairs and in the world of literature.

She had shared with him all the secrets of his literary activities from the beginning. She must have been one of the very few among his friends who really knew the full scope of his art and the variety of his literary powers. She had been allowed to share day by day in his experiences in the world of political intrigue, in his personal friendships and enmities, and in his comments as a very close observer on all the public events which took place during those last years of the reign of Anne. And she had been the first to share in the disappointment and the delays and then the final achievement of his long-promised preferment. When she heard of that it must have seemed to her that after all the comedy was working out to a pleasant ending, and that they would be together in Ireland for the rest of their lives, as he had so often protested that he wished to be. He had been living on the verge of the society of a court, he had been close friends with the leading men and women of the day, he had demanded that ladies of birth and fashion and even the reigning beauties of the hour should make overtures to him; and he had reported to her with the fullest freedom all his triumphs, and kept for her his secret comments of amusement, of scorn, or of pleasure.

But there was one episode which was quite different from the rest, which threatened to break up the play, or to turn it into a farce, or worse still to change everything into romantic tragedy. It had started innocently enough, and had been indeed a pleasant relaxation during the strain of Swift's struggle to hold the Ministry together, and prepare the public to accept the peace that was being offered them. He had grown interested in a promising girl, the daughter of a friendly neighbour, a Mrs. Vanhomrigh in whose household he had come to feel much at ease. He had found in Missessy (as he called her) the promise of wit and intelligence, and had been tempted to guide her reading and improve her mind, to bring her up as he had brought up Stella fifteen years earlier. But she was of a very different temperament; and she failed him. He had not begun her training soon enough; he could not cure her romantic disease. Nevertheless when he went back to London in the fall of 1713, after taking the oaths as Dean of St. Patrick's, Dublin, he made a determined effort to force this situation also into the stuff of comedy. The new Dean, who had hurried back to Windsor to be near the court, set to work first to write for Esther Vanhomrigh a dramatic poem which was to be perhaps his best work in verse, entitled *Cadenus and Vanessa*.

It was his foolish verse-writing that had caused this trouble; he would try this same method to exorcise it. He first erects a very elaborate and unreal classical structure from which emerges Vanessa in her bloom

> . . . like *Atalanta's* Star,
> But rarely seen, and seen from far:
> In a new World with Caution stept,
> Watch'd all the Company she kept,
> Well knowing from the Books she read
> What dangerous Paths young Virgins tread;
> Wou'd seldom at the Park appear,
> Nor saw the Play-House twice a Year;
> Yet not incurious, was inclin'd
> To know the Converse of Mankind.[14]

She naturally makes a bad impression on the fashionable fops and glittering dames, and boldly showed her disapproval of them.

> With silent Scorn *Vanessa* sat,
> Scarce list'ning to their idle Chat;
> Further than sometimes by a Frown,
> When they grew pert, to pull them down.
> At last she spitefully was bent
> To try their Wisdom's full Extent;
> And said, she valu'd nothing less
> Than Titles, Figure, Shape, and Dress;
> That, Merit should be chiefly plac'd
> In Judgment, Knowledge, Wit, and Taste;

[14] *Poems*, p. 696.

> And these, she offer'd to dispute,
> Alone distinguish'd Man from Brute:
> That, present Times have no Pretence
> To Virtue, in the Noblest Sense,
> By *Greeks* and *Romans* understood,
> To perish for our Country's Good.[15]

And here the portrait is neither fanciful nor unreal, for it has been pointed out that details are taken by Swift from a letter she wrote to him on June 23, 1713, a few months before—was it to mock at her sententiousness?

> Lord! how much we differ from the ancients, who used to sacrifice everything for the good of their commonwealth; but now our greatest men will at any time give up their country out of a pique, and that for nothing.[16]

Cadenus is at first delighted with her progress under his tutelage but becomes alarmed at a sudden change in her when she shows signs of weariness and distraction. He is modest enough to think she may be bored with him, and offers to leave her alone, thinking that naturally she would rather shine in the world. But she turns upon him with disdain, and reminds him of his own teaching, which had lifted her above vulgar forms and common standards:

> I knew by what you said and writ,
> How dang'rous Things were Men of Wit,
> You caution'd me against their Charms,
> But never gave me equal Arms:
> Your Lessons found the weakest Part,
> Aim'd at the Head, but reach'd the Heart.
>
> .   .   .   .   .
>
> *Cadenus* answers every End,
> The Book, the Author, and the Friend.
> The utmost her Desires will reach,
> Is but to learn what he can teach;
> His Converse is a System, fit
> Alone to fill up all her Wit;

[15] Ibid., p. 697.
[16] *Vanessa and Her Correspondence with Swift*, ed. A. M. Freeman, 1921, pp. 84-5.

> While ev'ry Passion of her Mind
> In him is center'd and confin'd.[17]

The rest of the story is told in two different versions—one a comedy in verse, the other a romantic tale in tragic prose. The first is Swift's account, in which he successfully maintains the tone of comedy to the end.

He recognizes that he is bound to be a victim of the jokes of the town:

> The Town wou'd swear he had betray'd,
> By Magick Spells, the harmless Maid;
> And ev'ry Beau wou'd have his Jokes,
> That Scholars were like other Folks:
> That when Platonick Flights were over,
> The Tutor turn'd a mortal Lover.
> So tender of the Young and Fair?
> It shew'd a true Paternal Care—
> Five thousand Guineas in her Purse?
> The Doctor might have fancy'd worse.—[18]

Nevertheless he is flattered at being preferred before a crowd of beaux; he cannot help approving her for such a judicious taste. Why should he not offer her in return his friendship?

> A constant, rational Delight,
> On Virtue's Basis fixed to last,
> When Love's Allurements long are past;[19]

But she will have nothing to do with such sublime conceits, and sets to work to be his tutor.

> Tho' she already can discern,
> Her Scholar is not apt to learn;
> Or wants Capacity to reach
> The Science she designs to teach:
> Wherein his Genius was below
> The Skill of ev'ry common Beau;[20]

[17] *Poems*, pp. 706, 709.
[18] Ibid., p. 707.
[19] Ibid., p. 711.
[20] Ibid., p. 712.

Then just at this moment when there is danger that a passionate outburst might disturb the comedy, he breaks off his tale, and leaves the
reader with a shrug and a smile:

> But what Success *Vanessa* met,
> Is to the World a Secret yet:
> Whether the Nymph, to please her Swain,
> Talks in a high Romantick Strain;
> Or whether he at last descends
> To like with less Seraphick Ends;
> Or, to compound the Business, whether
> They temper Love and Books together;
> Must never to Mankind be told,
> Nor shall the conscious Muse unfold.[21]

During the next ten years the story continued to unfold itself in a
series of letters, in which Swift struggles to keep the same light tone,
but is driven by her increasing emotional violence either into warnings or anger, or sometimes into tenderness and pity. He had tried to
fit her for the way of the world, to bring her up, like Stella, to play
her part with discretion and with wit and humour. But she failed
him. She could play only a tragic role, and from her insupportable
misery and solitude she pours out her agony in words which inevitably
bring to our remembrance the passionate lament of Eloisa for Abelard:

> I was born with violent passions, which terminate all in one—that un-
> expressible passion I have for you. . . .
> I firmly believe, could I know your thoughts (which no human
> creature is capable of guessing at, because never any one living thought
> like you), I should find that you have often in a rage wished me re-
> ligious, hoping then I should have paid my devotions to Heaven. But
> that would not spare you, for was I an enthusiast, still you'd be the
> deity I should worship. But what marks are there of a deity but what
> you are to be known by? You are present everywhere; your dear image
> is always before my eyes; sometimes you strike me with that prodigious
> awe, I tremble with fear; at other times a charming compassion shines
> through your countenance, which revives my soul.[22]

Even Swift falters occasionally in his role. In the midst of advice

[21] Ibid., p. 712.
[22] *Vanessa and her Correspondence with Swift*, p. 129.

he gives her to take more care of her health, by company and exercise, he gravely and quietly speaks of his constant affection.

> Cadenus assures me he continues to esteem and love and value you above all things, and so will do to the end of his life, but at the same time entreats that you would not make yourself or him unhappy by imaginations.[23]

Stella alone, if we may believe the tradition, succeeded in maintaining the tone of comedy, even during that episode. At least, afterwards, when the poem was published, and someone said that Vanessa must have been very attractive to have inspired so fine a poem, she replied that it was well known that the Dean could write wittily even about a Broomstick.

The correspondence between Swift and Stella in those same years was probably not very considerable, though we hear of letters written to her during his visits to friends in the country. None of them are known to have survived. But there are some autographs in Stella's handwriting, which are a positive witness to the steady continuance of their close companionship, and his reliance on her judgment, and his trust in her critical ability, which he later acknowledged in such extravagant terms.

> She had a true taste of wit and good sense, both in poetry and prose, and was a perfect good critic of style: neither was it easy to find a more proper or impartial judge, whose advice an author might better rely on, if he intended to send a thing into the world, provided it was on a subject that came within the compass of her knowledge. Yet, perhaps, she was sometimes too severe, which is a safe and pardonable error.[24]

One manuscript is an early draft of the beginning of *An Enquiry into the Behaviour of the Queen's last Ministry*, which they evidently started together, working perhaps with the help of detailed information recorded in the *Journal*.[25]

The best of the Stella autographs are contained in a small quarto volume, into which she had copied eighteen of Swift's poems, the last being the verses written for her birthday in March 1722. The volume

[23] Ibid., p. 132.
[24] *Prose*, V, 231.
[25] (*Ms. of Enquiry*) *Prose*, VIII, Frontispiece, & pp. v, xxxiv.

is in the Duke of Bedford's Library at Woburn Abbey, and it contains a note by the fourth Duke explaining how it came into his possession:

> This Manuscript was given me, by Sr. Archibald Acheson at Bath November 2nd 1768. It was given to his Father, by the Dean of St. Patrick, and is of the hand writing of Stella, Mrs. Johnson.[26]

Sir Harold Williams used it in preparing his edition of Swift's *Poems,* and in the second volume gives a facsimile of a couple of its pages.

It is useless to conjecture why Stella did not continue to copy into her book any poems after 1722, not even the verses she received regularly for her birthday. Perhaps she did not like the trick Swift played upon her in the long poem, addressed *To Stella, Who Collected and Transcribed his Poems,* in which he challenged her to set down in her own hand the only criticism that he ever made of her. The date has been given as 1720; but it seems to me more likely to have been written later, in 1722 or 1723, either just before or just after the death of Vanessa, when there was a good deal of unpleasant gossip in Dublin, which may well have roused Stella's anger. The poem begins with compliments and with an acknowledgment of her share in any merit his poems may have; for they had been prompted by her friendship. But now he has one thing to complain of, a weakness which, he implies, has been exposed by accident:

> *Stella,* when you these Lines transcribe,
> Lest you should take them for a Bribe,
> Resolv'd to mortify your Pride,
> I'll here expose your weaker Side.
>
> Your Spirits kindle to a Flame,
> Mov'd with the lightest Touch of Blame,
> And when a Friend in Kindness tries
> To shew you where your Error lies,
> Conviction does but more incense;
> Perverseness is your whole Defence:
> Truth, Judgment, Wit, give Place to Spite,
> Regardless both of Wrong and Right.
> Your Virtues, all suspended, wait

[26] *Poems,* pp. l-li.

> Till Time hath open'd Reason's Gate:
> And what is worse, your Passion bends
> Its Force against your nearest Friends;
> Which Manners, Decency, and Pride,
> Have taught you from the World to hide:[27]

There can be no doubt that the intention of the poem was to turn aside the full force of her anger, which had blazed up dangerously against him:

> Yet when I find your Passions rise,
> And Anger sparkling in your Eyes,
> I grieve those Spirits should be spent,
> For nobler Ends by Nature meant.[28]

He pursues his theme until we wonder whether he will not spoil it all by this persistent though restrained censure; but at the end he turns it back dextrously into the tone of comedy:

> Say, *Stella,* when you copy next,
> Will you keep strictly to the Text?
> Dare you let these Reproaches stand,
> And to your Failing set your Hand?
> Or if these Lines your Anger fire,
> Shall they in baser Flames expire?
> Whene'er they burn, if burn they must,
> They'll prove my Accusation just.[29]

Stella did not copy out this poem, but apparently she did not burn it; for after her death, Swift wrote from England, where he was staying with Pope, to ask Sheridan to send him a copy of it to print in the volume of *Miscellanies,* which was published in 1727.

If there was a quarrel between them, it was made up at the end of the summer of 1723, when Swift returned from his travels in the south of Ireland, and Stella came back to Dublin after spending the summer with Charles Ford at Wood-Park. For about that time he wrote a gay amusing poem, in which he pictures Stella's distress, when the fatal day of October 3rd arrived, and she was obliged to pack

[27] Ibid., p. 730.
[28] Ibid., p. 731.
[29] Ibid., p. 732.

up and leave behind the splendours of Wood-Park for her own miserable quarters in Dublin. It is really a welcome back to Dublin, disguised under the tone of raillery, and hidden beneath all the details of the little comic drama which Swift imagines.

First he describes the splendour and magnificence of Ford's hospitality:

> She look'd on Partridges with scorn,
> Except they tasted of the Corn:
> A Haunch of Ven'son made her sweat,
> Unless it had the right *Fumette*.
> Don *Carlos* earnestly would beg,
> Dear Madam, try this Pigeon's Leg;
> Was happy when he could prevail
> To make her only touch a Quail.[30]

Then in a manner reminiscent of the peculiar play of fancy which gives such vivid reality to some of the episodes in *Gulliver's Travels,* which Swift was writing at this time, he describes her return to Dublin:

> The Coachman stopt, she lookt, and swore
> The Rascal had mistook the Door:
> At coming in you saw her stoop;
> The Entry brusht against her Hoop:
> Each Moment rising in her Airs,
> She curst the narrow winding Stairs:
> Began a Thousand Faults to spy;
> The Ceiling hardly six Foot high;
> The smutty Wainscot full of Cracks,
> And half the Chairs with broken Backs:[31]

However, to keep up her spirits she invites her Dublin friends to sup and dine, until after a week's lavish expense, she has run through all her savings, and is ready to return to her former ways—"Small Beer, a Herring, and the Dean."

That is the whole story; but at the end, to avoid the possibility of offence, he explains that it is all a jest, and insists on drawing a moral from it:

[30] Ibid., p. 750.
[31] Ibid., p. 751.

> Yet, when you sigh to leave *Wood-Park*,
> The Scene, the Welcome, and the Spark,
>
> .   .   .   .   .
>
> We think you quite mistake the Case;
> The Virtue lies not in the Place:
> For though my Raillery were true,
> A Cottage is *Wood-Park* with you.[32]

There are several copies of this poem in Ford's handwriting, and
it has been suggested that it may well have been written at Wood-
Park, where Swift had probably joined the party just before they
were to leave. Ford was Swift's closest friend, and one of the very few
who were well acquainted with both Stella and Vanessa.

The following Christmas they were all in the country again, but
under quite different circumstances, staying with Sheridan at Quilca,
though Swift wrote very cheerfully about it to Ford after their return
—they had had "good Fare, warm Rooms with Mirth: all of us well
in going, residing and returning, without any Accident or other offence than abundance of Dirt and Wit." The place is described with
loving vigor in a poem written by Swift later, entitled *"To Quilca, a
Country House in no very good Repair, where the supposed Author,
and some of his Friends, spent a Summer, in the Year 1725."*[33]

But it was Sheridan who, on the occasion of this Christmas visit,
wrote a long account in verse of all their various activities, contrasting
the glories of the former wit and courtier with his present tasks, and
his present helpers.

> O what a mighty fall is here!
> From set'ling Governments & Thrones
> To splitting Rocks & piling Stones
> Instead of Bolinbroke & Anna,
> Shane Tunelly & Bryan Granna,
> Oxford & Ormond he supplies
> In ev'ry Irish Teague he spies;
> So far forgetting his old Station
> He seems to like their Conversation.
> Conforming to the tatter'd Rabble
> He learns their Irish Tongue to gabble,

[32] Ibid., p. 752.
[33] Ibid., pp. 1034-5.

And what our Anger more provokes
He's pleas'd with their insipid jokes.
Then turns & asks them who does lack a
Good Plug, or Pipe full of tobacca,
All cry they want, to ev'ry Man
He gives extravagant a Span.
Thus are they grown more fond than ever,
And he is highly in their Favour.
    Bright Stella Quilcah's greatest Pride
For them he scorns, & lays aside;
And Sheridan is left alone
All day to gape & stretch and groan,
While grumbling poor complaining Dingly
Is left to Care & Trouble singly.

    At Night, right loath to quit the Park,
His work just ended by the Dark
With all his Pioneers he comes,
To make more Work for Whisks & Brooms.
Then, seated in an elbow-chair,
To take a Nap he does prepare,
While two fair Damsells from the Lawns
Lull him asleep with soft Cronawns.
    Thus are his Days in Delving spent,
His Nights in Musick & Content.
He seems to gain by his Distress
His Friends are more, his Honours Less.[34]

I make no apology for quoting at length from these trifling verses, because I think they are little known, and yet they are important evidence of a constantly prevailing tone of easy comedy which runs through all the record even of the latter part of Swift's life in Ireland, so often obscured by being entirely seen in the light of some savage or cynical phrase, sufficiently violent to have caught the attention of biographers and critics. And I would emphasize that these trifles belong exactly to the years when he was writing *Gulliver's Travels*, of which the first complete draft was finished during the summer of 1725, which Swift spent at Quilca. And at the same time, or earlier, Swift and Stella were amusing themselves together by reading a vast

[34] Ibid., pp. 1040-1.

amount of travel literature which was much in vogue, "abundance of
trash," as he had called it in a letter to Charles Ford, of July 1722; but
the best he picked out for Stella's reading, for he says of her:

> She had read carefully all the best books of travels, which serve to open
> and enlarge the mind.[35]

She was, moreover, not wholly unprepared for some of the experiences
Gulliver met with, for she had had some training in the literature of
satire. She read French easily and Swift had bought for her a French
translation of Lucian when he was in London; later he had brought
back a considerable library from England when he settled at the
Deanery. He had also proposed to equip her with a microscope, an
instrument not without its effect upon some of the details of the
earlier part of *Gulliver's Travels*.

> Never—he says—was any of her sex born with better gifts of the mind,
> or more improved them by reading and conversation. Yet her memory
> was not of the best [this defect she shared with him], and was impaired
> in the latter years of her life. But I cannot call to mind that I ever once
> heard her make a wrong judgment of persons, books, or affairs. Her
> advice was always the best, and with the greatest freedom, mixed with
> the greatest decency. She had a gracefulness, somewhat more than
> human, in every motion, word, and action. Never was so happy a con-
> junction of civility, freedom, easiness, and sincerity.[36]

We are reminded of the ideal which Steele had in mind when he
discusses in the *Tatler*, No. 42, the difference between the women
characters in the comedies of Shakespeare's time and those in Congreve; and he draws the conclusion that in the earlier age women had
not the same freedom in conversation, and their characters were only
that they were mothers, sisters, daughters, and wives. That is to say,
they were dependents, not equals in a free society. He admits that this
new freedom was responsible for all sorts of folly and affectation, as
ironically indicated in this passage:

> There were not then among the Ladies, shining Wits, Politicians, Vir-
> tuosae, Free-Thinkers, and Disputants; nay, there was then hardly such
> a creature ev'n as a Coquet.[37]

[35] *Prose*, V, 231.
[36] Ibid., pp. 228-9.
[37] *Tatler*, 1710, I, 345.

But on the other hand it was the mark of a new sort of civilization, with new possibilities. It could produce such a character as the Lady Elizabeth Hastings, who "adds to the Severity and Privacy of the last Age all the Freedom and Ease of this."[38]

Swift is more precise in describing Stella's conversation. It was an art which he had studied carefully for many years, though he did not publish his treatise on *Polite Conversation* until ten years after the death of Stella. If we may accept his own statement in a letter to Pope written June 12, 1732, that he had begun it over twenty-eight years ago, and a similar calculation which he made in the Preface, he must have begun to collect his observations quite early in the century, and could have drawn his material from his own very varied experiences in all kinds of society. No one has ever so patiently and scrupulously examined the fatuities and sillinesses of common chat, and no one could have been more sensitive to every deficiency in the art. Nevertheless he has nothing but praise for her conversation. She was entirely free from pedantry and ostentation, so that some were disappointed at their first meeting with her, and would say that they found her like other women.

> But wise men, through all her modesty, whatever they discoursed on, could easily observe that she understood them very well, by the judgment shewn in her observations, as well as in her questions.[39]

One particular quality, Swift notes, she admired in Addison and shared with him:

> when she saw any of the company very warm in a wrong opinion, she was more inclined to confirm them in it, than oppose them. The excuse she commonly gave, when her friends asked the reason, was, that it prevented noise, and saved time.[40]

This is the very triumph of the comic spirit, the product of wit and urbanity; here is the wisdom that will not strive or cry, but in its own way is able to make strife and anger contemptible. And here, on the other hand, are the positive virtues of kindliness and patience and understanding, by the exercise of which in a civilized society men and

[38] Ibid., p. 346.
[39] *Prose*, V, 236.
[40] Ibid., p. 235.

women may live together in mutual esteem, and cultivate the delights
of friendship.

> She never had the least absence of mind in conversation, nor given to
> interruption, or appeared eager to put in her word, by waiting impa-
> tiently until another had done. She spoke in a most agreeable voice, in
> the plainest words, never hesitating, except out of modesty before new
> faces, where she was somewhat reserved: nor, among her nearest
> friends, ever spoke much at a time. . . .
>
> But she rather chose men for her companions, the usual topics of
> ladies' discourse being such as she had little knowledge of, and less
> relish. Yet no man was upon the rack to entertain her, for she easily de-
> scended to any thing that was innocent and diverting.[41]

Their friendship lasted more than thirty years; and then, in his
sixtieth year she failed him, and left him to go on with the comedy
alone. If he had not been treated thus unfairly, he would perhaps
never have been so intensely aware of the violence (it is his own
word) of the friendship he had allowed to grow. We have still to
examine how this strong feeling found its expression in the form of
sentiment.

[41] Ibid., pp. 230, 235.

SENTIMENT

It is a coincidence which I had overlooked until reminded last week by the members of my seminar at Smith College that this day, on which I am to give my last lecture on Stella, is March 13, the date of her birthday, so often celebrated in her later years by Swift with the gift of these verses, which we are considering.

Under these circumstances I cannot well begin this lecture in any other way than by reading to you a few lines of the verses written for her last birthday, March 13, 1727.

> This Day, whate'er the Fates decree,
> Shall still be kept with Joy by me:
> This Day then, let us not be told,
> That you are sick, and I grown old,
> Nor think on our approaching Ills,
> And talk of Spectacles and Pills;
> To morrow will be Time enough
> To hear such mortifying Stuff.
> Yet, since from Reason may be brought
> A better and more pleasing Thought,
> Which can in spite of all Decays,
> Support a few remaining Days:
> From not the gravest of Divines,
> Accept for once some serious Lines.[1]

I hope, too, that the reading of these lines will save me a great deal of explanation as to the topic of this lecture, which I have called

[1] *Poems*, pp. 763-4.

sentiment. For I am using the term simply to describe the feeling and the tone of this poem, and of all those other passages in which Swift writes to Stella or about Stella in this mood, when "not the gravest of Divines" drops his tone of satire or raillery or irony or mere fun, and offers her instead "some serious lines."

I use the term sentiment also because, in his grave way, and with the utmost restraint, Swift nevertheless succeeds in charging with emotion such simple bare rhymes, and in using the ordinary forms of conventional prose to express feelings of tenderness and affection.

I have hitherto dealt with qualities in his work which in relation to Stella have, I think, not been sufficiently noticed. I have reserved for our consideration now this quality which has been more frequently commented on, as something in him delicate and rare, like flowers growing out of a rock or blooming among the snows on a high mountain.

But do not be alarmed. I am not going to talk about the relic which, according to Sir Walter Scott, was in the possession of Dr. Tuke of St. Stephen's Green, an envelope, containing a lock of hair, on which was inscribed in Swift's hand "only a woman's hair." Too much has been written about it already. Nor am I going to do more than warn you against the inexcusably mawkish sentimentality of that perverse and misguided purveyor of false pathos, William Makepeace Thackeray, whose fraudulent reputation as a critic of the eighteenth century I feel it my bounden duty to expose whenever I have an opportunity.

Listen to this, for instance, from a mere footnote:

One may say that the book of Swift's life opens at places kept by these blighted flowers![2]

and this, from the text of his lecture on Swift:

Who hasn't in his mind an image of Stella? Who does not love her? Fair and tender creature: pure and affectionate heart! Boots it to you, now that you have been at rest for a hundred and twenty years, not divided in death from the cold heart which caused yours, whilst it beat, such faithful pangs of love and grief—boots it to you now, that the whole world loves and deplores you? Scarce any man, I believe, ever thought of that grave, that did not cast a flower of pity on it, and write over it a sweet epitaph. Gentle lady, so lovely, so loving, so unhappy!

[2] *Works of Thackeray*, ed. George Saintsbury, 1908, XIII, p. 497n.

you have had countless champions; millions of manly hearts mourning for you. From generation to generation we take up the fond tradition of your beauty; we watch and follow your tragedy, your bright morning love and purity, your constancy, your grief, your sweet martyrdom. We know your legend by heart. You are one of the saints of English story.[3]

It is this kind of criticism, and there is a lot more of it, in equally extravagant language, which makes it almost impossible for anyone to write normally on the subject of the *Journal to Stella*. The only way to get free from the effects of it is to go back and read again the poems, the Journal and the other letters, and gradually to regain one's composure under the influence of their quiet gravity.

The earliest record we have of Swift's regard for Stella is a passage, of a grave serious sort, in a letter which he wrote from London to the Rev. William Tisdall, who was at that time proposing to marry Stella himself. Swift writes in the manner of her guardian, as one knowing them both well, and able to speak with complete freedom.

. . . my conjecture is, that you think I obstructed your insinuations, to please my own, and that my intentions were the same with yours; in answer to all which, I will, upon my conscience and honour, tell you the naked truth. First, I think I have said to you before, that, if my fortunes and humour served me to think of that state, I should certainly, among all persons on earth, make your choice; because I never saw that person whose conversation I entirely valued but hers; this was the utmost I ever gave way to. And, secondly, I must assure you sincerely, that this regard of mine never once entered into my head to be an impediment to you: . . . nor shall any consideration of my own misfortune of losing so good a friend and companion as her, prevail on me, against her interest and settlement in the world, since it is held so necessary and convenient a thing for ladies to marry; and that time takes off from the lustre of virgins in all other eyes but mine.

. . . though it hath come in my way to converse with persons of the first rank, and of that sex, more than is usual to men of my level, and of our function; yet I have nowhere met with a humour, a wit, or conversation so agreeable, a better portion of good sense, or a truer judgement of men and things. . . .[4]

He wrote that careful judgment of Stella, when she was twenty-

[3] Ibid., pp. 497-8.
[4] Corr., I, 46-7.

three, just at the time when he was busy preparing for the publication
in London of *A Tale of a Tub*, in his thirty-seventh year. On his next
visit to England three years later, the ladies also spent part of a winter
in London; but we have no record of that episode, and the letters that
we know he wrote to them after their return to Dublin have all been
lost.

Then, during his long separation from them from September 1710
until June 1713, we have the record of the sixty-five letters, commonly known as the *Journal to Stella*. I have already had occasion to
refer to the ease and familiarity he maintains throughout, and the
intimacy of a perfectly free conversation between them. Even in those
early letters, which we possess only after they have been clipped and
pruned by their first editor, there is among the more arid matters of
fact and comment upon the ministers and their policies, a good deal
of affectionate pleasantry at the expense of the St. Mary's ladies; and
out of this persiflage breaks from time to time a flash of sentiment, a
feeling of a deeper tone, even though the actual expression is never
allowed to become emotional.

> And so you kept Presto's little birth-day, I warrant: would to God I
> had been at the health, rather than here, where I have no manner of
> pleasure, nothing but eternal business upon my hands. I shall grow
> wise in time; but no more of that: only I say Amen with my heart and
> vitals, that we may never be asunder again ten days together while
> poor Presto lives.[5]

But that is quickly dismissed as "splenetick talk."

During that first Christmas spent away from them in London, there
is a constant sense of her very vivid presence with him:

> I think I am bewitched to write so much in a morning to you, little
> MD. Let me go, will you? and I'll come again to-night in a fine clean
> sheet of paper; but I can nor will stay no longer now; no, I won't, for
> all your wheedling: no, no, look off, don't smile at me, and say, Pray,
> pray, Presto, write a little more. Ah! you're a wheedling slut, you be
> so. Nay, but prithee turn about, and let me go, do: 'tis a good girl,
> and do.
>   . . . I walked home for exercise, and at eleven got to bed, and all

[5] *Journal*, January 1, 1710-11, p. 85.

the while I was undressing my self, there was I speaking monkey things in air, just as if MD had been by, and did not recollect myself till I got into bed.[6]

It is really the same mood, so differently expressed, as that in Sidney's verses demanding news of his Stella:

> When I demaund of *Phenix Stella's* state,
> You say forsooth, you left her well of late.
> O God, thinke you that satisfies my care?
> I would know whether she did sit or walke,
> How cloth'd, how waited on, sighd she or smilde,
> Whereof, with whom, how often did she talke,
> With what pastime, time's journey she beguilde,
> If her lips daignd to sweeten my poore name.
> Say all, and all well sayd, still say the same.[7]

This attitude of devotion, of humility, which exalts her to the state of a heavenly being, journeying for awhile amid mere mortals, that is to say, the language of the courts of love, is changed in Swift to the affectionate tones of household speech, the intimate enquiries of a familiar friend. As he reads over their letter, his imagination fills out the scene:

Now, madam Stella, what say you? you ride every day; I know that already, sirrah; and if you rid every day for a twelvemonth, you would be still better and better . . . O Lord, how hasty we are, Stella can't stay writing and writing; she must write and go a cock-horse, pray now. Well; but the horses are not come to the door; the fellow can't find the bridle; your stirrup is broken; where did you put the whips, Dingley? Marg'et, where have you laid Mrs. Johnson's ribband to tie about her? reach me my mask: sup up this before you go. So, so, a gallop, a gallop: sit fast, sirrah, and don't ride hard upon the stones.—Well, now Stella is gone, tell me, Dingley, is she a good girl? and what news is that you are to tell me? . . . O madam Stella, welcome home; was it pleasant riding? did your horse stumble? how often did the man light to settle your stirrup? ride nine miles? faith you have galloped indeed. Well, but where's the fine thing you promised me? I have been a good boy, ask Dingley else. I believe you did not meet the fine-thing-man: faith you

---

[6] Ibid., January 4, 1710-11, p. 90.
[7] *Astrophil and Stella*, 92. See *Poems of Sidney*, p. 225.

are a cheat. So you'll see Raymond and his wife in town. Faith that riding to Laracor gives me short sighs, as well as you. All the days I have passed here, have been dirt to those.[8]

There is nothing left of the formality of prose or even of normal conversation here; and it may be that it is this sense of being inside such defences, overhearing things unawares that adds to the effect of what we read. As we go on reading even the barest skeleton of a record of where he had been, where dined and who was there, it becomes a symbol of his need for this daily meeting with them:

> As hope saved, nothing gives Presto any sort of dream of happiness but a letter now and then from his own dearest MD. I love the expectation of it, and when it does not come, I comfort myself, that I have it yet to be happy with. Yes, faith, and when I write to MD, I am happy too; it is just as if methinks you were here and I prating to you, and telling you where I have been: Well, says you, Presto, come, where have you been to-day? come let's hear now. And so then I answer; etc. etc.[9]

He had promised to write something every day, so that they would be always "in conversation" with one another. Perhaps she would be pleased to know how he passes his time in her absence. But,

> I am thinking what scurvy company I shall be to MD when I come back: they know everything of me already: I will tell you no more, or I shall have nothing to say, no story to tell, nor any kind of thing. . . . What shall Presto do for prittle prattle to entertain MD?[10]

Thus far I have quoted from the earlier letters of which we have only the printed text as edited by Mr. Deane Swift of Goodrich in 1768. It is evident that he allowed himself a good deal of liberty in preparing the original manuscript for the printer. But of the last twenty-five letters the original manuscript is in the British Museum, and as close a reproduction of it as is possible in type is easily available in the Everyman edition. Even so we cannot read it exactly as it came into Stella's hands, for in a good many places the manuscript itself has been obliterated, so that some words are entirely blotted out.

---

[8] *Journal,* June 30, 1711, pp. 189-90.
[9] Ibid., January 16, 1710-11, pp. 98-9.
[10] Ibid., October 9 & 13, 1710, pp. 24, 27.

Emil Pons has indeed argued in a very charming paper[11] that some of these lighter erasures (such as occur in other manuscripts of Swift which could not have been tampered with later), which consist of a series of lightly drawn interlocking circles, covering the word without making it totally illegible, were in the original letters, and were a kind of intimate play which Swift indulged in at the time of writing. It is true that the manuscript was written in a very tiny script, tightly packed into the large sheets without margins, as though not to invite inspection, if by chance it should ever be opened at the post office. And Swift remarks in an early letter:

> Methinks when I write plain, I do not know how, but we are not alone, all the world can see us. A bad scrawl is so snug, it looks like a PMD [i.e. a monogram of the three initials which he uses for their pet names].[12]

It is further all written in a sort of telegraphic style, with every possible kind of abbreviation. For instance, *You* is always indicated by a flourish that looks like a *y; the* looks like a *t* or *te,* and names and titles are generally given in the shortest possible abbreviations. It is an almost insoluble problem for an editor, even now, to know what to do with such a text; especially as the state of the manuscript makes a complete photographic facsimile impossible.

I have spoken of this matter of the text here, because I think it has some bearing on the impression which we get of the so-called "little language." In the manuscript itself with all its abbreviations and its erasures and its partial illegibility, it is much less surprising suddenly to come upon phrases written in a sort of nursery code, followed by strings of letters, MD FW Me or Lele, Leles.

It is extremely difficult to say anything about the little language without running into the danger of being either very solemn or very stupid; and the chief difficulty in a lecture is that it is quite impossible to quote it without a ludicrous effect. The best one can do is to quote Swift's remark about it:

> Do you know what? when I am writing in our language I make up my mouth just as if I was speaking it. I caught myself at it just now.[13]

---

[11] "Du Nouveau sur le *Journal à Stella," Études anglaises,* No. 3, May 1937.
[12] *Journal,* November 3, 1710, p. 43.
[13] Ibid., March 7, 1710-11, p. 127.

It is obvious enough that it was for him an escape from his public life
of struggle and political intrigue, into that snug retreat which he had
made for himself in their company. And there in his lodgings in London, as he writes morning and evening, he refreshes himself with
those pleasing memories. When his room is very cold on a winter's
morning, before his fire has burnt up, he begins his letter with an
exclamation—Starvation, starvation, and a series of sounds, which
accompany a shivering and a rubbing of the hands. And he falls back
happily upon remembered associations:

> Don't you remember I used to come into your chamber, and turn Stella
> out of her chair, and rake up the fire in a cold morning, and cry, Uth,
> uth, uth? etc.[14]

It is just the same with his longing for his country cottage at Laracor:

> Oh, that we were at Laracor this fine day! the willows begin to peep,
> and the quicks to bud. My dream's out: I was a-dreamed last night that
> I eat ripe cherries.—And now they begin to catch the pikes, etc.[15]

Perhaps it is just a necessary relief from the comedy of civilized society, as Virginia Woolf remarked:

> In any highly civilised society disguise plays so large a part, politeness
> is so essential, that to throw off the ceremonies and conventions and
> talk a 'little language' for one or two to understand, is as much a neces-
> sity as a breath of air in a hot room. The reserved, the powerful, the
> admired, have the most need of such a refuge. Swift himself found it
> so. The proudest of men coming home from the company of great men
> who praised him, of lovely women who flattered him, from intrigue and
> politics, put all that aside, settled himself comfortably in bed, pursed
> his severe lips into baby language and prattled to his 'two monkies', his
> 'dear Sirrahs', his 'naughty rogues' on the other side of the Irish
> Channel.[16]

Even though he tells them all that he is doing in such detail, and
fills his letters with news of public affairs as well as his own part in
them, he does not seem to wish them to share wholly in his public
life. He professes to find it ridiculous when he catches himself talk-

[14] Ibid., January 22, 1710-11, pp. 101-2.
[15] Ibid., March 19, 1710-11, p. 134.
[16] Virginia Woolf, *The Common Reader*, 2nd Series, 1935, p. 67.

ing politics to them, and boasts that he never knew what their politics were:

> I think it pretty extrdy, & a great Complment to y; & I believe never 3 People conversed so much with so little Politicks.[17]

And he is curiously angry about their interest in the premature gossip about his preferment. When that letter came, he tells them he just read it and then sealed it up again, and would not read it again at least for a twelvemonth. Though the town was full of such talk and the Court vexed him by congratulating him without reason, he seemed to resent more deeply their talking glibly of it as if the thing were really done. "You might be sure," he says, "I would have let you know as soon as it was done." It was not until six months later at the beginning of February 1713, that he had anything to tell them on the subject. The death of the Bishop of Dromore had opened a number of possibilities in Ireland. First he removes their fears that now he might not want preferment in Ireland.

> I did not write to Dr. Coghill that I would have nothing in Ireld; but that I was solliciting nothing any where, & that is true: I have named Dr. Stearn to Ld Tr, Ld Bolingbr and D. Ormd for a Bishoprick: and I did it heartily; I know not what will come of it; but I tell y as a great Secret, that I have made D. Ormd promise me to recommend nobody till he tells me; and this for some Reasons too long to mention.[18]

A month later nothing has been done and he is promising her fiercely that if he is not provided for he will pack up bag and baggage and return. Finally it is settled and the warrants signed and he knows that the news will give her pleasure.

> I suppose MD is malicious enough to be glad & rathr have it than Wells. . . . Pray write to me a good humored Lettr immediatly, let it be ever so short.[19]

The verses addressed to Stella belong to a later time after he had been settled in Dublin for some years and continue until just before her death in 1728. They are naturally less informal than the *Journal* but were also written in the first place for her pleasure and for the

[17] *Journal*, March 7, 1712-13, p. 418.
[18] Ibid., February 4, 1713, pp. 404-5.
[19] Ibid., April 23, 1713, p. 440.

amusement of their circle of close friends. Nevertheless, Swift himself allowed them to be published; and they appeared in London just
before her death in a volume of *Miscellanies* which also contained
Cadenus and Vanessa and a number of pieces by Pope.

I have spoken of some of them already. Here I shall consider only
a few further examples in which the mood is serious and in which the
lines, however easy and conversational, carry some weight of sentiment. For instance, he compares her to a favorite old Inn where the
sign has grown decayed but which in spite of competition continues
to attract its old clients.

> Now, this is Stella's Case in Fact;
> An Angel's Face, a little crack't;
> (Could Poets or could Painters fix
> How Angels look at thirty six)
> This drew us in at first to find
> In such a Form an Angel's Mind
> And ev'ry Virtue now supplyes
> The fainting Rays of Stella's Eyes:[20]

In this kind of complimentary verse it would be embarrassing to
find too elaborate politeness, or any extravagance of feeling. Commonplace is more safely avoided by a touch of humour, or by a
simplicity which gives the impression of unstudied ease. And this is
the outstanding quality of what Swift called his serious lines. He
confesses that he is past his prime for poetry, even as she is past the
fitting age to inspire him to write:

> At Fifty six, if this be true,
> Am I a Poet fit for you?
> Or at the Age of Forty three,
> Are you a Subject fit for me?
> Adieu bright Wit, and radiant Eyes;
> You must be grave, and I be wise.
> Our Fate in vain we would oppose,
> But I'll be still your Friend in Prose:
> Esteem and Friendship to express,
> Will not require Poetick Dress;
> And if the Muse deny her Aid
> To have them *sung*, they may be *said*.

[20] *Poems*, pp. 734-5.

> But, *Stella* say, what evil Tongue
> Reports you are no longer young?
> That *Time* sits with his Scythe to mow
> Where erst sate *Cupid* with his Bow;
> That half your Locks are turn'd to Grey;
> I'll ne'er believe a Word they say.
> 'Tis true, but let it not be known,
> My Eyes are somewhat dimmish grown;
> For Nature, always in the Right,
> To your Decays adapts my Sight,
> And Wrinkles undistinguish'd pass,
> For I'm asham'd to use a Glass;
> And till I see them with these Eyes,
> Whoever says you have them, lyes.[21]

In the following winter, 1724, and not I think, as the poem is usually dated, in 1720, he acknowledges her care of him in his sickness. Writing to Ford on Nov. 27, 1724, he says he has not been out of doors for three months and adds:

> The Ladyes bear me company in my Illness, I can hear nothing but Trebbles. I have put Mrs. Johnson into a Consumption by squalling to me.

The poem takes on added significance when it is rightly placed. For he is here concerned to praise her honour and her courage. And this was the time of Swift's greatest danger when a price had been set on his head, as the author of the Fourth *Drapier Letter*. At this moment, when he was sick and perhaps for other reasons felt safer to remain within the Liberty of St. Patrick's, the ladies had courageously moved into the Deanery to take charge of him. Only if we know the immediate situation can we understand at all the significance of this reiterated praise of Stella's honour and fidelity.

> Heroes and Heroins of old,
> By Honour only were enroll'd
> Among their Brethren of the Skies,
> To which (though late) shall *Stella* rise.
> Ten thousand Oaths upon Record,
> Are not so sacred as her Word:
> The World shall in its Atoms end,

[21] Ibid., pp. 757-8.

> E'er *Stella* can deceive a Friend.
> By Honour seated in her Breast,
> She still determines what is best:
> What Indignation in her Mind
> Against Enslavers of Mankind!
> Base Kings and Ministers of State,
> Eternal Objects of her Hate.[22]

Not till the end of the poem do we find him referring to her care of him in his sickness in spite of her own ill health. And in the last paragraph he seems to have a presentiment of what was soon to happen:

> Best Pattern of true Friends, beware;
> You pay too dearly for your Care;
> If, while your Tenderness secures
> My Life, it must endanger yours.
> For such a Fool was never found,
> Who pull'd a Palace to the Ground,
> Only to have the Ruins made
> Materials for an House decay'd.[22]

Within two years her own illness had grown so serious that he almost despaired of her recovery.

In July 1726, while he was staying with Pope at Twickenham, he received alarming news from his Dublin friends of her condition. And he writes to the Rev. John Worrall on July 15:

> What you tell me of Mrs. Johnson I have long expected, with great oppression and heaviness of heart. We have been perfect friends these thirty-five years. Upon my advice they both came to Ireland, and have been ever since my constant companions; and the remainder of my life will be a very melancholy scene, when one of them is gone, whom I most esteemed, upon the score of every good quality that can possibly recommend a human creature. I have these two months seen through Mrs. Dingley's disguises. And indeed, ever since I left you, my heart has been so sunk, that I have not been the same man, nor ever shall be again; but drag on a wretched life, till it shall please God to call me away.[23]

[22] Ibid., pp. 725, 727.
[23] Corr., III, 317.

91

He writes in anguish and does not disguise his misery.

> Pray write to me every week, that I may know what steps to take; for
> I am determined not to go to Ireland, to find her just dead, or dying.
> Nothing but extremity could make me so familiar with those terrible
> words, applied to such a dear friend. Let her know I have bought her
> a repeating gold watch, for her ease in winter nights. I designed to have
> surprised her with it; but now I would have her know it, that she may
> see how my thoughts were always to make her easy. I am of opinion
> that there is not a greater folly than to contract too great and intimate
> a friendship, which must always leave the survivor miserable.

And then realizing how completely he has put off all restraint and
given himself away, he adds:

> When you have read this letter twice, and retain what I desire, pray
> burn it, and let all I have said lie only in your breast.[24]

A few days later he writes in the same way to another Dublin friend,
the Rev. James Stopford:

> I think there is not a greater folly than that of entering into too strict
> and particular a friendship, with the loss of which a man must be
> absolutely miserable, but especially at an age when it is too late to en-
> gage in a new friendship. Besides, this was a person of my own rearing
> and instructing, from childhood, who excelled in every good quality
> that can possibly accomplish a human creature. . . . Dear Jim, par-
> don me, I know not what I am saying; but believe me that violent
> friendship is much more lasting, and as much engaging, as violent love.
> Adieu.[25]

Stella, however, recovered and Swift returned to Dublin at the end
of the summer. The next year, 1727, he went to England for his last
visit there, and once again received alarming news of Stella's condition. He returned to Dublin in October and remained there until
she died a few months later.

On the day of her death he wrote:

> This day, being Sunday, January 28, 1727-8, about eight o'clock at
> night, a servant brought me a note, with an account of the death of
> the truest, most virtuous, and valuable friend, that I, or perhaps any

[24] Ibid., p. 318.
[25] Ibid., p. 322.

other person, ever was blessed with. She expired about six in the evening of this day; and as soon as I am left alone, which is about eleven
at night, I resolve, for my own satisfaction, to say something of her life
and character.[26]

Then follows a short account of her life until her illness, and he
breaks off—"Thus far I writ the same night between eleven and
twelve." The following day, January 29, he resumed his writing for
a page or two, breaking off again—"My head aches, and I can write
no more." It is almost as though he falls back instinctively into the
method of the *Journal*. The next night, Tuesday, January 30, he
continues again:

This is the night of the funeral, which my sickness will not suffer me
to attend. It is now nine at night, and I am removed into another
apartment, that I may not see the light in the church, which is just
over against the window of my bed-chamber.[27]

and he goes on writing of her courage, her kindness, her intelligence
and her generosity to her friends. Later from time to time he continued to add a sentence or two to this memorial of her.

There is no longer the note of anguish and despair as in his letters
before she died; no word here of violent friendship, as violent as romantic love. It is indeed a rare document among Swift's writings, in
its quiet, placid surface, unruffled and unbroken, without even a
touch of irony.

It is also a conventional tribute. It answers no questions and gives
away no secrets. It is like a smooth slab placed over her grave by one
who was content to say to all the world: "She was the truest, most
virtuous, and valuable friend, that I, or perhaps any other person,
ever was blessed with."

In a world which he did not value overmuch this at least escapes
condemnation and is untouched by his scorn—this kindly and familiar conversation between man and woman, even though it may
lead to a friendship which may grip and last and hold, until it is
caught in the net of human frailty and mortality, and in its useless
struggle reveals again the pathos of life.

In our observation of the quality of sentiment in Swift's work, we

[26] *Prose*, V, 227.
[27] Ibid., p. 229.

have confined ourselves to material which was mainly in the more personal and private forms of journals and letters, and occasional verse, the remaining piece being a sort of elegy in prose. Although Swift has been sometimes angrily called a sentimentalist, he has not, I think, ever been given a serious place in the development of sentiment in eighteenth century literature.

I would only venture to call your attention to the fact that the growth of sentiment in fiction seems to be closely associated with the use of these same journal and letter forms, and in poetry with the cultivation of the elegy; while in the theatre it flourished by simply domesticating and taming the wild spirit of comedy. I would also remind you that the letters of Swift from which I have been quoting, were first published at various times between 1745 and 1767, that the account of the life and character of Stella first appeared in 1765, and the *Journal to Stella* partly in 1766, and partly in 1768; they were all therefore first read by those who had delighted in the novels of Richardson and Sterne, and who were enjoying the sentimental comedies of Kelly and Cumberland.

I have tried to examine a small part of Swift's work, which has had a good deal of attention from his biographers, who have rummaged about in it either to find a few dates or to pick out statements about his illnesses with which to diagnose his malady. I have used a different method, a very simple one, which has enabled me to isolate and scrutinize certain qualities in Swift's mind and art, one after another. I have chosen three different coloured filters, as it were, which enable you to see only one colour at a time; and I have asked you to notice the pattern and the design which was revealed while we kept each colour isolated.

There is obviously a great disadvantage in such a method, because of the necessity of making these observations one after the other, without any means of keeping them side by side for comparison; whereas in fact, in the work itself, they always exist together, if not mingled together, at least contiguous. But at least I can claim that I have not arbitrarily chosen these particular colours, and imposed them upon the work. I have only drawn your attention to what Swift himself noticed there and frequently mentioned.

In his *Epistle to a Lady, who desired the author to write some verses upon her in the Heroic Style,* from which I have already quoted, he insists again and again that his Muse is the Muse of raillery and laughter. And then he uses an image which emphasizes the gaiety and sparkle and perhaps irresponsibility of his well-meaning Muse:

> Have you seen a *Rocket* fly?
> You would swear it pierc'd the sky:
> It but reach'd the middle Air,
> Bursting into Pieces there;
> Thousand Sparkles falling down
> Light on many a Coxcomb's Crown.
> See what Mirth the Sport creates!
> Sindges Hair, but breaks no Pates.
>   .   .   .   .
> Such a rocket is my Muse:[28]

And again:

> All your Eloquence will scarce
> Drive me from my fav'rite Farce.
>   .   .   .   .
> As my Method of Reforming
> Is by Laughing, not by Storming,
> (For my Friends have always thought
> Tenderness my greatest Fault.)
> Wou'd you have me change my Style?[29]

A mingling of satire and laughter and tenderness.

And at his best these three are gathered up and perfectly blended together in a form which becomes the most characteristic idiom of Swift's writing both in verse and in prose. Permit me to give you two examples, one from the poems and one from the *Journal.* I choose these particular examples because of their telling simplicity, and also because together they will serve to answer some of the criticism that has been rather irresponsibly flung at Swift, not by academic critics, but by those who would perhaps regard themselves as carrying on his work in my generation.

In an essay, almost as misguided as Thackeray's, which he published in a volume, entitled *Do What You Will,* in 1929, Mr. Aldous

---

[28] *Poems,* p. 638.
[29] Ibid., pp. 636, 637.

Huxley trumped up a charge against Swift, based on evidence collected from the *Poems* and the *Journal,* to prove that Swift hated with almost insane violence the physical reality of the world. I tried once before to show that it was ill-founded,—and I do not hesitate to protest again, because I have now further evidence against him which I had not noticed then. He says: "Like so many of the Fathers of the Church, Swift could not forgive men and women for being vertebrate mammals as well as immortal souls." Or again, "Swift's poems about women are more ferocious even than his prose about the Yahoos; his resentment against women for being warm-blooded mammifers was incredibly bitter." But then he adds that there is a reverse side to this, which is even more revolting:

> The reverse of this ferocious hater was, as so often happens, a sentimentalist—a sentimentalist, moreover, of the worst kind; for, in the writer of the baby-langauge which fills so much space in Swift's *Journal to Stella,* we see that most abject and repulsive type of sentimentalist (a type, it may be added, exceedingly common at the present time), the adult man who deliberately mimics the attitudes of childhood.[30]

It is, you will agree, a very nasty attack, and one which cannot fairly be ignored. For in all that I have said about Swift and Stella, I have assumed that Swift felt no bitterness against women for being warm-blooded mammifers. And for proof I shall refer you to my two examples from the *Poems* and from the *Journal,* probably overlooked by Mr. Huxley, where satire and comedy and sentiment meet together. And in both, I would remind Mr. Huxley, Stella is affectionately (and as far as I can see, without any incredible bitterness) compared to a warm-blooded mammifer of the animal kingdom.

In the spring of 1725, perhaps instead of the usual Birthday verses, he wrote *A Receipt to restore Stella's Youth,* in which he points to her need of a summer in the country, and elaborates the idea by comparing her in great detail to a cow exposed during the winter to wind and want and weather:

> Meager and lank with fasting grown,
> And nothing left but Skin and Bone;

But as the spring comes

[30] Aldous Huxley, *Do What You Will,* 1929, pp. 93f.

The famish't cow her Want supplies;
Without an Ounce of last Year's Flesh,
Whate'er she gains is young and fresh;
Grows plump and round, etc.

.   .   .   .   .

Why, *Stella,* should you knit your Brow,
If I compare you to the Cow?
'Tis just the Case: For you have fasted
So long till all your Flesh is wasted,
And must against the warmer Days
Be sent to *Quilca* down to graze;

.   .   .   .   .

The Nutriment will from within
Round all your Body plump your Skin;
Will agitate the lazy Flood,
And fill your Veins with sprightly Blood:
Nor Flesh nor Blood will be the same,
Nor ought of *Stella,* but the Name;
For, what was ever understood,
By human Kind, but Flesh and Blood?[31]

I cannot detect there either with reference to Stella or to the cow any of that almost insane violence with which Swift hated the physical reality of the world and its creatures.

My other example is the postscript, added to the short note he sent from Chester, when he was held up for a boat to cross to Dublin in June 1713, to be installed as Dean of St. Patrick's. They are the last words of the *Journal,* as we happen to have it and they have always seemed to me to give an artistic unity to the *Journal,* which a mere bundle of letters ought not properly to have; for they sum up so delightfully, so absurdly and with such tenderness the complete understanding that held them together. The words were written at the last moment just on the inside of the cover, as he finished reading her letter, which had so delighted him by some little joke it contained—

. . . when I read that Passage upon Chester walls, as I was coming into Town, and just receivd the Letter: I sd aloud—Agreable B—tch.[32]

There satire and sentiment are perfectly mingled, and we recognize

[31] *Poems,* p. 759.
[32] *Journal,* June 6, 1713, p. 445.

unmistakably the tones of the comic spirit. The phrase is to me a perfect blend of the tones I have been trying to distinguish and to consider separately. "Agreeable bitch."

In form and expression, in raillery and playfulness and warmth of feeling, no words could have been more like Jonathan Swift, and I dare to add, no compliment more pleasing to Stella.

THE SATIRE OF JONATHAN SWIFT

This book contains three lectures
delivered at Smith College in May 1946

CONTENTS

INTRODUCTION

> *Satyr is a sort of Glass, wherein Beholders*
> *do generally discover every body's Face but*
> *their Own; which is the chief Reason for that*
> *kind of Reception it meets in the World,*
> *and that so very few are offended with it.*[1]

Whether or not that is the reason for the reader's satisfaction there can be no doubt that it is for his satire that Jonathan Swift is read, and will continue to be read. And this explanation of the effect of satire does account for the fact that people of all parties can equally enjoy and even applaud the strokes of a satirist like Swift. Two hundred years after his death he is remembered not perfunctorily, not just by scholars or collectors, but by those who would use his satire for their own present purposes. In London and Dublin the echoes of his voice might be expected to reverberate from Marlborough's wars to Churchill's wars, from Dublin's struggle against dependency on the Whig government of George I to Dublin's present independent neutrality. But his satire is no less alive and satisfying to the reader in an America staggering beneath the weight of her destructive powers, and it is being equally acclaimed and widely disseminated in the Soviet Union where for the first time a Russian translation of *A Tale of a Tub* has been allowed to appear, and where *Gulliver's Travels* has been recently translated into twenty-eight different languages for the Soviet peoples.

I do not, therefore, feel it necessary to apologize for venturing to choose at this time for the subject of these lectures the satirical writings of one who was very decidedly a Tory and a Churchman, though often an embarrassment both to the Church and to the Tories, being (as a contemporary called him) "one of the greatest *Droles* that ever

[1] Preface to *The Battle of the Books: Prose*, I, 140.

appear'd upon the Stage of the World";[2] and who was also an Irishman, not merely in the sense that he was born and died there and
was Dean of St. Patrick's, Dublin, but so deeply concerned with the
Irish cause that he earned the name of Hibernian Patriot; and further,
like many another Irishman, provided very good arguments for the
Americans in their struggle for independence. He remains none the
less, and would wish to be regarded, an English gentleman, a close
associate of men like Sir William Temple, Lord Somers, Oxford and
Bolingbroke, and the friend of Pope, Arbuthnot and Gay. Most of his
books were published in London, and those that appeared first in
Dublin, including a great many that were mistakenly attributed to
him there, were quickly picked up by the London booksellers and
reprinted for a market in which he was a certain best-seller.

In the last two hundred years, moreover, since Swift's death, his
works have been repeatedly re-edited, and he has been the subject
of Remarks, Observations, Lives, Studies, and lectures which have
shown the different fashions of the time only in their varying attitudes; he has been admired and disliked with equal intensity, but
never ignored. And during the revival of interest in eighteenth-cen-
tury studies which has taken place in the last forty years, a great deal
of useful work has been done to establish more carefully the canon
of his writings, to provide for the first time a reliable edition of his
Poems, a well-arranged and fully annotated edition of his *Correspondence,* together with new editions and studies of the *Prose Works*
necessitated by the considerable amount of new manuscript material
and bibliographical information which has recently come to light.

I speak of these editions, of this textual and bibliographical work,
not, I hope out of any foolish sense of the importance of my trade as
an editor, but to emphasize that there is no excuse for us to neglect
the close study of Swift's own writings to follow the lure of such intriguing problems as his personal relationships with Stella and Vanessa, or to try and find some scientific explanation for the violence
of his dislike for certain qualities of the human species, or to theorize
about some dark secret of demoniacal possession or Freudian complex
according to the prevailing fashion of the day.

I shall speak, therefore, only of the main satirical writings of Swift

[2] Anthony Collins, *A Discourse Concerning Ridicule and Irony in Writing,*
1729, p. 39.

in which he continues to live most powerfully. I shall examine his
work at three different levels which happen to fall into three separate
periods of his life, according to a very simple pattern which almost inevitably shapes the work of every writer and artist. The first shows
him in his relation to his art and may be called aesthetic; the second,
in his relation to society and may be called political; the third, in his
relation to moral and permanent values and may be called ethical.
These parts or divisions of a writer's work are in fact never entirely
separate or found in a regular sequence. Nevertheless, I believe it is
not very dangerous and might not be unprofitable to risk such a simplification. For every craftsman must begin by an apprenticeship to
his own particular trade; he must first learn to handle his tools and to
know his materials. He will be interested in the work that the successful masters are doing; he will tend to pick up the particular language of the trade, the shop-talk. His world will be the world of his
art and of his fellowcraftsmen. He may extend that further by becoming interested in the craftsmanship of earlier generations or in new
technical devices, or in the common problems of those working in
other allied arts; or he may be interested in theoretical or practical
criticism. He will be practising his art and developing his technical
skill and his knowledge, enjoying the free play of mind and imagination in a world of its own, detached, a world of what may be called
aesthetic values.

There are some (artists and prophets), who remain so preoccupied
with the problems of their art or with their own visions that they continue to live apart and refuse to allow themselves to be involved in the
social struggles or the political factions of their own times. "Let no one
marvel," says Vasari, "that Michelangelo loved solitude, for he was devoted to art which claims man for itself alone; and because those who
study must avoid society, the minds of those who study art are constantly preoccupied, and those who consider this to be eccentricity are
wrong, for he who would do well must avoid cares and vexations,
since genius demands thought, solitude and comfort, and a steadfast
mind."[3] It must not be forgotten that many of those who have avoided
or spurned the burden of public office and refused to be wearied by
temporal power have not always been self-indulgent escapists, but
have often been stirring witnesses against the follies of their times and

[3] Georgio Vasari, *Lives of the Painters*, 1927 (Everyman ed.), IV, 171.

against man's inhumanity to man; they have left in their art a permanent memorial, a negative criticism as it were, of the political and social questions of their day. There are others, however (historians and philosophers as well as scholars and artists), who have been equally men of action, playing a central part in the public life of their time, or at least much in society, whose creative work has seemed to be but the flowering of a life of action. In public office or in the service of a cause they have used their gift as orators or writers for an immediate purpose. Their speeches and pamphlets have been acts intended to bring about certain events, to rouse their people to war or to change a mode of government. Such writings have their origin in the circumstances of the time. They may even have little to do with the expression of the individual genius of the artist; his spirit is subdued and bent to a purpose beyond his control, outside forces lend him their power. This kind of writing can only be done by one who actually has the responsibility of action, and by one who is living at the centre of affairs. This kind of art does not depend on comfort and could not proceed out of quiet and solitude.

This was the situation of Swift at the height of his political influence in London during the last years of Queen Anne's reign. In a letter addressed to him at that time Archbishop King reminded him that "a man's spirit is never more awakened nor his thoughts better, than in the intervals of a hurry of business" and encouraged him to continue to write on subjects suitable to his calling; quoting as examples Caesar, "who wrote under the hurry and fatigues of a general," and Erasmus, "whose life was almost a continual journey."[4] At that very time Swift was, like Caesar, writing his commentaries and in the midst of his press of business keeping an intimate journal of his activities; but he was also using to the utmost his satirical powers as well as his facility in popular verse, in performance of his official duties as, in modern terms, director of publicity for the Tory ministry.

He is writing no longer as a wit, a young gentleman much in the world, showing off his skill as he makes fun of the world of religion and learning; he is now using his pen to get certain things done. His work is affected by qualities of expediency. He must calculate its effect upon a particular audience at a particular moment; and as long as he is thus concerned with a party and a cause, and engaged in the

[4] *Corr.*, I, 298.

performance of his official duties, there will inevitably be limits to the scope of his work, however fully it may draw out all his powers. He will need to use some of his weapons with great care; sometimes he may have to ignore the subtleties of a situation and simplify his arguments almost to crudity to get the required effect. However enlightened he will have to take the risk of seeing his human sympathies narrowed, his values tarnished by being absorbed in a party campaign or in a national or popular cause. But if, like Milton or like Swift, he is fortunate enough later to be removed from the service of temporal power and left in retirement and isolation to observe and remember and set down a record for posterity, he may be freed again for a final creative effort, in which all the qualities of his genius will be given free play whether they appear clothed in the grandeur and dignity of an epic or masquerading in a volume of lying Travels.

It is only in this final stage that the writer wins complete freedom. He is established as a master of his craft and is unaffected by, or able to use as he wills, the fashions of the literary world in which he has gained his reputation; and he is completely master of his material, untroubled by any concern with the immediate effect on a party or a cause, writing for posterity and dealing with moral values and human qualities with a power which enables him to break through the boundaries of his own time and place and leave his work among the permanent memorials of the human spirit.

LITERARY SATIRE

'Tis own'd he was a *Man* of *Wit*—,
Yet many a *foolish thing* he writ—;
And, sure he must be *deeply* learn'd—!
That's more than ever I discern'd—;
I know his *nearest friends* complain
He was too *airy* for a *Dean*—.[1]

Before the publication of *A Tale of a Tub* in 1704, Swift had appeared
in his own person in the world of letters only as an editor of the *Letters of Sir William Temple*. The first two volumes were printed in
1700 with a dedication in which he humbly presents them to his Most
Sacred Majesty William III, describing himself as a domestic chaplain
to his Excellency the Earl of Berkeley, one of the Lords Justices of
Ireland. A third volume was printed in 1703. But he evidently felt
that in his role as a satirist, he would be hampered and restricted if he
were to appear in this way, wearing a parson's gown and associated
with such respectable connections. There had been, indeed, in the
seventeenth century, a splendid tradition among the most reverend
and eminent divines in their controversial treatises about serious
matters which would seem to sanction, as Anthony Collins pointed
out in his *Discourse concerning Ridicule,* the use of "Insult, Buffoonery, Banter, Ridicule, Irony, Mockery and bitter Railing"; and after
the Restoration this tendency was further encouraged by a Court
audience led by "a King who had a disposition to banter and ridicule
everybody" and "some of the greatest Droles and Wits that any Age
ever produc'd."[2] But tastes were changing at the end of the century,
and Swift himself was then under the influence of Sir William
Temple, who had solemnly and vigorously denounced the taste for
satire, and had probably prevented Swift from publishing *The Battle
of the Books* in 1698.

[1] *Poems,* p. 547.
[2] Anthony Collins, op. cit., pp. 5 f.

At any rate we know that Swift put aside this and other satirical papers of his own which he had been working at in 1696-7, and took precautions that when they did appear he would not necessarily be involved, until he could see what sort of reception they would have. He felt that he needed for his purpose the fullest freedom to range at will over the whole field of letters, for he wished to make sport with all the foibles of the Grub-street brotherhood as well as the societies of Gresham and of Wills, the hack-writers and fashionable poets, the virtuosos and the wits, and "to expose the numerous corruptions in religion and learning, which might furnish matter for a satire that would be useful and diverting." He chose therefore to appear as an unknown young gentleman of taste and learning dedicated to the high task of serving the Church and the State by diverting the attacks of the wits who occupy themselves in picking holes in the weak sides of religion and government; and in such a task—which he claimed should win him the approval of all good men—he would be justified in letting loose all his powers to expose the shams of the time and to make merry at the expense of all hypocrites and dullards. But his attack must be made in "a manner altogether new, the world having been already too long nauseated with endless repetitions upon every subject."[3]

The author of *A Tale of a Tub* is presented to us as at the maturity of his powers—"his invention at the height, and his reading fresh in his head, . . . a young gentleman much in the world, who wrote to the taste of those who were like himself."[4] He is not without a certain youthful insolence, contemptuous alike of stupidity, dullness and pedantry, addressing himself to those who have enough wit to appreciate irony, and enough knowledge to recognize parody. He has had sufficient experience to know that he need not be afraid of those who will be provoked to anger and fury by his satire. They deserve only his scorn:

> There is a *Brain* that will endure but one *Scumming*: Let the Owner gather it with Discretion, and manage his little Stock with Husbandry; but of all things, let him beware of bringing it under the *Lash* of his *Betters*; because, That will make it all bubble up into Impertinence, and he will find no new Supply: Wit, without Knowledge, being a Sort

[3] *Prose*, I, 1.
[4] Ibid.

of *Cream,* which gathers in a Night to the Top, and by a skilful Hand, may be soon *whipt* into *Froth;* but once scumm'd away, what appears underneath will be fit for nothing, but to be thrown to the Hogs.[5]

This is still in the manner of the seventeenth century, in the true line of wit; the vivid image of the whipped cream, possibly picked up from his reading of François de Callières, who had used it simply as a symbol for writing "large in appearance but little in substance," but here elaborated and played with and worked to the utmost, until the froth vanishes and we are left with another even more powerful image of the skimmed milk fit only for the hogs. A careful contemporary reader would have recognized the method, and might have been reminded of another fantastic image of scorn in a popular satire of the preceding generation, which the author of *A Tale of a Tub* admired and referred to, *The Rehearsal Transpros'd* by Andrew Marvell. He also is describing the brain of his adversary:

> You have, contrary to all architecture and good economy, made a snow-house in your upper roome, which indeed was philosophically done of you, seeing you bear your head so high as if it were in or above the middle region, and so you thought it secure from melting. But you did not at the same time consider that your brain is so hot, that the wit is dissolv'd by it, and is always dripping away at the icicles of your nose. But it freezes again, I confess, as soon as it falls down; and hence it proceeds that there is no passage in my Book, deep or shallow, but with a chill and key-cold conceit you can ice it in a moment, and slide shere over it without scatches.[6]

There is the same playful extravagance and exuberant gaiety in these conceits, but Swift's sentences show an economy and strength, and a power of invention—to use the phrase of the time—which seems to me to justify his claim that his wit was all his own. He speaks of having read Marvell with pleasure, and evidently took good heed of his warnings addressed to those who would take upon themselves the envious and dangerous employment of being writers.

> For indeed, whosoever he be that comes in print, whereas he might have sate at home in quiet, does either make a treat, or send a challenge

[5] *A Tale of a Tub,* ed. A. C. Guthkelch and D. Nichol Smith, 1920, pp. 215-16.
[6] *The Rehearsal Transpros'd,* 1673, Part II, p. 255.

to all readers; in which cases, the first, it concerns him to have no scarcity of provisions, and in the other, to be compleatly arm'd; for, if anything be amiss on either part, men are subject to scorn the weakness of the attaque, or laugh at the meanness of the entertainment.[7]

There is no scarcity of entertainment in the fare Swift provides, no lack of weapons for the attack. The manner of his attack may seem at first sight very conventional, for it was a favourite conceit of the time to refer to the custom of seamen to throw out a tub when they meet a whale to divert it from attacking the ship. It must have been well known to all Swift's readers, as it occurs in such popular books as this satire of Marvell's I have been referring to:

> I only threw it out like an empty Cask to amuze him, knowing that I had a *Whale* to deal with, . . .[8]

and again in the prefatory Remarks to the Reader in Francis Osborn's *Works*, which had reached a seventh edition in 1673:

> . . . in immitation of Sea-men, I may perhaps by design have cast out some empty stuff, to find play for the Whale-mouthed gapers after Levity; lest they should spoil the Voyage.[9]

Swift's parable is very obvious, where the whale symbolizes Hobbes's *Leviathan* and the ship in danger the Commonwealth, though again he does not miss the opportunity to enlarge the conceit, rather confusing the picture, as the waters round the Leviathan positively seethe with tubs, namely "Schemes of religion and government, whereof a great many are hollow, and dry, and empty, and noisy, and wooden, and given to Rotation."[10] He will himself provide for the purpose *A Tale of a Tub*. Again neither the phrase nor its use as a title is new. Instances are given in the Guthkelch and Nichol Smith edition, to which I am indebted throughout, of its common use in the sixteenth and seventeenth centuries, in the sense of "an idle discourse," or as explained in the title of a lost work "a gallamaufrey of merriment."[11] Swift hooks the two ideas together and has a title for a gallimaufrey of merriment in which he can make fun of everything that catches his

[7] Ibid., pp. 26-7.
[8] Ibid., p. 115, quoted in *A Tale of a Tub*, p. xxviii.
[9] Francis Osborn, *Works*, 1673, p. (vi).
[10] *Prose*, I, 24.
[11] *Tale of a Tub*, pp. xxvi f.

fancy not only as he looks around him in the world of contemporary
controversy, but as he looks back across the troubled waters of the
Revolution and the Commonwealth and the Civil War to the serene
shores of that age immediately before the troubles which he always regarded with longing and pride as the time of England's highest glory
both in life and in letters.

For the real object of Swift's satire in the *Tale* is the corruption he
saw in English letters during the latter half of the seventeenth century, destroying what he felt had been its finest achievements. This
belief is repeatedly stated, and never modified. He first stated it in the
Tatler, dated September 28, 1710, satirizing current affectations of
language, and clearly setting forth what he regarded as the standards
of good taste in English, namely that simplicity which is unaffected
by modish fashions, such as "the writings of Hooker, a country clergyman, and of Parsons the Jesuit, both in the reign of Queen Elizabeth
. . . much more clear and intelligible than those of Sir H. Wotton,
Sir Robert Naunton, Osborn, Daniel the Historian, and several others
who writ later; but being men of the Court, and affecting the phrases
then in Fashion; they are often either not to be understood, or appear
perfectly ridiculous."[12]

He stated it very plainly in his *Letter to the Lord Treasurer*, emphasizing the corruptions in language "from the Civil War to this
present time"; first, the enthusiastic jargon prevailing during the
usurpation, and then the licentiousness which entered with the Restoration, which from infecting religion and morals fell to corrupt the
language, as shown in the plays and other compositions written for
entertainment during the next fifty years.[13] He stated it again in *A
Letter to a young Clergyman*, written in Ireland ten years later, and
again in a slightly different form in the *Essay on Conversation*, as,
for example:

> I take the highest period of politeness in England (and it is of the same
> date in France) to have been the peaceable part of King Charles I's
> reign.[14]

It is obvious from this on which side Swift would find himself in
the controversy between the Ancients and the Moderns which had

[12] *Prose*, II, 177.
[13] Ibid., IV, 10 f.
[14] Ibid., p. 94.

been sharpened by the recent claims for precedence made on behalf of the latest discoveries and developments in the world of science and letters. He was indeed inclined to be unduly sceptical of the importance and value of the new sciences and more aware of the corruptions than of the improvements in modern learning. He was not therefore led into the fray entirely to defend Sir William Temple against the attacks made on his *Essay upon the Ancient and Modern Learning,* although this episode provided him with an excuse to join with the Christ Church wits against Bentley and Wotton. At the same time it forced him to uphold a very weak case, as Temple had stated it in his Essay, and he was obliged to rely on the effectiveness of the literary devices he used to get the better of his opponents. The main device is indicated by the title—A Full and True Account of the Battle Fought last Friday, Between the Antient and the Modern Books in St. James's Library. This looked like an imitation of François de Callières's *Histoire poétique de la Guerre nouvellement déclarée entre les Anciens et les Modernes* though Swift afterwards said he had never heard of it. But there were many advantages in handling the subject in a mock heroic fashion as a battle between the actual volumes in the King's Library, which Bentley had confessed was in a state of dirt and confusion. The Homeric conflict takes place "on the plains of St. James's Library"—a phrase which is just enough to carry us into a mock heroic world remote from the actual controversy and the arguments over the genuineness of the Epistles of Phalaris. In this world Swift can play with the reader as he will; he has only to oppose Dryden to Virgil, describing Dryden's steed and his arms in Hudibrastian fashion:

> Behold, upon a sorrel Gelding of a monstrous Size, appear'd a Foe, issuing from among the thickest of the Enemy's Squadrons; But his Speed was less than his Noise; for his Horse, old and lean, spent the Dregs of his Strength in a high Trot, which though it made slow Advances, yet caused a loud Clashing of his Armor, terrible to hear.
> . . . the Helmet was nine Times too large for the Head, which appeared Situate far in the hinder Part, even like the Lady in a Lobster, or like a Mouse under a Canopy of State or like a shrivled Beau from within the Penthouse of a modern Periwig.[15]

In similar fashion he describes Bentley and Wotton "like two Mungrel curs prowling around" who steal the armour of Phalaris and

15 Ibid., I, 157.

Aesop while they are asleep; and the final exploit of Boyle who appears like a young lion, and hunts the two of them until finally his
lance pierces them together:

> As, when a skilful Cook has truss'd a Brace of Woodcocks, He, with
> Iron Skewer, pierces the tender Sides of both, their Legs and Wings
> close pinion'd to their Ribs; So was this Pair of Friends transfix'd, till
> down they fell, joyn'd in their Lives, Join'd in their Deaths.[16]

If this were all, however, we should feel that Swift had done no
more than provide a trivial diversion to draw attention away from the
real conflict. But again in the midst of the allegory, as in the *Tale*, he
introduces a digression: and a very fitting one, as the dispute was also
concerned with Aesop, who was praised by Temple as the most ancient of the ancients and was recognized by all ages as the greatest
master in this kind. Very fitly also in the dirt of St. James's Library,
Swift discovers a large spider's web, in which a bee, entering through
a broken pane of the window, has become entangled. This occasions
a dispute between them which is then interpreted by Aesop, who had
listened to them "with a world of pleasure."[17]

The fable and the interpretation of it are Swift's real contribution
to the debate between the Ancients and the Moderns; and it is not
surprising that a hundred and fifty years later, when the debate had
taken another form, Swift's phrase "sweetness and light" was carried
as a banner by a young apostle of culture as he advanced against the
hosts of the Philistines. It was also a triumphant vindication of the art
of Aesop, no matter what Bentley had done to his title page and half
of his leaves. The fable is made out of a proverb, evidently common,
as it is frequently turned to literary use in the seventeenth century:
"Where the bee sucks honey, the spider sucks poison." Here we can
observe it expanding into a lovely form, as it is dramatized in Bentley's
library, and elaborated with mock heroic language, and finally interpreted as a symbol of the dispute between the Ancients and the Moderns:

> For, pray Gentlemen, was ever any thing so *Modern* as the *Spider* in
> his Air, his Turns, and his Paradoxes? He argues in the Behalf of *You*
> his Brethren, and Himself, with many Boastings of his native Stock,

16 Ibid., p. 164.
17 Ibid., pp. 147 f.

and great Genius; that he Spins and Spits wholly from himself, and scorns to own any Obligation or Assistance from without. Then he displays to you his great Skill in Architecture, and Improvement in the Mathematicks . . . yet, if the materials be nothing but Dirt, spun out of your own Entrails (the Guts of *Modern* Brains) the Edifice will conclude at last in a *Cobweb*: The Duration of which, like that of other *Spiders* Webs, may be imputed to their being forgotten, or neglected, or hid in a Corner. . . . As for *Us*, the *Antients*. We are content with the *Bee*, to pretend to Nothing of our own, beyond our *Wings* and our *Voice*: that is to say, our *Flights* and our *Language*; For the rest, whatever we have got, has been by infinite Labor, and search, and ranging thro' every Corner of Nature: The Difference is, that instead of *Dirt* and *Poison*, we have rather chose to fill our Hives with *Honey* and *Wax*, thus furnishing Mankind with the two Noblest of Things, which are *Sweetness* and *Light*.[18]

It was a nice compliment to Temple to use the bee as the symbol of the Ancients; for some of Swift's readers would remember Temple's *Essay on Poetry*, where he compares the poet's art with the activities of the bees in a passage which Swift in that last sentence condensed with great precision:

[Bees] must range through Fields, as well as Gardens, chuse such Flowers as they please, and by Proprieties and Scents they only know and distinguish: They must work up their Cells with Admirable Art, extract their Honey with infinite Labour, and sever it from the Wax, with such Distinction and Choice, as belongs to none but themselves to perform or to judge.[19]

Some of Swift's readers would also remember this passage, to which Professor F. P. Wilson drew my attention, in Bacon's *Novum Organum*:

The men of experiment are like the ant; they only collect and use; the reasoners resemble spiders, who make cobwebs out of their own substance. But the bee takes a middle course, it gathers its material from the flowers of the garden and of the field, but transforms and digests it by a power of its own. Not unlike this is the true business of philosophy.

[18] Ibid., p. 151.
[19] *Tale of a Tub*, p. 232n.

In the *Battle of the Books* Swift shows what side he is on, and he succeeds by his wit and humour, and by the power of his style. But he does not reveal there as he does in the *Tale* the extent of the preparation he had undertaken so that in offering entertainment to his readers, he should not be criticized for any scarcity of provisions. As an undergraduate at Trinity College he had had no great reputation as a scholar; but we happen to have some interesting information about his reading during those years when he was planning and working on the *Tale*.

The list of his studies for the year 1697 indicates the breadth and variety of his reading, including, in addition to French and English authors, the Iliad and the Odyssey, Virgil twice, Lucretius three times, Horace, Cicero's Epistles, Petronius, Lucius Florus three times, Diodorus Siculus, Cyprian, Irenaeus and Sleidan's commentaries. "This —says Professor Nichol Smith—gives only a fraction of the reading that went to the making of the *Tale*," but "it admits us, as it were, to a secret view of Swift's habits of mind when he was gaining his full powers, and Swift never wrote anything that gives a greater sense of sheer power than some of the later sections of the *Tale*."[20]

It is unlike the rest of his writings, because it is so literary, so full of echoes from his reading, and so concerned with the world of letters, the world that at that time he knew best, because he had been living entirely in it. For he had been exercising himself in the art of writing as well as filling his mind. The *Tale* represents only a very small portion of all that he had written during the last ten years of the century. He had begun with a number of experiments in verse—Pindaric Odes in which he seems to have wished to compete with Cowley and experiments in heroic verse like the Lines addressed to Congreve, not much less restrained in manner. He soon discovered that such forms would not fit the kind of thing he wanted to say, and contemptuously turned away from these poetic exercises, not even including them in any of his later collections of verse. Nevertheless there is to be observed in them a force and energy, struggling with the too voluminous folds of flowing rhetoric and showing the ferment of thought in which he lived. In his attack on the extravagancies of the previous age, he benefited by these struggles in which he had won his freedom as per-

[20] *Tale of a Tub*, pp. li-lv.

haps every young writer has to do from the prevailing forces round
about him, in order to shape his art to fit his own individual purpose.
These Odes, addressed to the King, to Sir William Temple, to Archbishop Sancroft, and the Epistle to Mr. Congreve begin in a dignified
strain of compliment, and were evidently intended to serve the same
purpose as those later presented by Congreve on suitable occasions as
an offering to the King on his taking of Namur, or lamenting the
Death of our late Gracious Queen Mary of ever blessed Memory. But
unlike the cool marbled smoothness of Congreve's lines, Swift's gather
a tempestuous motion and quickly become roughened by moods of
anger and satire, and he breaks off apologizing for his unfitting outbursts:

> Perish the Muse's hour, thus vainly spent
> In satire, to my Congreve's praises meant;
> In how ill season her resentments rule,
> What's that to her if mankind be a fool?[21]

And in the last of these poems addressed to Temple in December
1693, he renounces the Muse as a delusion and a deceit,

> Troubling the chrystal fountain of the sight,
> Which darts on poets eyes a trembling light;
> Kindled while reason sleeps, but quickly flies
> Like antic shapes in dreams, from waking eyes:[22]

The experience, which he describes with such force in this poem,
where he turns away forever from the fond delusions of a youthful
poet's romantic dreams, is the source of the irony and gives a sort of
personal colouring to the triumphant scepticism of the Digression on
Madness in the *Tale*, where human happiness is defined as "a perpetual possession of being well deceived," and the same struggle between fancy and reason is examined:

> But when a Man's Fancy gets *astride* on his Reason, when Imagination
> is at Cuffs with the senses, and common Understanding, as well as
> common Sense, is kick't out of Doors; the first Proselyte he makes, is
> Himself.[23]

---

[21] *Poems*, pp. 47, 48.
[22] Ibid., p. 54.
[23] *Prose*, I, 108.

I have tried to indicate briefly how well prepared Swift was in 1697, as a young man of thirty, for the role of the Author of *A Tale of a Tub,* not only by his hard reading and study and contemplation, but also by the vigorous exercise of his imagination and his skill in the various forms of his art. Now I should like to examine the *Tale* itself to try and show the devices he used to gather into it so much of the spirit of the century that was nearing its close, its enthusiasm, its pedantry, its shams, its conceits, and all the richness and extravagance and variety of its strange faiths and hopes and delusions. For the paradox is—and it would miss its purpose if it were not paradoxical— that the work is a product of the seventeenth century, entirely characteristic in form and manner, and at the same time a repudiation and criticism of all the most vigorous literary fashions of the previous sixty years.

For example in its outward shape and form it obviously resembles the work of those writers whom Swift repudiates, rather than the work of those like Hooker and Parsons, whose style he admired. And it is equally unlike himself, as Dr. Johnson pointed out, going so far as to question indeed whether Swift could have written it: "It has so much more thinking, more knowledge, more power, more colour, than any of the works which are indubitably his."[24] This impression that the *Tale* is unlike Swift in having more colour, more evidence of his reading and knowledge of literature, is due to the fact that he has put into it so much material from the world of letters in order to make play with it and to shake himself free from it. It is also due to the element of parody in its whole design, a feature indeed constant in Swift's satire and he would say inevitably so, because he believed that it would be impossible for any satirist to imagine or create affectations which could serve his purpose as well as those plentifully to be found in life or literature. And parody to be perfect should be as close to the original as possible. Therefore since certain affectations in the world of letters usually appeared in certain particular places, e.g. in *Dedications,* or *Digressions,* or *Prefaces,* or *To The Readers,* what could be more fitting than to fit out the *Tale* with all these append- ages, so that the proper place would be available to exhibit and expose such follies? In order to make sure that his method would not be mis- understood by later readers, Swift was careful in the *Apology,* which

[24] *Lives of the Poets,* ed. G. Birkbeck Hill, 1905, III, 10, n. 6.

he added as a further preface in 1710, to explain exactly what he was
doing and who were his victims.

> There is one Thing which the judicious Reader cannot but have ob-
> served, that some of those Passages in this Discourse, which appear
> most liable to Objection are what they call Parodies, where the Author
> personates the Style and Manner of other Writers, whom he has a
> mind to expose. I shall produce one Instance, it is in the 51st Page.
> Dryden, L'Estrange, and some others I shall not name, are here levelled
> at, who having spent their Lives in Faction, and Apostacies, and all
> manner of Vice, pretended to be Sufferers for Loyalty and Religion. So
> Dryden tells us in one of his Prefaces of his Merits and Suffering,
> thanks God that he *possesses his Soul in Patience*: In other Places he
> talks at the same Rate, and L'Estrange often uses the like Style, and I
> believe the Reader may find more Persons to give that Passage an
> Application: But this is enough to direct those who may have over-
> look'd the Authors Intention.[25]

As a sample of Dryden's complaints, I will quote a sentence from
his *Discourse concerning Satire*:

> But being encouraged only with fair words by King Charles II, my
> little salary ill paid, and no prospect of a future subsistence, I was then
> discouraged in the beginning of my attempt; and now age has over-
> taken me, and want, a more insufferable evil, through the change of
> the times, has wholly disenabled me.[26]

But Dryden provided even better material in his translation of the
Works of Virgil, which appeared in the summer of 1697, while Swift
was probably working on the *Tale*. The volume was printed by Ton-
son in a handsome folio, adorned with a hundred sculptures, and a
list of the names of the subscribers to the cuts, each subscription being
five guineas; with a separate list of the second subscribers. It was
divided into three parts, containing the Pastorals, the Georgics and
the Aeneis, each part equipped not only with separate prefaces or
observations, but also with separate dedications—to Lord Clifford, the
Earl of Chesterfield and the Marquis of Normandy. Swift did not
miss his opportunity:

Our famous Dryden has ventured to proceed a Point farther, endeav-

---

[25] *Prose*, I, 3-4.
[26] *The Essays of John Dryden*, ed. W. P. Ker, 1900, II, 38.

ouring to introduce also a Multiplicity of God-fathers; which is an
Improvement of much more Advantage, upon a very obvious Account.[27]

It was such a good example that he would try it himself and therefore
divided his treatise into forty sections and approached forty Lords of
his acquaintance to stand, but they all made their excuses.

But in the Postscript to the Reader, Swift found a lovely sample of
Dryden's further acknowledgments to more god-fathers for all the encouragement and aids he had received in the course of his work, start-
ing with the assistance granted by the Almighty in the beginning,
prosecution and conclusion of his studies, and ending with his obligations to the whole Faculty of medicine, especially to those two ornaments of their profession, Dr. Guibbons and Dr. Hobbs. And finally
he assures the reader that his work will be judged in after ages to be
no dishonour to his native country, whose language and poetry he has
added to in the choice of words and in the harmony of numbers. This
Swift notes as an excellent method of advertisement:

> Our great Dryden . . . has often said to me in Confidence, that the
> World would have never suspected him to be so great a Poet, if he had
> not assured them so frequently in his Prefaces, that it was impossible
> they could either doubt or forget it.[28]

Finally all such affectations as are found scattered throughout these
prefaces and addresses to the reader, "all these wonderful civilities (as
Swift calls them) that have passed of late Years between the Nation
of Authors and that of Readers" are gathered up in the extravagant
travesty of the tenth section of *A Tale of a Tub,* where the author offers
his humble thanks to his Majesty, and both Houses of Parliament, the
Lords of the Privy Council, the Judges, clergy, gentry, and yeomanry
of the land, etc. for their approbation; expresses his happiness that
Fate has flung him into so blessed an age for the mutual felicity of
authors and booksellers, who produce and sell their wares so easily,
and promises entire satisfaction for every class of readers, the super-
ficial, the ignorant and the learned, and ends with throwing out some
bait for the latter group, by dropping some dark hints and innuendoes
of hidden meanings and profound mysteries, in the hope—as the
learned commentator puts it in a final note—of setting curious men

[27] *Prose,* I, 43.
[28] Dryden, op. cit., II, 240-45; *Prose,* I, 81-2.

a-hunting through Indexes, and enquiring for Books out of the common Road. I may add that there are probably very few of us who
have tried to edit or comment on this *Tale*, who have not been tricked
in this manner, and I can only commend to any of you who may be
looking for a subject for research with unlimited possibilities, that
you should investigate the qualities of *Acamoth*, which you may, or
may not, find illuminated in the work of the dark authors of the
seventeenth century.

The method of parody is also used in the ridicule of Bentley and
Wotton, which occurs in the Digression on Critics when he sets out
gravely to search for particular descriptions of the True Critick in the
writings of the Ancients, and brings together very much in the manner of Bentley a series of quotations proving that these Ancients generally fixed upon the same hieroglyph, as the subject was too dangerous to be treated except by types and figures. Thereupon the symbol of the ass is introduced with the help of two quotations from
Pausanias. "But Herodotus, holding the very same Hieroglyph, speaks
much plainer and almost *in terminis*. Upon which relation Ctesias yet
refines, etc." And even the three Maxims which provide a devastating
close for the chapter are ornamented with a number of similitudes, in
which the prevalent witty conceit is sharpened so that it may become
an effective weapon for satire. I will instance only the first of these
where the irony is so nicely balanced that an early compositor added
a negative which has confused the sentence as it now stands in many
editions:

> Criticism, contrary to all other Faculties of the Intellect, is ever held
> the truest and best, when it is the very *first* Result of the Critick's
> Mind: As Fowlers reckon the first aim for the surest, and seldom fail
> of missing the Mark, if they stay [not] for a Second.[29]

I have spoken at such length about the parody in the book, because
it explains its unlikeness to much of Swift's later work, and because it
is, I think, the source of that extraordinary richness and variety in the
style which is so much concerned with an examination of the books
of the previous generation that inevitably it preserves so many of
their tricks and mannerisms. But it contains also quite clearly and
fully developed the qualities which most distinctively mark Swift's

[29] *Prose*, I, 60, 63;

satire, "an Irony which runs through the Thread of the whole Book"
and a sardonic wit which is a perfect vehicle for a scepticism not less
profound and not less complete than that which perhaps more plainly
and nakedly reveals itself in his latest writings.

Consider for instance his answer to the problem why satire is likely
to be less dull than panegyrick. The solution, he says, is easy and
natural.

> For, the Materials of Panegyrick being very few in Number, have been
> long since exhausted: For, as Health is but one Thing and has been
> always the same, whereas Diseases are by thousands, besides new and
> daily Additions; So, all the Virtues that have been ever in Mankind,
> are to be counted upon a few Fingers, but his Follies and Vices are
> innumerable, and Time adds hourly to the Heap.[30]

That last phrase is so characteristic. It prevents the sentence from
falling flat, like some stale drab moralist's jibe. It thrusts it home, revealing the endless possibility of mankind's follies mounting higher
hour by hour. It reminds us of the *Dedication to Prince Posterity,*
where beneath the gay raillery of his tone as he bears witness to the
actual reputation of his illustrious contemporaries at the minute he is
writing, there can be heard the theme of Time and Mortality, and his
sentences are caught for a moment and held by that insistent rhythm
which had been dominant for a hundred years:

> I enquired after them among Readers and Booksellers, but I enquired
> in vain, *the Memorial of them was lost among Men, their Place was no
> more to be found;* and I was laughed to scorn . . .[31]

And then inexorably other echoes float into his mind and bring him
more images for his purpose, and, as we read, his sentences are disturbed and rock a little beneath the powerful swell of this very different rhetoric:

> Sometime we see a cloud that's dragonish;
> A vapour sometime like a bear or lion,
> A tower'd citadel, a pendent rock,
> A forked mountain, or blue promontory
> With trees upon't, that nod unto the world,

[30] Ibid., p. 30.
[31] Ibid., p. 21.

And mock our eyes with air; thou hast seen these signs;
They are black vesper's pageants.
                            Ay, my lord.
That which is now a horse, even with a thought
    The rack dislimns.[32]

Here is what Swift makes of it. I do not quote it as an example of
parody, but to show his mind in this way also enriched by his reading,
and subduing it to his purpose.

If I should venture in a windy Day, to affirm to *Your Highness,* that
there is a large Cloud near the *Horizon* in the Form of a *Bear,* another
in the *Zenith* with the Head of an *Ass,* a third to the Westward with
Claws like a *Dragon;* and *Your Highness* should in a few Minutes
think fit to examine the Truth, 'tis certain, they would all be changed
in Figure and Position, new ones would arise, and all we could agree
upon would be, that Clouds there were, but that I was grossly mistaken
in the *Zoography* and *Topography* of them.[33]

Professor Sherburn has drawn attention to a striking aspect of the
Tale, often overlooked, as it reveals Swift's "dislike of the deluding
powers of perverted reason," or, more specifically, his dislike of
proselytizing, of people who wish to force their opinions upon others.

Whoever hath *an Ambition to be heard in a Crowd*—so, with contempt, begins his Introduction to the *Tale;* and in the climactic Digression on Madness, the lunatics are the founders of states by conquest,
the founders of new systems of philosophy, and the founders of sects in
religion.[34]

This is very true, but even in this there is an element of irony, which
I think Swift was not unaware of, though it was at his own expense.
For he also had an ambition, and a very powerful ambition, to be
heard, and while he makes fun of those who exalt themselves above
the crowd by mounting upon one of those three wooden machines for
the use of orators who desire to talk much without interruption, he
has nevertheless devised his own Tub to provide a platform for his

[32] *Anthony and Cleopatra,* IV, xiv, 2-10.
[33] *Prose,* I, 21.
[34] George Sherburn, "Methods in Books about Swift," SP, xxxv (Oct. 1938),
650.

own special wit and genius. And it cannot be denied that he has sometimes endeavoured to satisfy the "Whale-mouthed gapers after Levity," and has taken advantage of "the liberty of these Times, which hath afforded Wisdom a larger Passport to travel, than was ever able formerly to be obtained, when the World kept her fettered in an implicite Obedience, by the three-fold Cord of Custom, Education and Ignorance." Even when Swift is most directly attacking the sects, and may be in part influenced by his own experience among the Presbyterians in Ireland, he is still writing not as a churchman or a politician, but as a wit and as a man of letters. That is perhaps the fundamental difference between the *Tale* and the roughest controversial satires of the bishops and their opponents. They are always at certain points protected and restrained by their official status. But the author of the *Tale* is completely free, unhampered by political or practical considerations. He is concerned with words; his wit is conceit; and he did not always realize perhaps the power and the effect of the weapons he was using.

In his handling of the allegory of the three brothers, for instance, he is inclined to dramatize their actions rather in the manner of the contemporary stage, and their language and gestures remind us of the world of Sir Novelty Fashion and Lord Foppington. And the symbol of the coats, meaning "the Doctrine and Faith of Christianity," is full of obvious dangers, though it not only lends itself to the necessary dramatization, but also may be neatly reversed and elaborated into a satire on the real religion of the fashionable world, its god the tailor, and its system of belief according to which the universe is a large suit of Clothes and man himself but a micro-Coat, the acquirements of his mind furnishing an exact dress:

> Is not Religion a Cloak, Honesty a Pair of Shoes, worn out in the Dirt, Self-Love a Surtout, Vanity a Shirt, and Conscience a Pair of Breeches?[35]

The whole of this passage is like a string of puns and conceits held together by a thread of irony. The dangers of Swift's satire on the corruptions of religion, whether in the allegory itself, or in the account of the sect of the Aeolists and the Fragment on the mechanical operation of the Spirit, arise out of the verbal play of his wit, which does

[35] *Prose*, I, 47.

not hesitate to make a sort of punning game with all the words which had become, it is true, soiled and bent by the usage they had received at the hands of hypocrites and fanatics, but which had nevertheless also been upon the lips of saints and prophets and remained for the devout Christian sacred symbols of his faith. It is not merely that the book contains "several youthful Sallies," or that "no one Opinion can fairly be deduced from it, which is contrary to Religion or Morality"— it is rather that the Author of *A Tale of a Tub* with an audience of "the greatest Droles and Wits that any Age every produced," set out to establish his reputation among them by outdistancing them all in the variety of his drollery and the reach and penetration of his wit.

In this he succeeded. None of them went farther in their probing, none of them journeyed farther in the exploration of a rationalist's complete scepticism, none of them opened their minds so freely and without prejudice to all that was being thought and said, none of them—not even Sir Thomas Browne—more eloquently expressed that experience of following the mind of man through all its magnificent and fantastic vagaries during the century. Here Swift shows what he could have done, had he wished to write like them. Here is a tour de force, a superb imitation of their most exalted rhetorical periods, soaring into the empyrean in circling parodies of their favourite cosmic images, only to burst at last into an explosive flash of wit, as he compares man's fancy to the brightly plumaged bird of paradise that was reputed to live only in the heights of the air.

AND, whereas the mind of Man, when he gives the Spur and Bridle to his Thoughts, doth never stop, but naturally sallies out into both extreams of High and Low, of Good and Evil; His first Flight of Fancy, commonly transports Him to Idea's of what is most Perfect, finished, and exalted; till having soared out of his own Reach and Sight, not well perceiving how near the Frontiers of Height and Depth, border upon each other; With the same Course and Wing, he falls down plum into the lowest Bottom of Things; like one who travels the East into the West; or like a strait Line drawn by its own length into a Circle. Whether a Tincture of Malice in our Natures, makes us fond of furnishing every bright Idea with its Reverse; Or, whether Reason reflecting upon the Sum of Things, can, like the Sun, serve only to enlighten one half of the Globe, leaving the other half, by Necessity, under Shade and Darkness: Or, whether Fancy, flying up to the imagination of what is Highest and Best, becomes over-shot, and spent, and weary, and suddenly falls like a dead Bird of Paradise, to the Ground.[36]

But no one has more lightly tossed aside these metaphysical conjectures to argue triumphantly in the cause of reason and common sense, ironically exposing the delusions of the imagination, and the dangers of all philosophical anatomizing, and showing the wisdom of contenting ourselves with the superficies of things, only to bring us to this conclusion:

> This is the sublime and refined Point of Felicity, called, *the Possession of being well deceived*; The Serene, Peaceful State of being a Fool among Knaves.[37]

And no one has gone quite so far—not even that "absolute Lord of Wit," the Earl of Rochester, who was indeed quite unhampered in his profanity and little concerned with man's dignity—as the Author of *A Tale of a Tub* when he recommends as a very noble undertaking to Tory members of the House of Commons that they should appoint a commission (who shall be empowered to send for Persons, Papers, and Records) to examine into the merits of every student and professor in Bedlam, so that they might be properly used for all the offices in the state, ecclesiastical, civil and military. Various suitable candidates are vividly described and their special fitness for various occupations indicated; and the irony is pressed home in a characteristically thorough manner, by the evident manifestation that "all would very much excel, and arrive at great Perfection in their several Kinds." In case anyone should doubt this, the author of these momentous truths modestly claims to have had the happiness of being for some time a worthy member of that honourable society, and by that one plain instance clinches his argument, admitting gravely that he is "a Person, whose Imaginations are hard-mouth'd, and exceedingly disposed to run away with his *Reason*," which he had observed "from long experience, to be a very light Rider, and easily shook off."

Dr. Johnson relates that "when this wild work first raised the attention of the publick, Sacheverell, meeting Smalridge, tried to flatter him by seeming to think him the author; but Smalridge answered with

[36] Ibid., p. 99.
[37] Ibid., p. 110.

indignation, 'Not all that you and I have in the world nor all that ever we shall have, should hire me to write the *Tale of a Tub*.' "[38] Perhaps there is some reason for such an attitude, not because the *Tale* is sometimes unconventional, or even profane; but because it reveals so fully through all the parody and wit and irony the intellectual experience of the author. Though there were chasms in the manuscript, where we are told certain passages were omitted, the book as printed gives the impression of holding nothing back. It is in the tradition of the century that was closing as it was written; it is in the direct line of Wit, and it may not be altogether extravagant to say that it makes an effective epilogue, and leaves the stage clear for a new and rather different set of actors. And perhaps it almost meets on a different level the requirements of one of the most notable wits in the company for whom Swift wrote, the Duke of Buckingham, who at the end of the century challenged his generation to produce another writer of such sincerity, as he who from the beginning of the century had exercised so much influence in England,—the incomparable Montaigne. "Yet," he says, "whenever any great Wit shall incline to the same free way of writing, I almost dare assure him of success; for besides the agreeableness of such a book, so very sincere a temper of mind needs not blush to be exposed as naked as possible."[39] In spite of all their differences and in spite of the novelty and originality of *A Tale of a Tub* and the violence and exuberance which make it so unlike the tone and manner of Montaigne, it was nevertheless written by one who was inclined to "the same free way of writing" and of "so very sincere a temper of mind" that it reveals as nakedly and as fearlessly as possible the intellectual experience of a man of letters, who had reached the age of thirty a little before the turn of the century together with what might not too fancifully be called the first generation of the modern world.

[38] *Lives of the Poets*, III, 10-11.
[39] *Miscellanea*, Haworth Press, 1933, pp. 82-3.

POLITICAL SATIRE

He was an *honest man* I'll swear—:
Why Sir, I differ from you there,
For, I have heard another Story,
He was a most *confounded Tory—!*[1]

In examining Swift's political satire we shall be concerned mainly
with his writings during two periods of four years; the first, when he
wrote for the Tory Ministry of the last four years of Queen Anne's
reign, for an English audience in London under the name of "Examiner"; and the second, when he wrote for an Irish audience in
Dublin, particularly from 1720 to 1724, when he assumed the name
and manner of a Dublin linen draper, though he continued later after
his last visit to England in 1727 from time to time to play a part in
Irish affairs.

Swift was of course no stranger to the world of politics before he
entered the service of the Tories. As secretary to Sir William Temple
and as editor of his works, he had been at a point of vantage to observe the course of affairs since the Revolution; and the first printed
work of which he was proud, though rather an academic performance,
received great approbation, and brought him as soon as he was known
to be the author the acquaintance of Lord Somers and Lord Halifax.
But the best account of this is provided by Swift himself in his *Memoirs relating to that change in the Queen's Ministry in 1710:*

> Although I had been for many years before no stranger to the court,
> and had made the nature of government a great part of my study, yet
> I had dealt very little with politics, either in writing or acting, till about
> a year before the late *King William's* death; when, returning with the
> Earl of Berkeley from Ireland, and falling upon the subject of the five
> great Lords who were then impeached, for high crimes and misde-

[1] *Poems*, p. 547.

meanours, by the House of Commons, I happened to say, That the
same manner of proceeding, at least as it appeared to me from the
views we received of it in Ireland, had ruined the liberties of Athens
and Rome; and that it might be easy to prove it from history. Soon
after I went to London; and, in a few weeks, drew up a discourse,
under the title of *The Contests and Dissensions of the Nobles and
Commons in Athens and Rome, with the Consequences they had upon
both those States*.

. . . I soon grew domestic with Lord Halifax and was as often with
Lord Somers as the formality of his nature (the only unconversable
fault he has) made it agreeable to me.

It was then I first began to trouble myself with the difference between
the principles of Whig and Tory; having formerly employed myself in
other, and I think much better speculations. I talked often upon this
subject with Lord Somers; told him, that, having been long conversant
with the Greek and Roman authors, and therefore a lover of liberty, I
found myself much inclined to be what they called a Whig in politics;
and that, besides, I thought it impossible, upon any other principle, to
defend, or submit to the Revolution: But, as to religion, I confessed
myself to be a High-churchman, and that I did not conceive how any
one, who wore the habit of a clergyman, could be otherwise.[2]

He then goes on to point to the pamphlets he had written two years
before he was first introduced to Harley, in which he had opposed the
party then in power and, in particular, had written against the measures which it was expected the Earl of Wharton would undertake to
get the Sacramental Test removed in Ireland. But the first three of
these tracts are hardly political satire; two of them indeed seem to
have been written for the volume of *Miscellanies* which did not even-
tually appear until 1711. In *The Sentiments of a Church-of-England
Man with Respect to Religion and Government* he definitely proposes
to write in such a way as would be liable to the least objection from
either party; he satirizes only the spirit of faction and recommends to
those who desire "to preserve the Constitution entire in Church and
State . . . to avoid the Extreams of *Whig* for the Sake of the former,
and the Extreams of *Tory* on Account of the latter."[3] And in the
Argument against Abolishing Christianity he writes still in the character of a Wit and a young gentleman much in the world and there-

[2] *Prose*, VIII, 119-20.
[3] Ibid., II, 25.

fore needing to rely wholly on irony to uphold such an unpopular
cause as the Established Church, against the arguments of the free-
thinkers and the men of pleasure and the politicians who are all bent
upon its destruction. There are many passages which remind us of
A Tale of a Tub, for instance:

> There is a Portion of Enthusiasm assigned to every Nation, which if it
> hath not proper Objects to work on, will burst out, and set all in a
> Flame. If the Quiet of a State can be bought by only flinging Men a
> few Ceremonies to devour, it is a Purchase no wise Man would refuse.
> Let the Mastiffs amuse themselves about a Sheep-skin stuffed with
> Hay, provided it will keep them from worrying the Flock.[4]

I would almost say that it is written with such enjoyment of the play
of irony, and with such an indulgence in wit, or on the other hand,
with such contempt of the ways of the world, and occasionally with
such double-edged scorn, that it hardly succeeds in its defence of the
Establishment or in its support of the dignity of the clergy, "who are
the only great Restorers of our Breed"; having been "reduced by the
wise Regulations of Henry the Eighth, to the Necessity of a low Diet,
and moderate Exercise."[5] And even that Tory tract, the *Project for the
Advancement of Religion* addressed to the Countess of Berkeley, and
printed in 1709, though advocating that the Court should exert its
full authority and employ in the government and the offices of State
only orthodox members of the Church party, was so clothed in the
language of morality that a good Whig like Steele took occasion to
commend it highly in the *Tatler.*

But in the other tract that Swift later mentions with justifiable
pride as a proof of his attitude while the Whigs were still in power,
which appeared as *A Letter from a Member of the House of Commons of Ireland concerning the Sacramental Test,* he appears for the
first time in action as a political satirist, writing on a specific matter on
behalf of the High-Church party and at the same time in his impersonation of an Irish M.P., surprising us by a curious foreshadowing of
his later role as a Hibernian patriot. Here already is that fierce indignation, strengthened by the double force of his feelings *for* Ireland
and *against* an English policy he hated on its own account. Often—

[4] Ibid., p. 35.
[5] Ibid., pp. 30-31.

he says—since he had read Cowley's Love Verses at the age of fifteen, he had imagined these lines to be spoken by Ireland:

> Forbid it Heaven my Life should be
> Weigh'd with her least Conveniency.

If your little Finger be sore, and you think a Poultice made of our *Vitals* will give it any Ease, speak the Word, and it shall be done;[6]

The pamphlet was written as a warning against the designs of which the Earl of Wharton was suspected to get the Test Act first repealed in Ireland; and it bore also the weight of Swift's personal dislike, since Wharton had received him so coldly over the matter of remitting the First Fruits to the Irish clergy, and had appointed Lambert, a Whig Low-Churchman, to be his chaplain. During the course of his government in Ireland, Swift remained aloof, and his dislike of Wharton turned to distrust and hatred and contempt, which found expression in a violent attack, dater from London, August 30, 1710, and entitled *A Short Character of his Excellency Thomas Earl of Wharton, Lord Lieutenant of Ireland.*

In all his political satire in both England and Ireland Swift made full use of his personal dislikes to destroy the public reputation of the leaders of the opposing party. His method is to adopt the role of a cold impartial examiner, patiently and thoroughly exposing the wretched and corrupt state of his victims in a mood which reminds us of the remark of the author of *A Tale of a Tub,* when he is warning us against the danger of anatomizing: "Last Week I saw a Woman flay'd, and you will hardly believe, how much it altered her Person for the worse." In the process of his examining of Thomas, Earl of Wharton, he confesses that he enters on the work with more cheerfulness because it is not possible to make him angry or hurt his reputation, as he is entirely without the sense of shame or glory; and then with considerable precision he delineates the character of an unscrupulous, intriguing, lying, foulmouthed politician driven by three predominant passions not usually found together, "Love of Power, Love of Money, and Love of Pleasure, but since he went to Ireland . . . most disposed to the second . . . having gained by his Government of under two Years, five and forty thousand Pounds by the most favourable Computation, half in the regular Way, and half in the prudential."[7]

[6] Ibid., p. 114.
[7] Ibid., III, 181.

But it was even more important in the interest of the Queen and her
new ministers to strike at the powerful group they had supplanted by
undermining the reputation of the great general himself. Swift did
not hesitate before the difficulty of such a task, or allow his private
opinions to modify the force of those arguments which were necessary to justify the action taken by the Ministry in setting aside the
Duke. In the *Journal to Stella* for January 1, 1712, he tells her that
he had dined with the Secretary,

> and it is true that the Duke of Marlborough is turned out of all.
> . . . If the Ministry be not sure of a Peace, I shall wonder at this step,
> and do not approve it at best. . . . however it be, the world abroad
> will blame us. I confess my belief that he has not one good quality in
> the world besides that of a general, and even that I have heard denied
> by several great soldiers. But we have had constant success in arms
> while he commanded. Opinion is a mighty matter in war, and I doubt
> the French think it impossible to conquer an army that he leads, and
> our soldiers think the same; and how far even this step may encourage
> the French to play tricks with us, no man knows. I do not love to see
> personal resentment mix with publick affairs.[8]

Nevertheless, once the step had been taken, it was his duty to
justify it thoroughly in order to prepare the way for a peace with
France by discrediting Marlborough's later handling of the campaign
in the Netherlands. The main argument is that England ought not to
have committed herself so deeply to support the Dutch by land, but
should have taken the opportunity to build up her own sea power and
impoverish France and Spain by attacks on their shipping and colonies. But unfortunately the sea was not the Duke of Marlborough's
element, and such a plan would not have contributed to his prestige
and profit.

Indeed, Swift does not hesitate to follow the method which he
had proved and continued to use in all controversies, the method
which he frankly described in this simple formula:

> In all Contests the safest way is to put those we dispute with as much
> *in the Wrong* as we can.[9]

So, a month later, he set to work to put Marlborough as much in the

[8] *Journal*, pp. 295-6.
[9] *Prose*, VIII, 96.

wrong as he could, by exposing his two weaknesses—his ambition, which led him to ask to be made general for life, and his avarice, which Swift deals with so subtly in his *Letter to Marcus Crassus*, published in the *Examiner*, February 8, 1710–11. It is a masterpiece of detraction, masked with opening phrases of compliment and genuine praise of the great qualities of the general which lead naturally to the question why he has not gained the love of the army abroad or the people at home. This is because, though he is the richest person in the land, he is "deeply stained with that odious and ignoble Vice of *Covetousness.*" If he does not believe it let him disguise himself and go among his soldiers and among the common people and listen to what they say about him; or let him ask his own nearest friends. And then the epistle concludes with this neat sentence:

> The moment you quit this Vice, you will be a truly Great Man; and still there will Imperfections enough remain to convince us, you are not a *God*. Farewell.[10]

It would be tempting to quote the satirical Elegy that Swift wrote at the time of Marlborough's death; but that was too late to be of any use as political satire. It indicates however something rather significant in Swift's own conception of himself as an impartial examiner; he seems so sure of himself in that role that he wished also to be the historiographer of the time, officially appointed to provide a true and impartial record for posterity. It was this that led him to pursue his enemies beyond the grave, so that the evil they committed would still stand as a judgment against them, or as he pleasantly puts it in justifying his attack later on the Lord Chief Justice of Ireland:

> it is certain, that People distinguished for their *Villainy*, have as good a Title for a Blast from the *proper Trumpet*, as those who are most renowned for their *Virtues*, have from the other; and have equal Reason to complain, if it be refused them.[11]

Certainly Swift undertook this double duty in the *Examiner*, a paper which the ministry had launched "to provide just reflections upon former proceedings and defend the present measures of her Majesty." Bolingbroke, Atterbury, Prior and a few friends were responsible for

10 Ibid., III, 85.
11 *An Answer to a Paper called a Memorial*, 1728. See Prose, XII, 23.

it at first, but Harley proposed to Swift that he should take it over entirely, and seems to have made some promise that he should be established in England. Thus for about eight months he wrote these weekly papers entirely himself, from the beginning of November 1710 to the middle of June 1711.

By the end of the eight months he could boast that his work was done, "the main body of the Whigs entirely subdued, and that there only remained to be dealt with a few wretches who had nothing left but their bare good will towards Faction and Mischief." And as far as he was concerned they could be disposed of in a final conceit:

> For my own particular, those little barking Pens which have so constantly pursued me, I take to be of no further Consequence to what I have writ, than the scoffing Slaves of old, placed behind the Chariot, to put the General in Mind of his Mortality; which was but a Thing of Form, and made no Stop or Disturbance in the Show. However, if those perpetual Snarlers against me had the same Design, I must own they have effectually compassed it; since nothing can well be more mortifying, than to reflect, that I am of the same Species with Creatures capable of uttering so much Scurrility, Dulness, Falshood and Impertinence, to the Scandal and Disgrace of Human Nature.[12]

He had throughout his campaign taken every opportunity to dissociate himself from these mere party hacks by maintaining a middle ground between the High-fliers and the Dissenters, between the *Rehearsal* and the *Medley;* and he had frequently tried to expose the use of "the cant-words, Whig and Tory," which had so often varied their significance in their thirty years' history, and to prove that the new ministry had wide-spread and national support, while their opponents were a mixture of heterogeneous factions which could not conceivably be brought together in the unity of a single party.

As these *Examiner* papers are not often carefully studied except by those who are concerned with the political history of this period, it might be well to look more particularly at No. 34, dated March 29, 1711, in which Swift very simply and clearly exposes the method of his irony. We can observe his success in using it as a device to convince his readers of the reasonableness of his own middle position, as a fair impartial examiner, who was completely protected against his

[12] *Prose*, III, pp. 171-2.

opponents from either extreme. It is a device which can be recommended in political debate, because it works by a process of simplification, setting over against one another certain antithetical ideas and propositions, and breaking down the whole complicated pattern into a few plain figures in black and white, which can be easily brought together for comparison and contrast.

In this paper he begins by confessing that he has grown weary of the job of examining and has therefore been led to take stock of his position, and to consider what would become of him, *if Times should alter;* but after mature consideration he decides that there is no cause for anxiety:

> what I have said upon Occasion, concerning the late Men in Power, may be called Satyr by some unthinking People, as long as that Faction is down; but if ever they come into Play again, I must give them warning beforehand, that I shall expect to be a *Favourite,* and that those pretended Advocates of theirs, will be Pilloried for *Libellers.*[13]

In like manner he had imagined that he had been complimenting the present ministry, when he had spoken of their loyalty to the Queen and the old constitution in Church and State, and their desire for an honourable peace.

> But it seems I am mistaken, and they reckon all this for Satyr, because it is directly contrary to the Practice of all those whom they set up to defend, and utterly against all their Notions of a good Ministry. Therefore I cannot but think they have Reason on their side: For, suppose I should write the Character of an Honest, a Religious, and a learned Man, and send the first to *Newgate,* and the second to the *Grecian Coffee-House,* and the last to *White's;* would they not all pass for *Satyrs,* and justly enough, among the Companies to whom they were sent?
> Having therefore employed several Papers in such sort of *Panegyricks,* and but very few on what they understand to be *Satyrs;* I shall henceforth upon Occasion be more Liberal of the latter; of which they are like to have a Taste in the remainder of this present Paper.[14]

He can appeal to the simple irony in the situation to justify his examination of the facts; he is as impartial as the Recording Angel; it is

13 Ibid., p. 117.
14 Ibid., p. 119.

but calling things by different names—panegyric or satire—and both parties equally approve, and applaud his excellent strokes. It is a neatly balanced performance which cannot be upset within the limits of the stage he has arranged. And the argument is so strongly woven that there is nothing to get hold of and twist out of shape. As a political satirist he is always concerned to rally his supporters, and to over-run all opposition, never to win over his opponents by persuasion or by concession. He has nothing of the temper of that real exponent of the via media, and Trimmer, the Marquis of Halifax; and though he was "for some time domesticate with him," shows little of his influence, none of his wise caution and scepticism, when he gives advice on the way to handle a political argument:

> there is hardly a single Proposition to be made, which is not deceitful, and the tying our Reason too close to it, may in many Cases be destructive. Circumstances must come in, and are to be made a part of the Matter of which we are to judge; positive *Decisions* are always dangerous, more especially in *Politicks*. A Man, who will be Master of an Argument, must do like a skilful General, who sendeth Scouts on all sides, to see whether there may not be an Enemy. So he must look round to see what Objections can be made, and not go on in a streight Line, which is the ready way to lead him into a mistake.[15]

Swift never looks round, or lets us look round if he can help it, to see what objections can be made, and he always prefers to move in a straight line, attacking directly straight down the middle, dividing his enemies to the left and to the right, passing through them unharmed and leaving them to their mutual destruction. And he would doubtless retort that it was not his fault if events within a very few years turned some of the *Examiner's* compliments to the new ministry and the new parliament into very bitter satire indeed.

Meantime he continued to provide the ministry with clear statements confidently justifying their policy in a series of pamphlets designed to win approval for the conclusion of a peace with France—*The Conduct of the Allies, The Barrier Treaty,* etc. That was his most dignified and important role, for he contributed a clear and reasonable analysis of the situation, which had immediate effect in producing the necessary change of opinion both in the House of Com-

15 *The Works of George Savile,* pp. 170-71.

mons and in the country. Again in these pamphlets he assumes with extraordinary conviction his role as impartial Examiner, though he trusts in fact to his favourite method of detraction, of proving in the wrong the Whig ministers who had bribed the Dutch to continue the war by offering them all the advantages of the Barrier Treaty instead of taking the perfect opportunity which had been presented them to make a completely satisfactory peace for Europe. Similarly he exposes the short-sightedness and selfishness of the Dutch in using the position for their own benefit, and so convincingly proves them in the wrong that he almost seems to justify the dishonourable betrayal of their Allies which the Tory ministry was actually planning. And finally he attempts to discredit them both—the Whigs and the Dutch alike—as belonging to a solemn League and Covenant devoted to their own base interests at the expense of the true welfare of the people of England:

> I have here imputed the Continuance of the War to the mutual Indulgence between our General and Allies, wherein they both so well found their Accounts; to the Fears of the *Mony-changers,* lest their *Tables should be overthrown;* to the Designs of the *Whigs,* who apprehended the Loss of their Credit and Employments in a Peace; and to those at home, who held their immoderate Engrossments of Power and Favour, by no other Tenure, than their own Presumption upon the Necessity of Affairs. The Truth of this will appear indisputable, by considering with what Unanimity and Concert these several Parties acted towards that great End.[16]

At the same time, he did not neglect other levels of attack, coming to the relief of the ministry with a squib giving a mock account of Prior's journey to Paris when that diplomatic secret mission was prematurely discovered, tossing hints to his aides and assistants in party journalism, and putting out ballads and popular verses against the Earl of Nottingham and the Duchess of Somerset, or the Duke of Marlborough. They were usually tried out first for the private amusement of the Brothers Society, and then, if approved, printed off on a half sheet the next day for the benefit of the public. In the pages of the *Journal to Stella,* we can watch him triumphantly at work, enjoying the excitement of public life and the invigorating experience of success in political action, seeing the results of his skilful plans. But

[16] *Prose*, VI, 43.

before the death of the Queen—after his return from Dublin when
he was installed as Dean in 1713, the growing division in the Ministry made it impossible for him to help them any longer:

> By Faction tir'd with Grief he waits a while,
> His great contending Friends to reconcile.
> Performs what Friendship, Justice, Truth require:
> What could he more, but decently retire?[17]

His retirement from active politics was to last for six years. During
that time he was to write only memoirs, histories and verses—'all
Panegyricks.' But in a letter addressed to Charles Ford, in December 1719, there is a strong hint that this period of inaction is nearly
over.

> . . . as the World is now turned, no Cloyster is retired enough to keep
> Politicks out, . . .

There was indeed noise enough that winter in Dublin to disturb
Swift in the corner of his Deanery, and when in March 1720 the
*Act for the better securing the Dependency of the Kingdom of Ireland
upon the Crown of Great Britain* was passed, taking away the juris-
diction of the Irish House of Lords, the general discontent spread to
all parties.

> I do assure you I never saw so universall a Discontent as there is
> among the highest most virulent and anti-church Whigs against that
> Bill and every Author or Abetter of it without Exception. They say
> publickly that having been the most loyall submissive complying Sub-
> jects that ever Prince had, no Subjects were ever so ill treated.[18]

Swift's comment shows the fundamental position he took throughout in all his activities as the Dublin linen draper: "The Question is
whether People ought to be Slaves or no."

In all his writings concerning Irish politics his object was to prevent collaboration and to keep alive the spirit of independence which
would resist by every possible means all further encroachments of the
British government in London on the liberties of Ireland. He could
not hope to do much with the leaders of the Church in Ireland or the
men in public employment, because they were appointed by the

[17] *Poems*, p. 196.
[18] *Letters to Ford*, pp. 82, 86.

Crown or under the influence of the Lord Lieutenant; therefore, his only chance was to rouse a popular campaign among the shopkeepers and country people of Ireland.

He began his campaign with a Proposal for the universal use of Irish Manufacture, in clothes, and furniture of Houses, etc., utterly rejecting and renouncing everything wearable that comes from England. This appeal to the public to boycott all goods from England, or as he put it in the popular phrase of the moment, "to burn everything that comes from England except their People and their Coals,"[19] was printed in Dublin just before the celebrations arranged for May 28, 1720, in honour of the sixtieth birthday of King George. Though it is written with wit and humour, and though he attacks the Irish Parliament for their neglect of the state of the nation and the shopkeepers for their lack of common sense, though he adds a final word of contempt for the project of a Bank in Dublin, his main purpose was perfectly clear—to attack again his old political enemies, the Whig ministers and the moneyed men, to rouse the feelings of the Irish people against them, and stir their resentment against them on account of the universal oppression which was evident throughout the whole land.

Like all his Irish Tracts, this was no mere literary production—it was political satire and political action; and it brought Swift into conflict with the Lord Chancellor and with the Chief Justice of Ireland. The printer was brought to trial immediately, and the Chief Justice did his utmost to get him convicted, sending back the jury nine times, and finally postponing the case until the next term. Swift was able to get the matter settled by using the influence of his friends in England upon the Duke of Grafton, the Lord Lieutenant, but he never forgave Whitshed, whom he was to meet again and to defeat on a more serious occasion.

Although this proposal for a boycott did not have any direct result, Swift adopted the same tactics four years later to meet another questionable project in English dealings with the people of Ireland. In 1722 a certain William Wood obtained a patent to coin and send into Ireland a limited amount of copper coinage. In spite of immediate protests against the patent from the Commissioners of the Revenue in Dublin, agreements were quietly made in 1723 for the delivery of

19 *Prose*, IX, 17.

the first consignments of the copper coins to Ireland. This aroused violent opposition, and, soon after the arrival of the Duke of Grafton as Lord Lieutenant in August of that year, both houses of Parliament drew up Addresses condemning the patent. This forced the British government to order an enquiry in the spring of 1724. At this moment Swift took action by printing *A Letter to the Shopkeepers, Tradesmen, Farmers and Common People of Ireland* by M. B. Drapier, in the form of a penny pamphlet, copies of which were available for distribution at a special rate of three dozen for two shillings.

This was the first of the series of letters which appeared during the year 1724, when Swift happened to be kept in Dublin throughout the summer because he was building a wall round part of his property, and so as it were by chance became involved in this episode of Wood's copper coinage. These letters were not, however, mere bagatelles for the amusement of the Dean and his friends, though they doubtless served that purpose excellently. But again they were a form of direct political action just the same as if he had gone out into the streets and addressed the people. They were written with the single purpose of persuading the people of Ireland to boycott Wood's coinage, and force the Crown to cancel the patent.

He had pointed out in his *Letter to a young Clergyman* in 1720 that the constant design of the great orators of Greece and Rome in all their speeches "was to drive some one particular Point; either the Condemnation, or Acquittal of an accused Person; a persuasive to War, the enforcing of a Law, and the like: which was determined upon the Spot, according as the Orators on either Side prevailed."[20] And he had there expressed his preference for the method of Demosthenes, who relied on the strength of his arguments offered to the understanding and the reason. But his Dublin audience was a simple one, and the formal methods of oratory were not to his taste; so he translates his argument into the plain unlearned speech that might be supposed to be the voice of a linen draper of Dublin. Yet through the mask he is careful that you should, if you are clever enough, recognize who is speaking. The opening sentences of Letter I, to readers in Dublin in March 1724, would, I think, at once be recognizable as having the tone which they were accustomed to hear from the pulpit

[20] Ibid., p. 69.

of St. Patrick's.[21] And as if to make sure of this he associates himself on the very next page with the *Proposal*, that had appeared four years earlier, which in Dublin was certainly known to have been written by him. The rest of the Letter is a plain statement of facts about the proposed coinage, and the laws governing coinage, which justified the rejection of Wood's copper—ending with an argument very direct in its appeal:

"Any person may expect to get a Quart of Two-penny Ale for Thirty Six of them."[22]

The second letter did not appear until August, when the rumours of the new modified proposal began to appear in the newspapers. It ended with a sample Declaration against Wood's coinage which Swift proposed should be signed by two or three hundred leading gentlemen of the Kingdom. The third followed shortly after, as soon as the Report of the Committee was published. These letters contain an attack on the London Committee's enquiry, a close examination of their Report, and are enlivened by some of Swift's best invective against Mr. Wood and indirectly against Walpole.

And *he defied the Armies of the Living God. Goliah's* Conditions of Combat were likewise the same with those of *Wood: If he prevail against us, then shall we be his Servants*: But if it happen that I *prevail* over him, I renounce the other part of the Conditions; he shall never be a *Servant* of mine; for I do not think him fit to be trusted in any *honest* Man's Shop.[23]

He then proceeds to outline a plan for carrying out the boycott:

i. Declarations against Wood's coinage by all public bodies and by all tradesmen.
ii. A boycott of all tradesmen who should accept the coin.

There remained however the danger that as soon as the new Lord Lieutenant should arrive, he would succeed by the usual bribery and pressure in winning over the influential people to back the scheme. Swift therefore prepared another letter, this time addressed to the

[21] *Drapier's Letters.* See *Prose*, X, 3.
[22] Ibid., p. 12.
[23] Ibid., p. 48.

whole People of Ireland, and got it printed ready for circulation in the
streets of Dublin on the very day that Carteret landed.

Here his method is entirely different. This is not the time for invective, and Lord Carteret for whom he had great admiration could
not be attacked. Instead of that, he meets him with compliments and
at the same time takes care very subtly to warn the Irish leaders
against the sort of methods that might be employed to win them
over. He reminds them that, however liable to temptation they may
be, Lord Carteret has really very little to tempt them with, as all the
good posts in the government were already given to Englishmen. But
the real sting of the pamphlet was to be found in the passage dealing
with the question of Ireland's dependence upon England.

> I have looked over all the English and Irish Statutes without finding
> any Law that makes Ireland *depend* upon England, any more than
> England does upon Ireland. We have indeed obliged our selves to have
> *the same King with them;* and consequently they are obliged to have
> the *same King with us.* For the Law was made by *our own Parliament;*
> and our Ancestors then were not such *Fools (whatever they were in
> the Preceding Reign)* to bring themselves under I know not what *De-
> pendance,* which is now talked of without any ground of *Law, Reason*
> or *Common Sense.*
>
> Let whoever think otherwise, I *M. B. Drapier,* desire to be excepted,
> for I declare, next under God, I *depend* only on the King my Sover-
> eign, and on the Laws of my own Country; and I am so far from
> depending upon the People of England, that if they should ever *rebel*
> against my Sovereign (which God forbid) I would be ready at the first
> Command from his Majesty to take Arms against them, as some of *my*
> Country men did against *theirs* at *Preston.* And, if such a Rebellion
> should prove so successful as to fix the *Pretender* on the Throne of
> *England,* I would venture to transgress that *Statute* so far, as to lose
> every Drop of my Blood, to hinder him from being *King* of Ire-
> land.[24]

This was going very near to high treason. Carteret took immediate
action, by calling the Privy Council together, and persuading them
to offer a reward of £300 for the discovery of the author, and to arrest
the printer. It was a comic situation, for he and everyone else at the
Castle knew pretty well who the author was. And for a time Swift

24 Ibid., p. 62.

apparently thought of coming forward and challenging the authorities to arrest him. He was probably advised not to do this.

The declarations continued to come in and the whole business of Parliament was held up. When the case of the printer came before the Grand Jury, Swift put out a paper giving them advice how to act and attacking Whitshed; and when this was also proceeded against, he provided them with a declaration, which was read out in court to the scandal of the judges, in which they used the opportunity of declaring their opposition to Wood instead of proceeding against Swift's printer. Verses were hawked in the streets against the Chief Justice, and the people of Dublin repeated the words of the Book of Samuel.

> And the people said unto Saul, Shall Jonathan die, who hath wrought this great salvation in Israel? God forbid: as the Lord liveth, there shall not one hair of his head fall to the ground, for he hath wrought with God this day. So the people rescued Jonathan, that he died not.[25]

Carteret saw that nothing could be done, and in due time on his advice the patent was withdrawn. In the meantime Swift published another letter addressed to an enlightened liberal peer, Lord Molesworth, in which with gentle irony he reviews the course of the whole controversy and his part in it, using the terms of his own trade as a draper. It is perhaps the wittiest of the letters, published at a time when it was no longer necessary for him to use his more powerful weapons. There is a sort of triumphant gaiety about it, fitting the mood of a Dublin which began to believe in the success of the opposition they had made, and was inclined to enjoy the fun of it. But it was also important in the campaign—he might have gone too far. It contained also an appeal from the Dean to other Dublin leaders to stand by him.

It is exciting to read the official documents of the time as they were sent in by all sorts of different people to London, reporting each new surprise, as it took place. It was indeed not Swift alone who enjoyed the situation; the venerable Archbishop of Dublin made the most of it also in the House of Lords, carrying it to a fine finish, even after the patent was withdrawn, and when their Lordships were drawing up an address of thanks to his Majesty for his favour to them. He cleverly inserted in the Address the words *in his great wisdom* referring to his

[25] I *Samuel*, xiv, 45.

Majesty's withdrawal of the patent, and when it was accepted was heard to say with great satisfaction, that that would indicate that it was anything but great wisdom to have granted it in the first place. Whereupon the innuendo was noticed and the House of Lords debated the phrase for two days much to the enjoyment of Dublin.

Swift had prepared a final letter to the Irish Parliament to be ready for their opening, but when the news came of the withdrawal of the patent he wrote immediately to his friends to stop the printing:

> . . . Since Wood's patent is cancelled, it will by no means be convenient to have the paper printed, as I suppose you, and Jack Grattan, and Sheridan will agree; therefore, if it be with the printer, I would have it taken back, and the press broke, and let her be satisfied. The work is done, and there is no more need of the Drapier.[26]

He had written to get something done, not to show off his wit or amuse an audience. Therefore when the thing was done, the desired result obtained, there was no further need that what he had written should be read.

He continued to interest himself in the affairs of Ireland, however, and in 1727 seems to have hoped that in the new reign there might be some improvement. He even went to the trouble of explaining the needs of that wretched country to Walpole. But when nothing came of this direct effort, and when his continued warnings, even in Ireland, were unheeded, he abandoned political action and turned to irony and the satisfaction of personal invective in his verses against both Walpole and the Parliament in Dublin. And finally, when the Duke of Dorset came over as Lord Lieutenant to Ireland in the fall of 1731, Swift assured him that he need have no anxiety that the Drapier would cause him the least inconvenience during his term of office. He had also offered a further guarantee of his good behaviour in a letter to the Countess of Suffolk, written on October 26, 1731:

> If any state scribble writ here should happen to reach London, I entreat your Ladyship would continue to do me the justice of believing my innocence, because I lately assured the Duke of Dorset that I would never have a hand in any such thing, and I gave him my reason before his Secretary, that looking upon this kingdom's condition as absolutely desperate, I would not prescribe a dose to the dead.[27]

26 *Corr.*, III, 266.
27 Ibid., IV, 266.

MORAL SATIRE

Sir, our *Accounts* are diff'rent quite,
And your *Conjectures* are not right;
'Tis plain, his Writings were design'd
To *please,* and to *reform* Mankind;
And, if he often miss'd his Aim,
The *World* must own it, to their *Shame;*
The *Praise* is *His,* and *Theirs* the *Blame.*[1]

We have examined the method of Swift's satire, first, as he was concerned with the world of letters, the Author of *A Tale of a Tub,* writing as a wit with his reading fresh in his head, so that the result is very literary, full of parody and of echoes of seventeenth century literature; and second, as he was concerned with the world of politics, both in London and in Dublin, when he appeared in the role of Tory Examiner and Drapier—not to show off his wit or his literature, but to support a party and bring about certain political action.

We must now try to observe him at work on a satire which he hoped would vex the world, and which was intended not merely to show off his wit or to reach a London or a Dublin audience, but which as he said later to the French translator of *Gulliver's Travels,* would be equally well understood abroad, and which was addressed both to his contemporaries and to posterity. If we were right in considering *A Tale of a Tub* as the final product of the seventeenth century, paradoxically growing out of it and at the same time satirizing it and repudiating so much of its spirit, so in like manner we may well regard *Gulliver's Travels* as, both in form and in shape, wholly the product of the eighteenth century, while being at the same time the most violent satire of its hopes and dreams and a repudiation of much that it most valued. For it is typical of the century in a very general way, because it is, more than all Swift's so-called historical writings, his contribution to the favourite study of the age—history, not of course in the present sense of the term, but as it was practised by the eighteenth

[1] *Poems,* p. 550.

century philosophers whether in France or in England, who were concerned, as Carl Becker has shown so conclusively in his *Heavenly City of the Eighteenth Century Philosophers,* all of them with a particular thesis on human behaviour, which they set out to prove, whether by a study of the Decline and Fall of the Roman Empire, or by the study of the history of England, or by a study of the spirit or ideas of Law.

They also like Swift used many of the weapons of the satirist—wit and ridicule and irony, even though their travels were limited to parts and places well-known. And Swift, like Gibbon, had learned his idea of liberty and justice from a study of the writers of Greece and Rome; he had given a good deal of attention to the study of government, and by his own direct experience had arrived at as complete a scepticism as any of theirs. But these eighteenth century philosophers had "demolished the Heavenly City of St. Augustine only to rebuild it with more up-to-date materials"; they remained optimists enough to believe in the possible enlightenment and rescue of the human race from its folly and from its superstition. Swift had an answer very different from theirs, which has continued to shock successive generations, even though the course of later history has hardly proved him wrong. He thought of himself as different even from his friends, and he remained apart from and unlike most of the philosophers of the century. He could not share their beliefs, and he termed them "vous autres." Perhaps it was the purpose of Gulliver to prove this to them, and to their followers.

When his first political career was coming to an end, Swift like many other discarded statesmen turned to the writing of memoirs. He had wished to be appointed officially historiographer to the Queen, in order that he might leave a record for posterity. So after his return to Ireland in 1714, and indeed earlier in England after he left London, despairing of being of further use to the Ministry, he had immediately set to work to put down his own record of the history of the last four years of the Queen. There are various manuscripts surviving from this period, one—*The Enquiry into the Behaviour of the Queen's last Ministry*—begun in the hand of Stella with corrections in the hand of Swift, but none of these memorials were printed in Swift's lifetime, and it was perhaps natural or inevitable that he should try to find some form in which he could make his comment on human behaviour

for the benefit of his contemporaries as well as posterity. But this again
could only be done safely and adequately in some disguise. For this
purpose he could not appear as the London wit; a Bickerstaff would
be too provincial and too literary, the Tory Examiner too political, the
Dean too ecclesiastical, the linen draper of Dublin too Irish.

Once again he finds the solution by employing his favourite device
of parody. He would write a book of Travels, in imitation of the most
popular best sellers of the day, like Dampier's *Voyages*. It should not
be forgotten also that in 1719, when Swift seems to have begun work
seriously on *Gulliver's Travels*, that despised rival political pam-
phleteer, that secret henchman of Harley's, the fellow who was pil-
loried, whose name Swift could never remember, Daniel Defoe, delighted the world with his story of Robinson Crusoe. And so Swift
settled down to read a lot of this trash, and turned over the pages of a
seaman's manual in order to provide himself with the necessary flavour of nautical language, and emerged in an entirely new disguise,
the one in which he is best known to the whole world—as the seaman,
the plain honest traveller, not over learned or too literary (he had only
been three years at Emmanuel College and after that had had some
training as a surgeon and in navigation), a simple plain teachable
man of unspoiled intelligence, who could serve as a sort of *Everyman*.

My Father had a small Estate in Nottinghamshire; I was the Third of
five Sons. He sent me to Emanuel-College in Cambridge, at Fourteen
Years old, where I resided three Years, and applied my self close to my
Studies: But the Charge of maintaining me (although I had a very
scanty Allowance) being too great for a narrow Fortune; I was bound
Apprentice to Mr. James Bates, an eminent Surgeon in London, with
whom I continued four Years; and my Father now and then sending
me small Sums of Money, I laid them out in learning Navigation, and
other Parts of the Mathematicks, useful to those who intend to travel,
as I always believed it would be some time or other my Fortune to do.
When I left Mr. Bates, I went down to my Father; where, by the
Assistance of him and my Uncle John, and some other Relations, I got
Forty Pounds, and a Promise of Thirty Pounds a Year to maintain me
at Leyden: There I studied Physick two Years and seven Months,
knowing it would be useful in long Voyages.

. . . I was Surgeon successively in two Ships, and made several Voyages, for six Years, to the East and West-Indies; by which I got some
Addition to my Fortune. My Hours of Leisure I spent in reading the

best Authors, ancient and modern; being always provided with a good Number of Books; and when I was ashore, in observing the Manners and Dispositions of the People, as well as learning their Language; wherein I had a great Facility by the Strength of my Memory.[2]

This device would also provide him with a way to use all the hints and plans that had remained from the evenings of the Brothers Club, or the satirical papers of Martin Scriblerus, or, even before that, suggestions thrown out to Steele and Addison for a Tatler: e.g., *Journal to Stella,* April 28, 1711: "Yesterday the Spectator was made of a noble hint I gave him long ago for his Tatlers, about an Indian supposed to write his Travels into England. I repent he ever had it. I intended to have written a book on that subject." It is not fanciful to find here the first source in Swift's mind of some of the comments on English life of the King of Brobdingnag or of the criticism of English morals made by Gulliver's master in the land of the Houyhnhnms.

By employing the form of the travel book Swift was able to use the satirical methods which he had perfected in his earliest literary work, parody and raillery and irony, and to make use of all his experience of the world gained during his active political career, and make a masterpiece—the product of his mastery of his art together with his mastery of the business of life. It is this, I think, which gives such finality to his ethical judgments. It is sometimes said that Swift was not a great intelligence, that he was no profound scholar, no outstanding political thinker, and no really original genius. But at least that well-prepared, sceptical intelligence which showed itself in *A Tale of a Tub* had been given a rather complete and varied experience of the ways of the world and of the characters of men and women in those thirty years between his earliest writings and the appearance of *Gulliver's Travels.* He had met and known intimately the greatest and best men of his time, and he had likewise come up against and suffered from some of the cleverest and most ruthless scoundrels; he had had a price set on his head, and he had known what it was to be the idol of the mob, or, as he called them later, his good friends the common people of Ireland. He had indeed been himself a great traveller, and had learned many things; his problem was to find a way in which he could set down the most significant of his observations upon human life, so that the world might be forced to

[2] *Prose,* XI, 19-20.

read them. For even if he could not do any good, he might be able to
vex the world and perhaps amuse some of his friends.

In the first and the third books of *Gulliver's Travels* he manages
to include a great deal of satirical reference to the political events in
which he had taken part, both in England and in Ireland. Both of
these books are in fact confused and inconsistent, because they are
constantly twisted to suit his immediate satirical purpose, whether he
is concerned with the political situation or with very specific parody
and burlesque of the experiments of contemporary scientists or the
schemes of other projectors.

There is a good deal of fun in Lilliput, and with Gulliver we are
able to assume a certain superior detachment and amusement at the
ways of the pigmies. Like him we are protected from any serious
danger at the hands of the Lilliputians. We are provided as it were
with a buff jerkin, which is proof against all their arrows; we are on
good terms with them, and could not be unduly disturbed by anything
those little creatures might do, who could dance, five or six of them
at a time on the palm of one of our hands, or play at hide-and-seek in
our hair. Even the diversions of the court of Lilliput are therefore
inevitably observed by us with good humour, and we can laugh at
the antics of the rope-dancers, and the *leaping* and *creeping* of the
ministers as the Emperor advances or depresses his stick. It is just a
joke to watch them swearing an oath according to the strange method
prescribed by their laws:

> hold the right foot in the left hand, place the middle finger of the right
> hand on the crown of the head, and the thumb on the tip of the right
> ear[3]

—just another of the antics of these minute ballet-dancers. And even
the struggles between the High Heels and the Low Heels, and between those who break their Eggs at the Big End and at the Little
End, seem to be a matter for comedy; and that ugly ambition of the
Emperor to obtain all his enemy's ships, after their Navy had been
brought to him by Gulliver, in order to make himself monarch of the
whole world, does not frighten us unduly, especially as his ambition
is not approved by the wisest part of his ministry.

We are indeed made very subtly to share the innocence of Gulli-

[3] Ibid., pp. 42-3.

ver, his unwillingness to believe evil of princes, his unpreparedness
for their ingratitude and dishonesty. It was only after he had been
wrongly suspected of disaffection that he began to have doubts:

> This was the first time [he says] I began to conceive some imperfect
> Idea of Courts and Ministers.[4]

We cannot really believe any harm of them, as the Royal Family come
to dine with him, sitting in their chairs of state, with their guards
about them, on a corner of his table, just over against him; or as the
members of the Court visited him, remaining in their coaches drawn
by two horses gently round his table. Even when the articles of impeachment are drawn up against Gulliver, and the fierceness of his
enemies is disclosed, with their demand that he should be horribly
murdered, whereas the Emperor in his lenity and tenderness was
willing to condemn him only to the loss of his eyes, he is still able to
make use of the most delicate form of irony:

> Yet, as to myself, I must confess, having never been designed for a
> Courtier, either by my Birth or Education, I was so ill a Judge of
> Things, that I could not discover the *Lenity* and Favour of this Sen-
> tence; but conceived it (perhaps erroneously) rather to be rigorous than
> gentle. I sometimes thought of standing my Tryal; for although I could
> not deny the Facts alledged in the several Articles, yet I hoped they
> would admit of some Extenuations. But having in my life perused
> many State-Tryals, which I ever observed to terminate as the Judges
> thought fit to direct; I durst not rely on so dangerous a Decision, in so
> critical a Juncture, and against such powerful Enemies. Once I was
> strongly bent upon Resistance: For while I had Liberty, the whole
> Strength of that Empire could hardly subdue me, and I might easily
> with Stones pelt the Metropolis to Pieces; But I soon rejected that
> Project with Horror, by remembering the Oath I had made to the
> Emperor, the Favours I received from him, and the high Title of
> *Nardac* he conferred upon me. Neither had I so soon learned the
> Gratitude of Courtiers, to persuade myself that his Majesty's *present
> Severities acquitted me of all past Obligations.*[5]

It is almost as though the very scale of the Lilliputians obliges him
to handle them and their affairs with a sort of tenderness lest they

[4] Ibid., p. 54.
[5] Ibid., pp. 72-3.

break in pieces. The whole country remains inevitably in the imagination as a sort of toy-shop, invaded by a clumsy colossus who finds it
difficult to move about without overturning houses and trampling on
their inhabitants, unable even to see what is going on; amazed to observe "a cook pulling a Lark, which was not so large as a common fly;
and a young girl threading an invisible needle with invisible silk."
Only occasionally when Gulliver allows himself to make comments on
the laws and customs of the land, and on their system of education,
we sometimes forget the figure of Gulliver the colossus and the minute
figures he is discussing, and hear rather the familiar comments of
Dean Swift on education and life. It is surprising how easily the imagination is kept in leash if we are constantly given some one concrete
detail, a goose the size of a sparrow, or a forest tree the top of which
Gulliver can just reach with his closed fist; but likewise, a sentence or
two can completely dispel the scene and banish us from this tiny
commonwealth.

> In relating these and the following Laws, I would only be understood
> to mean the original Institutions, and not the most scandalous Corrup-
> tions into which these People are fallen by the degenerate Nature of
> Man.[6]

Phrases like "the degenerate nature of man," "the great laws of nature," "the miseries of human life" are somewhat too large for that
tiny world and break down the willing suspension of our unbelief;
and then it takes more than the word *Lilliputian* to restore it again.

Swift was to find a better way of handling this problem of keeping
in due balance the imagined scene and the real world in books II
and IV, so that he could use quite freely every phase of his experience,
and bring it to be weighed in the scales provided by his hosts.

But in the Third book, which as I have said is also somewhat confused and lacking in unity, his difficulty was not so much in forcing
his satire to adapt itself to the imaginary circumstances of the voyage;
it is rather that the material in part has never been thoroughly assimi-
lated through his own experience, and he seems sometimes to fall
back almost on the method of the *Tale* in making fun of the extravagancies of the virtuosos, and the strange experiments of the scientists
of the Royal Society. A great deal has been written about the details

[6] Ibid., p. 60.

of this book, to prove how closely he was parodying, when describing the experiments in the Academy of Lagado, the actual accounts he had read in the *Philosophical Transactions of the Royal Society.* In thus using his favourite method of parody which for full enjoyment requires an immediate recognition of the original, Swift was appealing more directly to his contemporaries and especially to his London audience, but he doubtless trusted that the absurdities he slightly exaggerated would serve as symbols which everyone could recognize of the spirit of research he was eager to expose. Professor Everett Case in his *Essays on Gulliver's Travels* published by the Princeton Press just preceding his death, is I believe correct in emphasizing that the satire upon Projectors in this book was not limited to virtuosos and scientists; for Swift was equally if not more concerned to warn his readers against the political projectors and speculators, who had been responsible for such schemes as the South Sea Bubble, and other trade swindles of this sort.

The real reason why so many readers have felt that the Third book is confused and less effective than the others is not simply that Swift was making use of old stuff remaining from the days of the Scriblerus Club; it is rather that he was adding even after the rest of the book was finished passages of political satire in which he was tempted to celebrate his recent success in Ireland, a section indeed which seemed to the printer to be of so immediate and dangerous significance that it was not even included by Faulkner in his Dublin edition published ten years after the events referred to. And further Marjorie Hope Nicolson's and Nora Mohler's studies of the sources of the experiments in the Lagado Academy would indicate the likelihood that Swift, caught by the spirit of parody which he could never resist, went on even as late as the spring of 1726, when he spent some weeks in the company of Dr. Arbuthnot, collecting information about actual experiments then being carried out in order to burlesque them for his main purpose. Sir Harold Williams in his introductory essay to my edition of *Gulliver's Travels* has drawn attention to Dr. Arbuthnot's letter of October 1725, in which he offers the latest information:

> . . . before you put the finishing touch to it, it is really necessary to be acquainted with some new improvements of mankind that have appeared of late, and are daily appearing. Mankind has an inexhaustible source of invention in the way of folly and madness.

But he assumes that Swift did not avail himself of this offer, because a few days after the book was printed Arbuthnot commented:

> I tell you freely, the part of the projectors is the least brilliant.[7]

I myself am tempted to interpret that in the opposite way, for it must be remembered that they were two rivals in irony, and I cannot imagine that Arbuthnot would have been so indelicate as to have written just then almost in reproach, if Swift had indeed rebuffed his offers to help. But what more natural if he had provided Swift with material and advice for this section, than that he should say "Of course the part of the book which I interfered with is the least brilliant"?

In any case, the construction of parts of this book is less satisfactory. The materials used have not been properly matured, the wood is too green; and one would have to admit also that the position of the satirist himself is not a very secure one in some of his attacks upon the physical scientists, and the whirligig of time has given them their revenge.

But the real greatness of *Gulliver's Travels* is to be found when we recognize it as the final and completest satire on human life of this Christian moralist. That is the reason why so many people have been disturbed by the book. Some have said: Do not listen to this fellow, because he is mad; or, He is a monster, uttering blasphemies against mankind; or, He is abnormal, incapable of ordinary affection and loyalties; do not trust anything he says.

It is written by one who did not like the way of the world and was not unwilling to set down his testimony against it. There are two passages which seemed to the original publisher so unveiled, such unrestrained invective that he employed a clergyman, the Rev. Andrew Tooke, to rewrite them in more cautious language; but Swift was careful to have them restored in the edition he prepared for his collected works. The first is a comment on English political life:

> The Bulk of the People consisted wholly of Discoverers, Witnesses, Informers, Accusers, Prosecutors, Evidences, Swearers; together with their several subservient and subaltern Instruments; all under the Colours, the Conduct, and pay of Ministers and their Deputies.[8]

[7] Ibid., XI, pp. xx-xxi.
[8] Ibid., p. 191.

The second is a comment on the legal profession, with which it must
be admitted Swift had had some unfortunate experiences: and perhaps it should also be remembered that Gulliver had been living some
time in the land of the Houyhnhnms, and had doubtless been influenced by their simple views, before making this explanation to his
master:

> I said there was a Society of Men among us, bred up from their Youth
> in the Art of proving by Words multiplied for the Purpose, that *White*
> is *Black,* and *Black* is *White,* according as they are paid. To this So-
> ciety all the rest of the People are Slaves.
> . . . Now, your Honour is to know, that these Judges are Persons ap-
> pointed to decide all Controversies of Property, as well as for the Tryal
> of Criminals; and picked out from the most dextrous Lawyers who are
> grown old or lazy: And having been byassed all their lives against
> Truth and Equity, are under such a fatal Necessity of favouring Fraud,
> Perjury and Oppression; that I have known some of them to have re-
> fused a large Bribe from the Side where Justice lay, rather than injure
> the *Faculty,* by doing any thing unbecoming their Nature or their
> Office.
> . . . In the Tryal of Persons accused for Crimes against the State, the
> Method is much more short and commendable: The Judge first sends
> to sound the Disposition of those in Power; after which he can easily
> hang or save the Criminal, strictly preserving all the Forms of Law.[9]

But there were other comments which occur in the second journey
when Gulliver was trying to explain the glories of western civilization
to the simple-hearted king of the Brobdingnagians, that the publisher
did not bother to change, though the author's intention and the possible effect might be considered dangerous, for they were carefully
covered in irony. Gulliver is still able to boast of the past history of
his own people and to try to describe to the King some of the more
important developments of society, becoming quite eloquent as anyone may easily do when abroad "to celebrate the Praise of our own
dear country in a style equal to its merits and felicity." It took five
audiences each of several hours, and then in a sixth his majesty, con-
sulting his notes, proposed many doubts, queries and objections upon
every article; and later he sums up his impressions in a fitting but unpleasant figure:

[9] Ibid., pp. 248, 249, 250.

I cannot but conclude the Bulk of your Natives, to be the most pre-
nicious Race of little odious Vermin that Nature ever suffered to crawl
upon the Surface of the Earth.

Great allowances of course have to be made for one living wholly se-
cluded from the world, unacquainted with the manners and customs
of other nations; and Gulliver adds another story to illustrate the
effect of narrow principles and short views, resulting from a confined
education:

I shall here insert a Passage which will hardly obtain Belief. In hopes
to ingratiate my self farther into his Majesty's Favour, I told him of an
Invention discovered between three and four hundred Years ago, to
make a certain Powder; into an heap of which the smallest Spark of
Fire falling, would kindle the whole in a Moment, although it were
as big as a Mountain; and make it all fly up in the Air together, with
a Noise and Agitation greater than Thunder. That, a proper Quantity
of this Powder rammed into an hollow Tube of Brass or Iron, according to its Bigness, would drive a Ball of Iron or Lead with such Violence and Speed, as nothing was able to sustain its Force. That, the
largest Balls thus discharged, would not only Destroy whole Ranks of
an Army at once; but batter the strongest Walls to the Ground; sink
down Ships with a thousand Men in each, to the Bottom of the Sea;
and when linked together by a Chain, would cut through Masts and
Rigging; divide Hundreds of Bodies in the Middle, and lay all Waste
before them. That we often put this Powder into large hollow Balls of
Iron, and discharged them by an Engine into some City we were be-
sieging; which would rip up the Pavement, tear the Houses to Pieces,
burst and throw Splinters on every Side, dashing out the Brains of all
who came near. That I knew the Ingredients very well, which were
Cheap, and common; I understood the Manner of compounding them,
and could direct his Workmen how to make those Tubes of a Size
proportionable to all other Things in his Majesty's Kingdom; and the
largest need not be above two hundred Foot long; twenty or thirty of
which Tubes, charged with the proper Quantity of Powder and Balls,
would batter down the Walls of the strongest Town in his Dominions
in a few Hours; or destroy the whole Metropolis, if ever it should pretend to dispute his absolute Commands. This I humbly offered to his
Majesty, as a small Tribute of Acknowledgment in return of so many
Marks that I had received of his Royal Favour and Protection.
    The King was struck with Horror at the Description I had given of

those terrible Engines, and the Proposal I had made. He was amazed how so impotent and groveling an Insect as I (these were his Expressions) could entertain such inhuman Ideas, and in so familiar a Manner as to appear wholly unmoved at all the Scenes of Blood and Desolation, which I had painted as the common Effects of those destructive Machines; whereof he said, some evil Genius, Enemy to Mankind, must have been the first Contriver. As for himself, he protested, that although few Things delighted him so much as new Discoveries in Art or in Nature; yet he would rather lose half his Kingdom than be privy to such a Secret; which he commanded me, as I valued my Life, never to mention any more.[10]

Book IV

But it is after all the fable of the Fourth book which has most shocked Swift's readers, though it is a simple and traditional moral tale, rather vividly dramatized with the help of animal symbolism. It is perhaps a little mediaeval in its extravagant and sometimes unpleasant burlesque of some of the qualities of man's brute nature, and in the complete separation of his rational qualities as they might conceivably exist in some utopian world. But the real source of our fear of Swift's satire is that we are progressively led on with Gulliver from a comparatively happy condition in which we were in that blessed state of being well deceived—the serene peaceful state of being a fool among knaves—until we have made the painful discovery of the knavery of human life and of the stupidity and malice of mankind. But many moralists and prophets and satirists have made this same discovery and travelled by this same road, and have found the world a wilderness and life a sorry condition, and they have turned to the past or the future or to another world for consolation, and in some way or other have justified the fact of life. But Swift leaves us no escape, no place for dreams or imaginings; he can see no reason for it at all. He has not been able to keep out at any point in his travels this plain dislike of human existence, the protest of the individual against the sum of things,

> a stranger and afraid
> In a world I never made.[11]

But his protest is put in a quite simple non-romantic way, some de-

[10] Ibid., pp. 132, 134-5.
[11] A. E. Housman, *Last Poems,* 1922, p. 28.

velopment of the theme stated in one of his own Pensées, printed under the title, *Thoughts on Religion*.

> Although reason were intended by providence to govern our passions,
> yet it seems that, in two points of the greatest moment to the being and
> continuance of the world, God hath intended our passions to prevail
> over reason. The first is, the propagation of our species, since no wise
> man ever married from the dictates of reason. The other is, the love of
> life, which, from the dictates of reason every man would despise, and
> wish it at an end, or that it never had a beginning.[12]

This colours that passage in the sixth chapter of the Voyage to Lilliput concerning the relations between parents and children:

> they will never allow, that a Child is under any Obligation to his
> Father for begetting him, or to his Mother for bringing him into the
> World; which, considering the Miseries of human Life, was neither
> a Benefit in itself, nor intended so by his Parents, whose Thoughts in
> their Love-encounters were otherwise employed. Upon these, and the
> like Reasonings, their Opinion is, that Parents are the last of all others
> to be trusted with the Education of their own Children:[13]

More dramatically and more memorably he plays with the same
theme at the end of the Fourth book, when, returning from his experience of a rational Utopia under the influence of beings who were
the perfection of nature, Gulliver freely confesses that the sight of his
wife and family filled him "only with Hatred, Disgust and Contempt;
and the more, by reflecting on the near Alliance [he] had to them."[14]

But even this is not such a violent satire upon "love of life" as Swift
reserved for the last episode of the third voyage, which may well have
been in point of composition the last chapter he wrote. For we know
that he wrote the Fourth book mainly in 1723, and did not complete
the Third—apart from final revisions—until 1725. It is a chapter entirely complete in itself—a perfect little irony. I cannot understand
why it has not been more praised, and used in anthologies, or in books
of piety. Swift himself draws particular attention to it, and evidently
considered it to be quite original. He says:

[12] *Prose*, IX, 263.
[13] Ibid., XI, 60.
[14] Ibid., p. 289.

I thought this account of the Struldbruggs might be some Entertain-
ment to the Reader, because it seems to be a little out of the common
Way; at least, I do not remember to have met the like in any Book of
Travels that hath come to my Hands.[15]

Gulliver is asked one day whether he had seen any of their immor-
tals, and after hearing an account of them, indulges in his most en-
dearingly innocent way in extravagant expressions of rapture at the
thought of a people so blessed. He is then asked by his amused hosts
what he would do if he were an immortal. After enlarging upon many
topics "which the natural desire of endless life and sublunary happiness could easily furnish," he is told what the Struldbruggs are
really like and finally has an opportunity to see five or six of them,
the youngest not above two hundred years old.

They were the most mortifying Sight I ever beheld . . . and my keen
Appetite for Perpetuity of Life was much abated.[16]

He would have been glad to send a couple home to arm people
against the fear of death, but that was forbidden by the laws of the
kingdom. Nevertheless, he tells us again with disarming innocence,
he was led to believe that if he were to write down a simple and
wholly truthful account of his travels, it might possibly do his countrymen some good. He can claim to be above any possible censure,
having avoided every fault commonly charged against writers of
travels:

I write for the noblest End, to inform and instruct Mankind, over
whom I may, without Breach of Modesty, pretend to some Superiority,
from the Advantages I received by conversing so long among the most
accomplished *Houyhnhnms*. I write without any View towards Profit
or Praise.[17]

Is Gulliver then after all only another moral tale, another rationalist's utopian dream to turn men from the folly of their ways and bring
about some improvement in human society? Swift indeed allows
Lemuel Gulliver to enter unsuspectingly the company of the eighteenth century philosophers, and to believe for a while, as even the

[15] Ibid., p. 215.
[16] Ibid., p. 214.
[17] Ibid., p. 293.

most sceptical of them did, even a Hume or a Voltaire, that humanity could enter into a heavenly city of its own if only it could be released from the bonds of superstition and ignorance. But Swift allowed Gulliver to go thus far only to undeceive him utterly, and take from him his last illusion.

When the book appeared for the first time pretty much as Swift had written it, published under his direction in Dublin in 1735, it had been provided with an epilogue, in the form of a letter from Captain Gulliver to his cousin Richard Sympson, who had been responsible for getting the book printed. In this final statement Swift is careful to separate himself from the other historians and philosophers, and even from the rest of the satirists, turning his satire full upon them and their vain hopes to do something to improve the human species:

> I do in the next place complain of my own great Want of Judgment, in being prevailed upon . . . very much against my own Opinion, to suffer my Travels to be published. Pray bring to your Mind how often I desired you to consider, when you insisted on the Motive of *publick Good;* that the Yahoos were a species of animal utterly incapable of Amendment by Precepts or Examples: And so it hath proved; for instead of seeing a full Stop put to all Abuses and Corruptions, at least in this little Island, as I had reason to expect: Behold, after above six Months Warning, I cannot learn that my Book hath produced one single Effect according to my Intentions: . . . And, it must be owned, that seven Months were a sufficient Time to correct every Vice and Folly to which Yahoos are subject; if their Natures had been capable of the least Disposition to Virtue or Wisdom.[18]

Swift could not escape from this final irony. He did not wish to prescribe for the sickness of humanity, having no hope of its recovery; but he could not refrain from probing, anatomizing and diagnosing its malady, though convinced that the further he went the more he would find to stir his indignation and his pity. And from his youth he had known it and written it down with a kind of foolish pride, that he was one

> . . . *whose lash just Heaven has long decreed*
> *Shall on a day make sin and folly bleed.*[19]

[18] Ibid., pp. 6-7.
[19] *Poems,* p. 47.

To the end it was his peculiar satisfaction as a moralist and a satirist, in all his various disguises, and employing all the tricks of his trades, to make us see what a world we live in, to make us feel its brutality and its degradation, to disturb all our complacencies and to leave us unreconciled to the "unestimable sum of human pain."

Although *Gulliver's Travels* is the one book by which Swift has been most widely and continuously known, it was not his last word as a moral satirist. For another twelve years he continued to write both in verse and in prose, stirred by the situation in Ireland, even when he had given up political satire as futile. For he could still give vent to his indignation, his bitterness and his scorn, even when he had no hope. He could continue to indulge in the luxury of satire, and find an escape from unprofitable political activity into pure irony.

He had 'been wearied out for many years with offering vain, idle, visionary Thoughts'; at length, 'utterly despairing of Success' he fell upon a Proposal 'wholly new,' of 'no Expense and little Trouble.'[20] which he proceeds very quietly to set out in great detail as a means wholly unexceptional *for preventing the Children of poor People from being a Burthen to their Parents or the Country, and for making them Beneficial to the Publick*. It is curious to note the similarity in tone, as he introduces us to his last irony, with the Apology, which he had written for *A Tale of a Tub,* twenty years before:

> He resolved to proceed in a manner, that should be altogether new, the World having been already too long nauseated with endless Repetitions upon every Subject.[21]

But there is also an important difference. Then, he promised his audience something altogether new, out of consideration for them, because of the endless repetitions they had been obliged to listen to. He was concerned with his audience, and with the effect of his wit upon them. Now, the irony is related to his own weariness with endless repetitions of projects and proposals, all impractical and stupid because they bear, as he knows too well out of long experience, no relation to the real state of affairs in Ireland, and because they take no account of the determined policy of the English government to impoverish the Irish people. Then, like a showman, he was con-

---

[20] *Prose,* XII, 117.
[21] Ibid., I, 1.

cerned to advertise an entirely novel entertainment; now, wearied out and hopeless, he nevertheless comes once more for the last time to challenge in public those responsible for the condition of the poor people in Ireland, by proposing a scheme to which no one in England or in Ireland could conceivably object. It meets all difficulties and would give universal satisfaction.

It is a very simple plan, and he is able to work out the economic and business details of the proposed new industry in a way which demonstrates very clearly that it would be profitable to all concerned. It would provide a new commodity for the rich and a modest living for the poor. He calculates that the children of the beggarly Irish can be reared to the age of twelve months at a cost of about two shillings to their parents, "rags included." Tolerably nursed, they should weigh at that age about twenty-eight pounds, and the carcass should make four dishes of excellent nutritive meat, which would not be dear at ten shillings. That would provide a reasonable profit, and further the plan would save the country the maintenance of a hundred thousand children, from two years and upwards, which would increase the nation's stock fifty thousand pounds annually. A further profit could be made out of the skin, which, "artifically dressed, will make admirable *Gloves for Ladies, and Summer Boots for fine Gentlemen.*"[22]

It might seem at first sight that this *Modest Proposal* should be considered a political satire, for it was carefully worked out for a particular situation in Ireland at that moment; and it was ostensibly an appeal to the people of Ireland to take certain immediate action. But Swift is here parodying himself. The irony is partly in the parody; but the weapon is in the hand of a moralist, not of a politician. The irony is also partly in the attitude adopted by the writer. He has learned that he has no longer any power as a politician; he is unable to influence the government, though he had once been a highly successful government apologist; he is unable to rouse the people, though he had once been acclaimed by them as their leader and they had banded themselves together for his defence. He has only one satisfaction left—to carry the case before a higher court, to appeal to the conscience of mankind and bear witness before posterity, leaving them to answer his irony, and to decide in such a case—for there would be many others like it—what answer they would make to his modest pro-

[22] Ibid., XII, 112.

posal, what alternative they would have to suggest, which he had overlooked. Let the sentimentalists shudder, if only the oppressors of mankind might feel for a moment the sting of his irony, and the oppressed
be stirred to madness; and justice and humanity be vindicated, even
though they should be banished from the earth.

MISCELLANEOUS ESSAYS

SWIFT'S VIEW OF POETRY

It is strange that Swift has not been given more attention both on account of what he has written in verse and of what he has written about poetry. For although he did not profess to be either a poet or a critic of poetry, he is nevertheless in his casual and contemptuous manner the most extreme example that we have ever had in England of reaction against the heroic or romantic view of the poet's function and art.

Dryden of course is rightly regarded as in theory and practice the great champion of the new poetry of his day, the character of which had been sketched so admirably—as we are reminded in Dr. Mark van Doren's study, *John Dryden* (1920)—in the introductory matter contributed by Waller, Denham, Hobbes, and Davenant to the latter's *Gondibert*, published in 1651. Yet Dryden never accepted fully the logical conclusion of these theories. "He spoke often, in common with his contemporaries, of the *furor poeticus;* he championed poetic license; and he tried to write like Shakespeare." Indeed throughout his whole career Dryden continued constantly to use the traditional language whenever he spoke of the art of poetry. He remained essentially a heroic poet, and loved to flaunt the pomp and colours of his cause:

> O gracious God! how far have we
> Profan'd thy heav'nly gift of poesy!
> Made prostitute and profligate the Muse,
> Debas'd to each obscene and impious use,

> Whose harmony was first ordain'd above
> For tongues of angels, and for hymns of love![1]

This *Ode to Mrs. Anne Killigrew* was probably written in 1685, but
again in the epistle prefixed to *Beauty in Distress* (1698), *To my
Friend Mr. Motteux* he speaks of

> That sacred art, by heav'n itself infus'd
> Which Moses, David, Salomon have us'd,[2]

And however little Dryden may have really believed in thus ascribing
to the art of poetry all the sacredness that Milton had claimed for it—
at least in its finest manifestations—he would probably have readily
accepted that noble claim made by Sir William Temple in his *Essay
on Heroick Virtue* (1690):

> "Among all the Endowments of Nature, or Improvements of Art
> wherein Men have excelled and distinguished themselves most in the
> World, there are Two only that have had the Honour of being called
> Divine, and of giving that Esteem or Appellation to such as possessed
> them in very eminent Degrees; which are, Heroick Virtue, and Poetry:
> For Prophecy cannot be esteemed any Excellency of Nature or of Art,
> but, wherever it is true, is an immediate Gift of God, and bestowed
> according to his Pleasure, and upon Subjects of the meanest Capacity;
> upon Women or Children, or even Things inanimate; . . ."[3]

This careful distinction here made in the use of the word "divine" as
applied to the inspiration of the poet and the prophet respectively
should be remarked. It seems to have been preserved in the eighteenth
century, so that, while the Deists and the sceptics were making an in-
creasingly violent attack upon the idea of the supernatural revelation
of the prophet, there was on the other hand an almost dogmatic in-
sistence on the true faith and the efficacy of the canonical books, i.e.,
the classics, in the tradition of poetry.

This is exactly the attitude of Pope. In his attempt to "trace for
English readers the just boundaries of taste in literature" in his *Essay
on Criticism*, he shows the mentality of a young priest of the strictest

[1] Ll. 56-61.
[2] Ll. 3-4.
[3] Sir William Temple, *Works*, 1740, I, 191.

orthodoxy, bold, proud, dogmatic, with nothing but scorn for those who are not of the true faith. He looks upon poetry as the special activity of a privileged and well-trained hierarchy, which professes and believes literally in a creed that has been handed down by the great founders and leaders of the order. They alone have the true faith—to them the revelation has been made of Nature, "the source, and end, and test of art."

> Those Rules of old discovered, not devis'd
> Are Nature still, but Nature methodiz'd:

Virgil found that "Nature and Homer were the same"—

> Learn hence for ancient rules a just esteem;
> To copy Nature is to copy them.[4]

He knows himself to be a faithful member of this true church, devoted to the work to which he has been called, delighting to do honour to the great fathers of the church, who are infallible:

> Nor is it Homer nods, but we that dream.

With fine rhetoric, and not without a flash of pride, he breaks out into a great hymn in honour of the temple of poetry, and the altars of the dead still green with bays:

> Still green with bays each ancient Altar stands,
> Above the reach of sacrilegious hands;
> Secure from Flames, from Envy's fiercer rage,
> Destructive War, and all-involving Age.
> See, from each clime the learn'd their incense bring!
> Hear, in all tongues consenting Pæans ring!
> In praise so just let ev'ry voice be join'd,
> And fill the gen'ral chorus of mankind.[5]

Finally he approaches humbly to take of the fire from off the altar, that he may go forth to speak a word to the people, and declare to them the glories they can admire but not share.

> Oh may some spark of your celestial fire,
> The last, the meanest of your sons inspire,

---

[4] Ll. 139-40.
[5] Ll. 180-88.

> (That on weak wings, from far, pursues your flights;
> Glows while he reads, but trembles as he writes)
> To teach vain Wits a science little known,
> T' admire superior sense, and doubt their own![6]

He has all the rigour and the sternness of the true priest; he would proscribe all field-preachers and nonconformists, and he would stamp out every heresy. He is careful to show that he is no sectarian, but a member of the true church, which is limited to no small corner of the earth, nor to a single generation, and he protests against those who would apply "wit"

> To one small sect, and all are damn'd beside.
> Meanly they seek the blessing to confine
> And force the sun but on a part to shine,
> Which not alone the southern wit sublimes
> But ripens spirits in cold northern climes.[7]

It is important to notice too his claim that so long as the poet belongs to the true lineage he may receive inspiration in many diverse ways. He does not receive his great gifts by any mechanical operation—by a mere following of Rules:

> Some beauties yet no Precepts can declare,
> For there's a happiness as well as care.[8]
>
>   .   .   .   .   .
>
> Thus Pegasus, a nearer way to take,
> May boldly deviate from the common track;
>
>   .   .   .   .
>
> And snatch a grace beyond the reach of art,
> Which without passing thro' the judgment, gains
> The heart, and all its end at once attains.[9]

Thus confidently, in spite of his youth and inexperience did Pope come forward, clothed already in the dignity and authority of his high calling, to preach to his generation, to saints and sinners alike,

[6] Ll. 195-200.
[7] Ll. 397-401.
[8] Ll. 141-2.
[9] Ll. 150-7.

to noble lords like Lansdowne and the Duke of Buckingham as well as outsiders like Dennis, what he believed to be the true nature and function of poetry.

Swift had none of this professional pride, and never showed the least inclination to set much value on the business of writing poetry. He was willing to use it either to gain a reputation and establish his influence or to force his views upon the public. He wrote always not as an artist but as a man of action, or else he wrote as a gentleman writes, to amuse himself and his friends. He refused to be considered as a writer or a poet professionally, and he emphasized the difference contemptuously in *Thoughts on Various Subjects continued*, 1726, "A copy of verses kept in the cabinet, and only shewn to a few friends, is like a virgin much sought after and admired; but when printed and published, is like a common whore, whom anybody may purchase for half-a-crown."

This may sound like the common affectation of an eighteenth century gentleman, who was rather expected to sneer at those who fiddle for pay, or write a prologue or a dedication for ten pound. But yet it would be a greater affectation still for the author of *A Tale of a Tub* to allow himself to be impressed by such idle fancies as the poet's claim to divine honours. Is it likely that the satirist of kings and courts, politicians and lawyers, scholars and scientists, will show respect before the less tangible dignity of a poet, however magnificently he may wrap his singing robes around him? In Bedlam he had found the poets so numerous and in such poor company, that they were not worth special mention: "I shall not descend so minutely, as to insist upon the vast number of beaux, fiddlers, poets and politicians, that the world might recover. . . ."

One of the main themes of *A Tale of a Tub* is of course an analysis of "enthusiasm," which is defined as a "lifting-up of the soul, or its faculties, above matter." And in the *Discourse on the Mechanical Operation of the Spirit* he adds a fantastic travesty of a mechanistic theory of the activity of the brain, which purports to be an explanation of the way in which poetry is written. The brain is to be considered as a crowd of little animals clinging together like bees in a perpetual swarm upon a tree:

That all Invention is formed by the Morsure of two or more of these Animals, upon certain capillary Nerves, which proceed from thence, whereof three Branches spread into the Tongue, and two into the right Hand. . . . Farther, that nothing less than a violent Heat can disentangle these Creatures from their hamated Station of Life, or give them Vigor and Humor to imprint the Marks of their little Teeth. That if the Morsure be Hexagonal, it produces Poetry; . . . .[10]

But perhaps the most fundamental attack upon "inspiration," which may be equally applied to the prophetical or poetical variety, is found in the preceding paragraph:

For, I think, it is in *Life* as in *Tragedy*, where, it is held a Conviction of great Defect, both in Order and Invention, to interpose the Assistance of preternatural Power, without an absolute and last Necessity. However, it is a Sketch of Human Vanity, for every Individual to imagine the whole Universe is interess'd in his meanest Concern. . . . Who, that sees a little paultry mortal, droning, and dreaming, and drivelling to a Multitude, can think it agreeable to common good Sense, that either Heaven or Hell should be put to the Trouble of Influence or Inspection, upon what he is about? Therefore I am resolved immediately to weed this Error out of Mankind, by making it clear, that this Mystery of vending spiritual Gifts is nothing but a *Trade* acquired by as much instruction and mastered by equal Practice and Application as others are.[10]

If he had needed support in thus challenging the notion of divine inspiration Swift might well have quoted Hobbes, who in his *Answer to Sr Will. D'Avenant's Preface Before Gondibert* (1650) had approved of his innovation in omitting "to invoke a Muse or some other Deity," for though he refuses to condemn that Heathen custom in them, yet

why a Christian should think it an ornament to his Poem, either to profane the true God or invoke a false one, I can imagin no cause but a reasonless imitation of Custom, of a foolish custome, by which a man, enabled to speak wisely from the principles of nature and his own meditation, loves rather to be thought to speak by inspiration, like a Bagpipe.

Time and Education begets experience; Experience begets memory; Memory begets Judgment and Fancy: Judgment begets the strength and structure, and Fancy begets the ornaments of a Poem.[11]

[10] *Prose*, I, 180-82.
[11] *Critical Essays of the Seventeenth Century*, ed. J. E. Spingarn, 1957, II, 59.

There, at any rate, is an intelligent explanation of the phenomenon
of poetry, which Swift may well have accepted; he would at least
have approved of Hobbes's point of view. It might even be said that
with all its limitations it is nevertheless sufficient to account for that
kind of poetry which Swift himself produced.

Swift amused himself in similar fashion in verse, by laughing at
the exalted flights of Grub-Street wits, when sufficiently freed from
the "Incumbrances of Food and Clothes," but whose inspiration immediately flags as soon as they have received their pay. It is a short
poem in very colloquial octosyllabic lines, called *The Progress of
Poetry*.[12] But it was followed much later by one of Swift's most vigorous and sustained efforts in verse, which he is said to have regarded
as one of his best pieces, *On Poetry: A Rhapsody*,[13] which was published anonymously in London on December 31, 1733.

Swift begins by looking over the whole commonwealth of letters,
and ridiculing the strange ambition of the human race, which drives
every fool to try to be a wit and a poet:

> But *Man* we find the only Creature
> Who, led by *Folly*, fights with *Nature*;
> Who, when *she* loudly cries, *Forbear*,
> With Obstinacy fixes there;
> And, where his *Genius* least inclines,
> Absurdly bends his whole Designs.

It is a strange and inexplicable malady, for nothing is more certain to
ruin a man's chance of success than a career which offers only one
single prize—the Laureate's pittance of just "one annual hundred
pound."

> Not Beggar's Brat, on Bulk begot;
> Nor Bastard of a Pedlar *Scot*;
> Nor Boy brought up to cleaning Shoes,
> The Spawn of *Bridewell*, or the Stews;
> Nor Infants dropt, the spurious Pledges
> Of *Gipsies* littering under Hedges,
> Are so disqualified by Fate

[12] *Poems*, p. 230.
[13] Ibid., p. 640.

> To rise in *Church,* or *Law,* or *State,*
> As he, whom Phebus in his Ire
> Hath *blasted* with poetick Fire.[14]

In an earlier and happier time perhaps a Congreve or an Addison could win his way to fame and success with a poem, but now the only profitable game is to sell yourself to a corrupt and venal court—

> From Party-Merit seek Support;
> The vilest Verse thrives best at Court.
> A Pamphlet in Sir Rob's Defence
> Will never fail to bring in Pence:
> Nor be concern'd about the Sale,
> He pays his Workmen on the Nail.[15]

Such then is the poet's fate: neither profit nor dignity nor pleasure can be found in the pursuit of poetical fame. In the world of letters, as everywhere else in life, Hobbes's view is justified that every creature lives in a state of war by nature, only here it is the lesser who prey upon the greater—a condition of things found in nature only among vermin.

> So, Nat'ralists observe, a Flea
> Hath smaller Fleas that on him prey,
> And these have smaller Fleas to bite 'em,
> And so proceed *ad infinitum.*[16]

Swift is of course not concerned in this poem with any poetic ideal; he is satirising directly the inhabitants of Grub-Street, and the conditions of society which make such a Grub-Street possible.

> In Bulk there are not more Degrees
> From *Elephants* to *Mites* in Cheese,
> Than what a curious Eye may trace
> In Creatures of the rhiming Race.
> From bad to worse, and worse they fall,
> But who can reach the Worst of all?
> For, tho', in Nature Depth and Height
> Are equally held infinite:

[14] Ibid., p. 641.
[15] Ibid., p. 646.
[16] Ibid., p. 651.

> In Poetry the Height we know;
> 'Tis only infinite below.[17]

In such a world what room is there for the sublime and the pathetic? There is nothing left to do but to rail, or simply to amuse oneself and one's friends. Swift was not one of those who could build a little private palace of art for himself, or find consolation in dreams of a better existence than the present; he was never willing to buy happiness at the price of being well-deceived, nor would he allow himself to be lulled into contentment by the soothing incantations or divine raptures of romantic poetry.

It would be easy of course to suggest that just as Swift's satire on politicians was largely due to his bitter hatred of Walpole and the Whigs, and his fall with the Tories from power and influence, so his satire on poets was due to his early disappointments and failures, and especially to Dryden's emphatic and rather brutal judgment on his attempts to gain attention by writing Pindaric Odes after the manner of Cowley. But Swift, however unable to forget such a remark, was hardly one to be crippled by it, and we have evidence enough to show how he came to scorn the poetic Muse, scoff at her claims for devotion, and turn his technical skill as a verse-writer to account in the service of a less romantic mistress.

Perhaps too much has been made of Swift's confession that he was devoted to Cowley's poetry while he was still at school, for he seems to have begun to write verse himself in a very different vein,—crude satirical doggerel intended to satisfy the taste of his fellow undergraduates at Trinity College. In Dr. Elrington Ball's study, *Swift's Verse*, reference is made to all the early verses attributed to Swift by Vice-Provost Barrett in his *Essay on the earlier part of the Life of Swift*, and later by Sir William Wilde on the evidence of the Christie volume—a sort of commonplace book of Swift's which dates from his undergraduate years. Whether we regard any of these verses as the work of Swift or not, perhaps more importance should be attached to the fact that here at any rate are verses which Swift copied out in his own hand, which show already that his taste was entirely for satire

[17] Ibid., p. 653.

and buffoonery and for occasional poems concerned with public affairs and political and religious controversy. Here is an early indication of Swift's natural bent; and this is very significant in showing that it was only after settling at Moor Park—and I suggest under the direct influence of Sir William Temple—that he turned aside and was persuaded to try to imitate Cowley, and indulge in what Dr. Ball very rightly calls a period of "Pindaric and Heroic Aberration." And a careful study of these pieces, which are not by any means as uninteresting or as weak as is often suggested, show Swift struggling with an unsuitable medium, and forced into an attitude, a pose which he soon recognized as an affectation, and then contemptuously abandoned. It is perhaps worth remarking that only the *Ode to the Athenian Society*,[18] was published in his lifetime. Dunton had printed it as the work of a country gentleman in the Supplement to the *Fifth Volume of the Athenian Gazette*, 1691, and it was printed again in pamphlet form in 1725 with the title—*Sphinx: A Poem ascrib'd to certain Anonymous Authors: By the Revd. Dean S—t*. The rest of these Moor Park poems were not printed in Swift's lifetime.

They are interesting because here we see Swift for the only time trying seriously to be a poet. His letters indicate that he set himself industriously to try for fame in the conventional manner following the example of Dryden and Cowley. He comes to pay his court to the accepted Muse, with panegyrics in Pindaric form. And the result is exactly what we should expect. What had he to do with writing the praise of great men, giving honour to noble deeds? Was the world that he knew, even at that time, a place for compliments and the praise of beauty and virtue?

But it was while he was making these experiments that he began to realize how much cant there is in all this talk of the divine inspiration of the poet.

> Thus the *deluding Muse* oft blinds me to her Ways,
> And ev'n my very Thoughts transfers
> And changes all to Beauty and the Praise
>   Of that proud Tyrant Sex of Hers.
>   The *Rebel Muse,* alas, takes part,
>   But with my own Rebellious Heart.[19]

[18] Ibid., p. 14.
[19] Ibid., p. 23.

And in the *Ode to Dr. William Sancroft,* written probably two years
later, panegyric turns already into scepticism and satire—

> No wonder, then, we talk amiss
> Of truth, and what, or where it is:
> Say, Muse, for thou, if any, know'st,
> Since the bright essence fled, where haunts the reverend ghost?[20]

This appeal to the Muse for guidance, with that little qualification,
"thou, if any, know'st" is very like Swift.
  And again:

> Forgive (Original Mildness) this ill-govern'd zeal,
> 'Tis all the angry slighted Muse can do
>   In the pollution of these days;
>   No province now is left her but to rail,
> And poetry has lost the art to praise,
>   Alas, the occasions are so few:[21]

Nevertheless in the *Ode to Sir William Temple* written about the
same time, he seems determined to put aside all doubts and try what
he can do. Here after an outburst in Temple's own manner against
"philosophy, the lumber of the schools" and the "ill-manner'd pedantry" of those who

> . . . purchase Knowledge at the Expence
> Of common Breeding, common Sense,
> And grow at once Scholars and Fools;[22]

he devotes himself to limitless adulation of his patron, and of that
quiet life in a country retreat which he has chosen, and launched in
full career boasts at last of his own slavery to the poetic Muse, and
even refers to the hopes and encouragements that have bound him
to her service.

> Nature the hidden Spark did at my Birth infuse,
> And kindled first with Indolence and Ease,
>   And since too oft debauch'd by Praise,
> 'Tis now grown an incurable Disease:
>   In vain to quench this foolish Fire I try

[20] Ibid., p. 35-6.
[21] Ibid., p. 38.
[22] Ibid., 27.

> In Wisdom and Philosophy:
> In vain all wholesome Herbs I sow,
> Where nought but Weeds will grow.
> Whate'er I plant (like Corn on barren Earth)
> By an equivocal Birth,
> Seeds and runs up to Poetry.[23]

This was the end of the Pindarics, though not of complimentary verse. It is almost as though Swift realized that this was in every way the least sincere piece he ever wrote. And in the two poems that follow, *To Mr. Congreve* and *Occasioned by Sir William Temple's late Illness and Recovery,* he is too much concerned with his own disillusionment to have much thought for his subjects. It is true that he talks of disappointment and despair, but I do not feel with Dr. Elrington Ball that he was despondent "because of his failure to succeed in the Cowleyan School." It is true too that for the next five years from 1693-8 he wrote no more verses—or at least none survive—but that may equally well be due to the fact that he had discovered, not that he could not write like Cowley or Dryden, but that he did not want to. There was no sign of lack of confidence surely in the famous lines:

> *My hate, whose lash just heaven has long decreed*
> *Shall on a day make sin and folly bleed;*[24]

nor in the lines quoted from a lost Ode, inscribed "The Poet":

> *Beat not the dirty paths where vulgar feet have trod,*
> *But give the vigorous fancy room.*
> For when like stupid alchymists you try
> To fix this nimble god,
> This volatile mercury,
> The subtle spirit all flies up in fume;
> Nor shall the bubbl'd virtuoso find
> More than a fade insipid mixture left behind[25]

It is hardly the voice of the disappointed worshipper, rejected by the Muse that he had patiently courted, but of one who is thoroughly disillusioned, and anxious to expose the cheat that he had detected, that we hear in such lines as these:

[23] Ibid., pp. 32-3.
[24] Ibid., p. 47.
[25] Ibid., p. 49.

> Malignant goddess! bane to my repose,
> Thou universal cause of all my woes;
> Say, whence it comes that thou art grown of late
> A poor amusement for my scorn and hate;
>
> . . . . . .
>
> Ah, should I tell a secret yet unknown,
> That thou ne'er hadst a being of thy own,
> But a wild form dependent on the brain,
> Scatt'ring loose features o'er the optic vein;
> Troubling the chrystal fountain of the sight,
> Which darts on poets eyes a trembling light;
> Kindled while reason sleeps, but quickly flies,
> Like antic shapes in dreams, from waking eyes:
> In sum, a glitt'ring voice, a painted name,
> A walking vapor, like thy sister fame.[26]

And finally, with a triumphant cry he breaks away, turning his back upon visionary dreams and fancies, eager only to gaze with untroubled sight upon a world of reality:

> There thy enchantment broke, and from this hour
> I here renounce thy visionary pow'r;
> And since thy essence on my breath depends,
> Thus with a puff the whole delusion ends.[27]

Instead of poetry Swift turned to prose satire, and in the following years until the death of Sir William Temple, was probably mainly occupied with the *Tale of a Tub*. When that finally appeared in 1704, its author must have felt that he had successfully evaded the power of the malignant goddess, who troubles the crystal fountain of the sight, and fills the brain with antic shapes while reason sleeps. And if further proof was required of his emancipation, it could scarcely have been better provided than in the volume of *Miscellanies*, published in 1711, in which he included thirteen poems, chosen out of a considerable amount of political and satirical verse, some already published as Broadsides. It seems almost as if he wished to flout the votaries of the heroic and romantic muse by ostentatiously placing at the very beginning of this little group the lines *Written in a Lady's*

[26] Ibid., pp. 53-4.
[27] Ibid., p. 55.

Ivory Table-book, 1698.[28] Here instead of compliment or a lover's devotion, he makes a collection of some of the stupidest of the senseless trifles it contains, and exposes them as a revelation of its owner's heart:

> Here you may read (*Dear Charming Saint*)
> Beneath (*A new Receit for Paint*)
> Here, in Beau-spelling (*tru tel deth*)
> There in her own (*far an el breth*)
>
> .   .   .   .   .
>
> Who that had Wit would place it here,
> For every peeping Fop to Jear.

And this is followed by the delightfully absurd chatter of *The humble petition of Frances Harris,*[29] with its vigorous caricatures of the servants in the Earl of Berkeley's household. It almost seems as if immediately Swift escaped from the restrained and dignified atmosphere of Sir William Temple's household, where he had tried to produce conventional poetry, and returned to Dublin in the train of the Earl of Berkeley, he found encouragement to indulge his own taste for ridicule and burlesque. Temple had particularly disapproved of this in his essay on *Ancient and Modern Learning:—*

> I wish the Vein of Ridiculing all that is Serious and Good, all Honour and Virtue, as well as Learning and Piety, may have no worse Effects on any other States: 'Tis the Itch of our Age and Climate, and has overrun both the Court and the Stage; enters a House of Lords and Commons, as boldly as a *Coffee*-House, Debates of Council as well as private Conversation; and I have known, in my Life, more than one or two Ministers of State, that would rather have said a Witty Thing, than done a Wise One; and made the Company laugh, rather than the Kingdom rejoice.[30]

And Swift himself in the *Battle of the Books* had upheld Temple in this, and gone on further to scoff at the characteristically modern claim for originality.

> For any Thing else of Genuine, that the *Moderns* may pretend to, I can-

---

[28] Ibid., p. 60.
[29] Ibid., p. 69.
[30] Sir William Temple, op. cit., p. 169.

not recollect; unless it be a large Vein of Wrangling and Satyr, much of a Nature and Substance with the *Spider's* Poison; which, however they pretend to spit wholly out of themselves, is improved by the same arts, by feeding upon the *Insects* and *Vermin* of the age.[31]

This was probably written in the latter part of 1697, and this scornful attitude towards even the genuine productions of the Moderns was doubtless intended to win the approval of his dignified patron. It is strange that none of Swift's critics, so far as I know, have turned this to account, by quoting it as a good description of a great deal of his own writing, which is certainly—as Swift liked himself to think— "spit wholly out of himself" and often improved "by feeding upon the insects and vermin of the age."

Few of Swift's biographers and critics have indeed troubled much with his poetry; like Dr. Johnson, they find little upon which to exercise their powers, and are content to compliment him on his facility and ease, or protest against his outspokenness, without indicating very clearly the character and significance of his work as a whole. They often give the impression that like Lord Orrery they would have been better pleased if his editors had not been so active in bringing together every trifle that may have come from his pen. "Many of them"— he says—"are spurious, and many more are trifling, and in every respect improper for the public view"; an attitude, which is of course in accord with his pompous conventionality, shown in his remarks on the "low humour" of the *Directions to Servants*:

> Superior talents seem to have been intended by Providence as public benefits, and the person, who possesses such blessings, is certainly answerable to Heaven for those endowments, which he enjoys above the rest of mankind. Let him jest with dignity, and let him be ironical upon useful subjects: leaving poor slaves to *heat their porridge* or *drink their small beer*, in such vessels as they shall find proper. The Dean, it seems, had not this way of thinking.[32]

He certainly had not; and it was with very different standards from those of his Lordship that Swift chose out of all the infinite variety of circumstance the particular occasion for poetry; and when the occa-

---

[31] *Prose*, I, 151.
[32] John Boyle, *Earl of Orrery, Remarks on the Life and Writings of Jonathan Swift*, 1752 (2nd edition, corrected), p. 180.

sion demanded, he never refused the challenge, and often answered
with surprising readiness and quickness. Most frequently his poetry
was prompted entirely from without, as was all the political verse,
and a great deal that belongs to his friendships and enmities. There is
no more struggle, as in his early attempts, at heroic verse. He never
courts the Muse, but turns instead to the laughing and irrepressible
demon of satire, always ready at his elbow to use anything or anybody
for its own disreputable purpose. It may be a mere Partridge—shoe-
maker, quack, and astrologer, who is given an elegy exalting him to a
place among the heavenly bodies, where he may still follow his calling. Or it may be Lord Cutts—who, while acting temporarily as a
Lord Justice in Ireland in 1705, was the first of many who held that
office to attract Swift's violent dislike—whose character and appearance are made to fit so admirably Pliny's description of a Salamander.
Or it may be a more pleasant joke, delightfully elaborated on the
subject of the tiny house that Vanbrugh, the architect and dramatist,
had built out of the profits of a play. Or even a street scene in the
City in the early morning, or when it is raining—the two perfect
sketches in heroic couplets, which Swift contributed to the *Tatler*.

It is interesting to note that the second of these—the *Description of
a City Shower*[33] had, as Dr. Elrington Ball points out, "an ulterior
motive, namely, to make the use of the triplet and alexandrine ridiculous," in these concluding lines:

> Sweepings from Butchers' Stalls, Dung, Guts, and Blood,
> Drown'd Puppies, stinking Sprats, all drench'd in Mud,
> Dead Cats, and Turnip-Tops come tumbling down the Flood.

It has perhaps not been clearly enough recognized that a good number
of Swift's pieces owe their existence entirely to such purely literary
motives. However true it may be that much of his writing is the work
of a man of action rather than a man of letters, yet Swift was always
very closely associated with the literary world, and keenly interested
in the work of his contemporaries. He was concerned moreover to
influence their taste, and to do that he employed his usual method of
satirizing what seemed to him to be the affectations and absurdities
of poetical fashions. He scorned above all the artificial conventions,
the outworn ornaments and false sentimentality, which are perhaps

[33] *Poems*, p. 136.

at all times the marks of minor poetry. His attitude towards such poetry is shown in a parody, written probably in 1733, *A Love Song in the modern Taste*.[34] All the usual tricks are here exposed—the ornamental epithet, the classical references, the personification, the alliteration, the sing-song lilt, the unreal language, the sentimental commonplaces, and all the dreary staleness of these false, imitated, poetical devices:

> *Cynthia*, tune harmonious Numbers;
>   Fair Discretion string the Lyre;
> Sooth my ever-waking Slumbers:
> Bright *Apollo* lend thy Choir.
>   .   .   .   .   .
> Melancholly smooth *Meander*,
>   Swiftly purling in a Round,
> On thy Margin Lovers wander,
>   With thy flow'ry Chaplets crown'd.

Again, in a reply to some complimentary verses by Dr. Delany, *News from Parnassus*—which reports that at a session of the poets on Parnassus, convened by Apollo on February 27, 1720, Swift was appointed his vicegerent on earth—Swift, assuming this new dignity, issues what he called *Apollo's Edict*,[35] and in a very easy pleasant manner proclaims therein what may and what may not be done by his vassals. Swift's own methods are of course to be imitated:

> Let his Success our Subjects sway
> Our Inspirations to obey,
> And follow where *he* leads the Way:
> Then study to correct your Taste,
> Nor *beaten* Paths be longer trac'd.

Then follows a list of things to be avoided—all the worn-out tags of poetic finery:

> No Simile shall be begun,
> With *rising* or with *setting* Sun: . . .
>   No Son of mine shall dare to say,
> *Aurora usher'd in the Day*,
> Or ever name the *milky Way*. . . .

---

[34] Ibid., p. 660.
[35] Ibid., p. 269.

> Your tragick Heroes shall not rant,
> Nor Shepherds use *poetick Cant:*

Even Denham's famous line so often quoted and so much admired is
forbidden:

> Nor let my Votaries show their Skill
> In aping Lines from *Cooper's Hill;*
> For know I cannot bear to hear
> The Mimickry of *deep yet clear.*

And especially of course he proscribes all the nonsense of love-poetry;

> When you describe a lovely Girl,
> No Lips of *Coral,* Teeth of *Pearl.*
>   *Cupid* shall ne'er mistake another,
> However beauteous, for his Mother:
> Nor shall his Darts at random fly
> From Magazeen in *Coelia's* Eye.

A more violent attack on poetic cant is made in a little group of
poems, which were included in the *Miscellanies* by Pope in 1727.
The first of these—*Phillis; or, The Progress of Love,* 1716[36]—which
gives the past history of the landlord and hostess of the Old Blue
Boar, at Staines, which Swift used to pass on his journeys to Windsor,
is possibly a version of some story he has heard; but even if that is
so, it is certainly at the same time a satire upon the popular notions of
romantic love and such attendant follies as a girl's elopement with
a servant to escape from a reasonable match properly arranged by her
parents. She leaves behind of course a note of explanation and an
appeal to her father for forgiveness:

> ('Tis always done, Romances tell us,
> When Daughters run away with Fellows)
>   .   .   .   .   .
> It was her Fate, must be forgiven;
> For Marriages are made in Heaven:
> His Pardon begg'd, but, to be plain,
> She'd do't if 'twere to do again.
> Thank'd God, 'twas neither Shame nor Sin,
> For John was come of honest Kin:

[36] Ibid., p. 221.

> Love never thinks of Rich and Poor,
> She'd beg with John from Door to Door:

The adventures which befell them are very rapidly sketched, until
at last

> Fate put a Period to the Farce;
> And with exact Poetick Justice:
> For John is Landlord, Phillis Hostess;
> They keep at Stains the old blue Boar,
> Are Cat and Dog, and Rogue and Whore.

It is worth while to compare with this poem a letter that Swift wrote
to Mrs. Swanton, a distant relative, on July 12, 1733 giving her advice how to deal with her daughter who had left her home in order
to be free to marry according to her own wishes.

> Although such an action in a daughter whom you have used so well can
> deserve no pardon, yet I would have you leave her without excuse.
> Send to her to come home; if she refuse, send a second and third time,
> and if she still refuseth, let her know in plain terms, that you will never
> have the least correspondence with her, and when she is ruined, as
> will certainly be the case, that you will never see her, nor give or leave
> her or her children, if she have any, a morsel of bread. Let her know
> you have given her fair warning, and if she will run into destruction
> with her eyes open, against common sense and the opinion of all ra-
> tional people, she hath none to blame but herself; and that she must
> not expect to move your compassion some years hence with the cries
> of half a dozen children at your door for want of bread. . . .[37]

In life and in literature Swift never ceased to protest against ideas and
conduct, which he considered "against common sense and the opinion of rational people."

The Progress of Beauty, 1720[38] shows how Swift is prepared to deal
himself with subjects, which have been sicklied o'er with the sentimentality of romantic poets. And I would suggest that some of the
unpleasant qualities of these poems, which have caused his admirers
so much difficulty, may have been due as much to his impatience
with poetic cant as to any unspeakable perversions in his mind. "No
lips of coral, teeth of pearl" he had already demanded; now he goes

[37] Corr., V, 11.
[38] Poems, p. 225.

a little further, and substitutes for the usual flatteries such lines as
these. Is it the beauty of the moon that the poets celebrate, then let
them look more closely:

> When first Diana leaves her Bed,
> Vapors and Streams her Looks disgrace,
> A frouzy dirty colour'd red
> Sits on her cloudy wrinckled Face.

And there is an exact parallel between earthly females and the moon:

> To see her from her Pillow rise
> All reeking in a cloudy Steam,
> Crackt Lips, foul Teeth, and gummy Eyes,
> Poor Strephon! how would he blaspheme!

It is only a matter of shifting the colours round, as he proceeds very
innocently to explain:

> Three Colours, Black, and Red, and White,
> So gracefull in their proper Place,
> Remove them to a diff'rent Lite,
> They form a frightfull hideous Face:
> For instance; when the Lilly slipps
> Into the Precincts of the Rose,
> And takes Possession of the Lips,
> Leaving the Purple to the Nose.
> So Celia went entire to bed,
> All her Complexions safe and sound;
> But, when she rose, the black and red,
> Though still in Sight, had chang'd their Ground.

The comparison is continued throughout, and Celia's fading beauties
given no longer date than the waning moon; the last stanza closes the
story with a gay little note, unusual in Swift.

> Ye Pow'rs who over Love preside,
> Since mortal Beautyes drop so soon,
> If you would have us well supply'd,
> Send us new Nymphs with each new Moon.

It may be said of course that these are all very slight productions,
and that it is not of much real significance that Swift amuses himself

thus in attacking the romantic attitude. The test comes only when he is actually confronted by those experiences in life which have inspired the poets with their most sublime utterances. Is there any evidence that at such moments Swift turned to poetry? Does he succeed then in still maintaining his complete control of himself? Is it true that he never touches "the sublime or the pathetic," is he never betrayed into sentimentality, or stirred to emotional fervour?

We should expect to find an answer in *Cadenus and Vanessa* and in the *Stella* poems which Swift allowed Pope to include in the Miscellanies in 1727. Fortunately we do not need here to repeat all the stories that have been written about the two women whom Swift loved. We are concerned only with the way in which he treats these personal experiences of love and friendship in his verse. We are concerned with the poems as literature, not as a clue to certain biographical problems, however intriguing. And *Cadenus and Vanessa*[39] is as literary as anything that Swift ever produced. Apart from the title, which alone removes it just outside the world of plain happenings, Swift has carefully framed it in a fantasy, in which gods and goddesses play their part, endowing Vanessa with graces and gifts rarely combined in women. And when this prodigy is finally introduced into the world, Swift indulges his usual banter at the expense of the "fashionable fops" and "glittering dames From around the purlieus of St. James':

> Both Sexes, arm'd with Guilt and Spite,
> Against *Vanessa's* Pow'r unite;
> To copy her, few Nymphs aspir'd;
> Her Virtues fewer Swains admir'd:[40]

But a few had better taste, whom she entertained with pleasing arts. Among these was Cadenus; and Cupid—piqued at his lack of success with her—determines to take revenge, by making her fall in love with him.

> *Cadenus* is a Subject fit,
> Grown old in Politicks and Wit;
> Caress'd by Ministers of State,
> Of half Mankind the Dread and Hate.

[39] Ibid., p. 686.
[40] Ibid., p. 700.

It is curious that Vanessa is represented as being particularly affected by some lines in a poem of Swift's:

> *Cadenus* many things had writ;
> *Vanessa* much esteem'd his Wit,
> And call'd for his Poetick Works;
> Mean time the Boy in secret lurks,
> And while the Book was in her Hand,
> The Urchin from his private Stand
> Took Aim, and shot with all his Strength
> A Dart of such prodigious Length,
> It pierc'd the feeble Volume thro',
> And deep transfix'd her Bosom too.
> Some Lines, more moving than the rest,
> Stuck to the Point that pierc'd her Breast;
> And, born directly to the Heart,
> With Pains unknown increased her Smart.[41]

As the episode referred to must have taken place in 1712 or 1713, when Swift's published verses were still very slight in bulk, it is tempting to speculate what these lines could have been—unless this specific detail is merely a little joke. Most of Swift's biographers agree that it probably happened sometime after his return to London, on September 9, 1713, on one of his visits to the court at Windsor, which continued until the end of December, 1713. On October 31, Swift had addressed some lines *To Lord Harley, on his Marriage*,[42] and in this poem there is at least a passage which might very well have served as an introduction to Vanessa's declaration of love. For there Swift in an unusual vein of happy compliment praises Harley's young bride, the daughter of the Duke of Newcastle, for her sensible choice of the virtuous and the learned Harley, in preference to the glittering crowd of fortunes and titles that had aspired to her. How aptly, if Vanessa had been reading this poem, could she have turned the argument to her own purpose. She too had been taught by Swift to despise the ordinary ways of the world:

> Terrestrial nymphs, by formal arts,
> Display their various nets for hearts:
> Their looks are all by method set,

[41] Ibid., p. 702.
[42] Ibid., p. 176.

> When to be prude, and when coquette;
> Yet, wanting skill and pow'r to choose,
> Their only pride is to refuse.
> But, when a Goddess would bestow
> Her love on some bright youth below
> Round all the earth she casts her eyes;
> And then, descending from the skies,
> Makes choice of him she fancies best, . . .[43]

Her taste was surely even more exalted, leading her to choose before all the Court a Dean twice her age. The latter part of the poem has always been regarded as a reliable account of what happened. Naturally when the poem was published in 1726, Swift wishing to dismiss it lightly, referred to it in a letter to Knightley Chetwode, April 19, 1726, as "a task performed on a frolic among some ladies at Windsor . . . for my own part, I forget what is in it, but believe it to be only a cavalier business . . . a private humorsome thing, which, by an accident inevitable, and the baseness of particular malice, is made public."[44]

That is perhaps hardly fair, and yet the phrases "a cavalier business" —"a private humorsome thing" are not inaccurate descriptions of the poem. Whatever the episode itself was—however charged with passion and pity, however difficult and dangerous—Swift treats it with as little emotion as possible; he is neither cynical nor sentimental, he detaches himself gently from it, and places it a little way off, and sees it as something separate, a private affair of Cadenus and Vanessa, a delicate subject to be touched carefully with wit and fancy and humour.

Nothing that Swift ever wrote shows more perfectly his mastery of himself and his art than these lines, describing at length the dispute between Cadenus and Vanessa. He recognizes the force of her argument, he is fairly caught, it is a "bite." But he may well be proud at her confession,

> Constr'ing the Passion she had shown,
> Much to her Praise, more to his Own.
> Nature in him had Merit plac'd,
> In her, a most judicious Taste.

In return he gladly offers her "friendship in its greatest height."

[43] Ibid., p. 178.'
[44] Corr. III, 306.

> His Want of Passion will redeem,
> With Gratitude, Respect, Esteem:
> With what Devotion we bestow,
> When Goddesses appear below.

But Vanessa has been taught too well by him; she knows the proper value of such "exalted strains"—

> The Nymph in sober Words intreats
> A Truce with all sublime Conceits.
> For why such Raptures, Flights, and Fancies,
> To her, who durst not read Romances;
> In lofty Style to make Replies,
> Which he had taught her to despise.[45]

She will have her turn to be tutor, and will teach him the science

> Wherein his Genius was below
> The Skill of ev'ry common Beau;

And now in this extremely delicate situation, Swift must avoid either the bathos of a happy ending, or a hint perhaps of the tragedy that was to follow. He preserves instead the "humorsome" tone perfectly, by ending in cavalier fashion—

> But what Success *Vanessa* met,
> Is to the World a Secret yet:
> Whether the Nymph, to please her Swain,
> Talks in a high Romantick Strain;
> Or whether he at last descends
> To act with less Seraphick Ends;
> Or, to compound the Business, whether
> They temper Love and Books together;
> Must never to Mankind be told,
> Nor shall the conscious Muse unfold.[46]

The poems to Stella are if possible both in subject and in style an even more complete triumph over any temptation to indulge in sentiment or romance; and it is surprising, as Dr. Elrington Ball remarks, "that Swift could have borne the publication of these verses, especially when he believed her to be dying and was writing to Sheridan in an

[45] *Poems*, p. 711.
[46] Ibid., p. 712.

agony of affliction." And he can only offer the not very convincing explanation that it was due to Swift's infatuation for Pope and his wish to leave the arrangement of the *Miscellanies* entirely in his hands. It may well be that Pope was anxious to have as much new material as possible in order to give some justification for the publisher's advertisement, which described the *Last Volume* as "consisting of several Copies of Verses, most of them never before printed." But it is perhaps equally reasonable to suppose that Swift definitely wished to include, and set over against the *Cadenus and Vanessa*, these plain records of his friendship with Stella.

The Birthday Verses belong to the last years of her life, 1719-1727, and are perfectly described by a phrase which Swift uses to describe the character of his poetry in some lines written *To Mr. Delany, Nov. 10, 1718*.[47]

> To you the Muse this Verse bestows,
> Which might as well have been in Prose;
> No Thought, no Fancy, no Sublime,
> But simple Topicks told in Rime

He might perhaps have gone further and said that he sometimes wrote verse because it was easier than to write prose. The doggerel trifles that he and Sheridan tossed off together were of course very much easier, as Sheridan admits in his verses *To the Dean, when in England, in 1726*:

> Because hot weather makes me lazy
> To write in metre is more easy.[48]

Sometimes Swift wrote down his verses with his left hand, while the other hand was at the same time writing letters of business, or (if we may believe his time-keeping) at the tremendous speed of 38 rhyming lines "Written, sign'd, and seal'd, five minutes and eleven seconds after the receipt of yours, allowing seven seconds for sealing and superscribing, from my bed-side, just eleven minutes after eleven, Sept. 15, 1718."[49] But in his best work too, Swift forces the rhymed octosyllabic couplet to serve him as a means of obtaining an effect of

[47] Ibid., p. 215.
[48] Ibid., p. 1042.
[49] Ibid., p. 980.

perfect spontaneity and ease, a medium of expression even less formal
than prose. Most poets use verse where prose would not be good
enough for their particular purpose. Swift seems almost to have used
it as a more familiar, more intimate way of communication. He could
do anything he liked with prose, except, I think, that he was not a
master of the familiar style; even in the *Journal to Stella* he is obliged
to fall back upon "little language."

And so, just as in dealing with his enemies in political controversy
he used verse for his roughest and least considered outbursts, tossing
off ballads and broadsides shaped to popular tunes, so in his friendships his most familiar manner of address was always in verse. What
could be more familiar—and at the same time an excellent parody on
the usual complimentary Birthday-Odes—than the first of the poems
written for *Stella's Birthday, March 13, 1718-19.*[50]

> Stella this Day is thirty four,
> (We won't dispute a Year or more)
> However Stella, be not troubled,
> Although thy Size and Years are doubled,
> Since first I saw Thee at Sixteen . . .

He delights always to emphasize that she is no longer either young or
beautiful—

> An Angel's face, a little crack't;[51]

he boasts that in all his addresses to her there had been only sincerity—
To Stella, who collected and transcribed his Poems, 1720[52]

> Thou, *Stella*, wert no longer young,
> When first for thee my Harp I strung:
> Without one Word of *Cupid's* Darts,
> Of killing Eyes, or bleeding Hearts:
> With Friendship and Esteem possesst,
> I ne'er admitted Love a Guest.
>   .   .   .   .   .
> Your Virtues safely I commend,
> They on no Accidents depend:

[50] Ibid., p. 721.
[51] Ibid., p. 734.
[52] Ibid., p. 727.

> Let Malice look with all her Eyes,
> She dares not say the Poet lyes.

There are a good many commonplaces, and too many repetitions on the birthday theme, which Swift himself seems to have tired of, for in 1724-5 he complains that he can no longer dance in rhyme:[53]

> Adieu bright Wit, and radiant Eyes;
> You must be grave, and I be wise.
> Our Fate in vain we would oppose,
> But I'll be still your Friend in Prose:
> Esteem and Friendship to express,
> Will not require Poetick Dress;
> And if the Muse deny her Aid
> To have them *sung,* they may be *said.*

Yet two years later, on Stella's last birthday, he offers her a splendid final poem, where without any change of tone these plain prosaic octosyllables take on real force and dignity.

In such verses we can perhaps best feel the limitations of Swift's poetry; for here in a line or two we can see them as it were just giving way. That severe plainness of speech, that unwillingness to allow words to become emotional or musical,—the flat tonelessness of many of the serious poems almost disappears, and we are half persuaded that we can distinguish tones from another kind of poetry in that last couplet:

> To morrow will be time enough
> To hear such mortifying Stuff.[54]

But still he limits himself to his particular theme, and allows nothing fanciful or extraneous to enter. It was doubtless Swift himself who chose the title for the volume of poems which Faulkner included in the first collected edition of the *Works,* 1735—*Poems on several Occasions.* It is a most accurate description—for all his verse is in the strictest sense occasional, and when the occasion is private, he rarely allows it to expand into general significance. This is partly because verses like these to Stella were written primarily for her and for their friends, without any consideration of a wider audience. When the

53 Ibid., p. 756.
54 Ibid., p. 763.

occasion is public, the poetry is often more powerful, for then it is generally aimed with a definite purpose at the larger public; with the result that it takes on a character which Scott has well described:

> Sometimes, however, the intensity of the satire gives to his poetry a character of emphatic violence, which borders upon grandeur. . . . [It] indicates rather ardour of temper than power of imagination. *Facit indignatio versus.* The elevation of tone arises from the strong mood of passion rather than from poetical fancy.

There was one great occasion which Swift took full advantage of— the death of the Duke of Marlborough. The poem was *A Satirical Elegy on the death of a late famous General,* 1722[55]

> His Grace! impossible! what dead!
> Of old age too, and in his bed!
>
> .   .   .   .
>
> Behold his funeral appears,
> Nor widows' sighs, nor orphans' tears,
> Wont at such times each heart to pierce,
> Attend the progress of his herse.
> But what of that, his friends may say,
> He had those honours in his day.
> True to his profit and his pride,
> He made them weep before he dy'd.
>
>   Come hither, all ye empty things,
> Ye bubbles rais'd by breath of Kings;
> Who float upon the tide of state,
> Come hither, and behold your fate.
> Let pride be taught by this rebuke,
> How very mean a thing's a Duke;
> From all his ill-got honours flung,
> Turn'd to that dirt from whence he sprung.

Is truth, or prejudice, too nakedly exposed? Must we therefore say that this cannot be poetry? If the imagination may trace the noble dust of Alexander till it is found stopping a bung-hole, may it not also triumph in the return of the ignoble to "that dirt from whence he sprung"?

Swift seems to delight to go through the whole realm of poetry,

[55] Ibid., p. 296.

turning everything upside down. If we look for elegies, fitting a
solemn moment, this is what we find; if we want sentiment and the
delicate play of fancy, we are offered a parody of Cowley's *Clad all in
White*—one of the Love-Verses from *The Mistress*. Swift changes the
title to *Clad all in Brown*,[56] and proceeds to cover with filth his detested and despised enemy Richard Tighe. This is again a poem
which can be regarded either as the product of a diseased imagination
or as a contemptuous revolt against poetic sentiment. Here are a few
lines of the original and the parody:

Fairest thing that shines below, . . .	Foulest Brute that stinks below, . . .
So clouds themselves like Suns ap-pear,	Not one Jot better looks the Sun
When the Sun pierces them with Light: . . .	Seen from behind a dirty Clout: . . .
So Lillies in a glass enclose,	So T - - ds within a Glass enclose,
The Glass will seem as white as those. . . .	The Glass will seem as brown as those. . . .
Such robes the Saints departed wear,	Old carted Bawds such Garments wear,
Woven all with Light divine. . . .	When pelted all with Dirt they shine; . . .

It is little to be wondered at that some of his contemporaries declared that there was no traditional name for such a writer as this. In
Gulliveriana, 1728, Dean Smedley describes Swift's verse as follows:

> Low, groveling Poetry all of it; and I challenge all the World, to show
> one good *Epic, Elegiac* or *Lyric* Poem of his; one *Eclogue, Pastoral,* or
> anything like the *Antients;* and as he can't write like them, so they
> had no name for such a Writer as he is: And his *Doggerel* and *Bur-
> lesque* had Banish'd him *Rome,* notwithstanding he is so often huzza'd
> in *Dublin.*

In 1733 Swift wrote an admirable reply to this criticism of his practice of poetry; it is a long piece, entitled *An Epistle to a Lady, who desired the Author to make Verses on Her, in the Heroick Style.*[57] She
asks him to

[56] Ibid., p. 786.
[57] Ibid., p. 629.

> suspend a While
> That same paultry, *Burlesque* Stile;
> Drop, for once, your constant Rule,
> Turning all to Ridicule;

She will provide him with material, and he is to try instead to sing her praise in strain sublime. But the attempt is vain; he allows her due praise, but instinctively turns to give her advice, and then offers this apology:

> To conclude this long Essay;
> Pardon if I disobey:
> Nor, against my nat'ral Vein,
> Treat you in Heroick Strain.
> I, as all the Parish knows,
> Hardly can be grave in Prose:
> .   .   .   .   .
> From the Planet of my Birth
> I encounter Vice with Mirth.[58]

Then he turns to have a fling at kings and courts, and corrupt ministers, but here too constantly insists that his only method of treating all such things is ridicule.

> Safe within my little Wherry,
> All their Madness makes me merry:
> Like the Watermen of *Thames,*
> I row by, and call them Names.
> Like the ever-laughing Sage,
> In a Jest I spend my Rage:
> (Tho' it must be understood,
> I would hang them if I cou'd;)[59]

And he concludes:

> For your Sake, as well as mine,
> I the lofty Stile decline.
> I shou'd make a Figure scurvy,
> And your Head turn Topsy-turvy.[60]

[58] Ibid., p. 634.
[59] Ibid., p. 635.
[60] Ibid., p. 637.

When Faulkner published the volume of collected poems, it was prefaced by an *Advertisement,* dated Dublin 1734, which must have been approved if not written by Swift. The collection is said to consist chiefly "of Humour or Satyr, and very often of both together." And the one claim that is made for the Poems is that at any rate they do not follow the old well-trodden paths: "the Author never was known either in Verse or Prose to borrow any Thought, Simile, Epithet, or particular Manner of Style: but whatever he writ, whether good, bad, or indifferent, is an Original in itself."

Twenty years later, it was pointed out in the *Connoisseur* (No. 67) that a great age in literature is always marked by variety and originality, and its authors are distinguished by cultivating different branches of poetry from each other. "We admire Swift, Pope, Gay, Bolingbroke, Addison, etc., but we admire each for his particular beauties separate and distinguished from the rest." At least during the eighteenth century it was not forgotten that the poetry of the Augustans was both original and varied; the differences were never merged together under some stupid generalization, merely for the convenience of the historian in contrasting them with something else. Even Dr. Elrington Ball is inclined, I think, to give too much importance to Swift's association with Addison and Prior, though strangely enough he makes no reference whatever to Samuel Butler. If we wish to account for the particular quality of Swift's verse, if we wish to place him in a tradition, we shall have to investigate first of all what he owed to *Hudibras,* and to the popular verse-satire of the seventeenth century.

Swift was, however, like his contemporaries in claiming that all his satire, whether concerning public affairs or the manners of society, "hath no other Aim than to reform the Errors of both Sexes." Many of his critics, as well in the eighteenth century as in the twentieth, have not been satisfied with this explanation of such poems as *The Lady's Dressing Room, A beautiful young Nymph going to Bed,* and *Strephon and Chloe.* I will pass over the usual objections, and consider only a very recent attack from an unexpected quarter; for it is particularly interesting to find that Aldous Huxley and D. H. Lawrence were distressed by these poems.

The latter objects in an essay entitled *Apropos of Lady Chatterley's Lover* (1930), that Swift in *The Lady's Dressing Room* (which he refers to in a very misleading fashion as a poem "to his mistress Celia") gives evidence of a mind diseased by "terror of the body."

> A great wit like Swift could not see how ridiculous he made himself. . . . Think of poor Celia, made to feel iniquitous about her proper natural function, by her lover. It is monstrous. And it comes from having taboo words, and from not keeping the mind sufficiently developed in physical and sexual consciousness.

And yet of course Swift had no taboo words, and shocked even some of his eighteenth century readers because he manifests that so clearly in this very poem, and because he was willing to bring so much at any rate of the physical into consciousness. The whole significance of these poems lies in the fact that Swift hated the sentimentality of the ordinary romantic love-stuff. He is repeating here—even more drastically—what he had done in the poems already referred to, *The Progress of Beauty,* and *Clad all in Brown.* Instead of rapturously describing the beauty of the body, or the poetry of dress, and all that stimulates desire, he is as usual turning things upside down, and with complete lack of restraint exposing the ugliness and unpleasantness of certain physical functions, and of certain aspects of private life in English fashionable society of the time, which were usually kept hidden. What squeamish people really object to is that in such poems Swift, as he readily admits, mingles humour with satire. They cannot forgive him because, in the very act of uncovering these unsavoury things, instead of making a horrified grimace, he is able to grin; it is in accordance with his experience—

> Thus, I find it by Experiment,
> Scolding moves you less than Merriment.
> I may storm and rage in vain;
> It but stupefies your Brain.
> But with Raillery to nettle,
> Set your Thoughts upon their Mettle:[61]

Aldous Huxley's essay on *Swift* (included in *What You Will,* 1929) is a brilliant elaboration of the same point. It is suspicious, however, in the first place because of the violence of his language. He quotes a casual remark of Swift's from a letter to Stella "(I hate the word bowels)" and then continues excitedly:

[61] Ibid., p. 636.

Yes, how he hated it! And not the word only—the things too, the harmless necessary tripes—he loathed and detested them with an intensity of hatred such as few men have ever been capable of. It was unbearable to him that men should go through life with guts and sweetbreads, with liver and lights, spleens and kidneys. . . . All this was "a source of excruciating suffering" . . . his resentment was incredibly bitter.

Did it ever occur to Mr. Huxley in the first place that the word "bowels" had been used (in its metaphorical and sentimental sense) throughout the seventeenth century by all the canting preachers whom Swift most detested, till the very sound of it must have been unendurable in his ears? Even the few references given in the *New English Dictionary* are significant enough. There is a Parliamentary Proclamation for 1651, which refers to "Want of bowels in preaching towards them who are in hazard to perish." Fuller could not resist quoting a horrible pun in 1655: "Bloody Bonner . . . full (as one said) of guts, and empty of bowels." And this continued into the eighteenth century, as for instance in this delightful phrase from the *London Gazette* just a little earlier than Swift's protest: "To shew their bowels for their country."

I doubt very much Mr. Huxley's remark that Swift loathed "the things too, the harmless necessary tripes." It seems to me only a proof of the extreme sensitiveness of the twentieth century humorist that accounts for his abhorrent disgust at Swift's unsavoury jokes. And, I am sure, a little further acquaintance with Swift would prevent Mr. Huxley from writing such a sentence as this: "Swift's greatness lies in the intensity, the almost insane violence of that "hatred of bowels" which is the essence of his misanthropy and which underlies the whole of his work." Is this not to forget a little too obviously that the Dean of St. Patrick's was in the first place a wit and a humorist?

But, to return to the poems, is it fantastic to suggest that *Strephon and Chloe* can be most fairly judged, if it is regarded as a burlesque Epithalamium? At least it is a satire on a subject which always drove Swift to violent ridicule—romantic nonsense about marriage, a poison which he always feared as a great menace to human happiness. Whenever he speaks of marriage it is with almost incredible detachment and cold reasonableness. In one of his earliest letters it will be remembered that he had written to Varina to make a proposal of marriage. After a long list of questions, which he had always resolved to put to her with whom he meant to pass his life, he concludes: "whenever you can heartily answer them in the affirmative, I shall be blessed to have you in my arms, without regarding whether your person be beautiful, or your fortune large. Cleanliness in the first, and competency in the other, is all I look for."[62] Again when asked for advice about getting married by his friend Knightley Chetwode, Swift replied (Feb. 12, 1729-30):

> As to changing your single life, it is impossible to advise without know-ing all circumstances both of you and the person. Archbishop Sheldon advised a young Lord to be sure to get money with a wife, because he would then be at least possessed of one good thing."[63]

At any rate Swift always felt that it was a dangerous business, and he endeavours repeatedly in his poem *Strephon and Chloe*[64] to make his moral purpose clear. He allows full play to his satirical wit in pic-turing Strephon's fall out of the clouds of romance, but constantly interrupts his story to give advice of the plainest kind:

> Since Husbands get behind the Scene,
> The Wife should study to be clean;
>
> .   .   .   .
>
> Authorities both old and recent,
> Direct that Women must be decent;
> And, from the Spouse each Blemish hide
> More than from all the World beside.[65]

And the concluding moral is almost too commonplace and serious:

> On Sense and Wit your Passion found,
> By Decency cemented round;
> Let Prudence with Good Nature strive,
> To keep Esteem and Love alive.
> Then come old Age whene'er it will,
> Your Friendship shall continue still;
> And thus a mutual gentle Fire,
> Shall never but with Life expire.[66]

We are reminded of a splendid tribute to Swift, in one of Arbuthnot's letters, written on September 20, 1726:

[62] *Corr.*, I, 35.
[63] Ibid., IV, 123.
[64] *Poems*, p. 584.
[65] Ibid., pp. 588, 591.
[66] Ibid., p. 593.

I had a great deal of discourse with your friend, her Royal Highness. She insisted upon your wit, and good conversation. I told her Royal Highness, that was not what I valued you for, but for being a sincere honest man, and speaking truth when others were afraid to speak it.[67]

But it was that indeed which was the very source of Swift's wit; he needed only to say with his perfect simplicity and directness what he saw to be true, and to most of his readers who live perpetually in a world of romance and sentiment, it seemed the most biting irony. To them he appeared a mad fellow indeed, turning everything to wit and foolery—friendship and hate, love and marriage, and at last, death and judgment.

Even Lucretius, in his argument against the fear of death, allows that death brings grief for those who are left behind:

> But we, thy friends, shall all those sorrows find,
> Which in forgetful death thou leav'st behind;
> No time shall dry our tears, nor drive them from our mind.[68]

But Swift turns even this to scorn, with his motto from La Roche-foucauld, which he takes as his theme for the *Verses on the Death of Dr. Swift*, published in 1739:[69]

> In all Distresses of our Friends
> We first consult our private Ends,
> While Nature kindly bent to ease us,
> Points out some Circumstance to please us.

The poem is an "apologia pro vita sua," and characteristically concerned more with what he was and did, than with what he wrote. He does, however, repeat once more his favourite boast that "what he writ was all his own" and

> . . . with a moral View design'd
> To cure the Vices of Mankind:[70]

but he finally admits:

[67] *Corr.*, III, 343.
[68] Dryden's translation of the latter part of the Third Book, included in *Sylvae*, 1685, ll. 92-4.
[69] *Poems*, p. 553.
[70] Ibid., p. 565.

> Perhaps I may allow, the Dean
> Had too much Satyr in his Vein;
> And seem'd determin'd not to starve it,
> Because no Age could more deserve it.[71]

But that does not restrain him from one last stroke—beautifully expressive of the way in which so often he mingled generosity and contempt.

> He gave the little wealth he had
> To build a House for Fools and Mad:
> And shew'd by one satyric Touch,
> No Nation wanted it so much:[72]

There is not much further scope left for wit and satire. But after his death there was found among his papers, in his own handwriting, a poem on *The Day of Judgment*.[73] It was very fitting that it was first printed as quoted by Lord Chesterfield, in a letter to Voltaire, dated August 27, 1752.

It describes the Last Day, with the world standing trembling before Jove's throne, and then gives very shortly the epilogue to the whole comedy of life:

> Offending Race of Human Kind,
> By Nature, Reason, Learning, blind;
> You who, thro' Frailty step'd aside,
> And you who never fell-*thro' Pride;*
> You who in different Sects have shamm'd,
> And come to see each other damn'd;
> (So some Folks told you, but they knew
> No more of Jove's Designs than you)
> The World's mad Business now is o'er,
> And I resent these Pranks no more.
> I to such Blockheads set my Wit!
> I damn such Fools!—Go, go, you're bit.

Here is the complete triumph of the Comic Spirit, unabashed and unafraid, delighting to overthrow all mankind's claims to dignity and importance, and "ending with a puff" the whole heroic and romantic delusion.

[71] Ibid., p. 571.
[72] Ibid., p. 572.
[73] Ibid., p. 578.

SWIFT AND THE PEDANTS

Under the engaging but misleading title that I have chosen for this study, I wish to treat of a part of Swift's work, and to stress some of his favourite interests, so as to correct a bias and alter an emphasis which persist in much that has been written about him, and which continue to keep alive a romantic legend largely due to the desire of most of his biographers "to point a moral or adorn a tale."

Swift, of course, is himself to blame for providing eccentricities and mysteries enough for the legend to flourish upon easily. He was an Anglo-Irishman, full of outspoken contempt for Ireland, who yet gained the reputation of being one of the greatest Irish patriots; he was in Anglican orders and became Dean of St. Patrick's Cathedral, yet he was also the author of *A Tale of a Tub*; he was a Tory High-churchman, not as a place-seeker, but by conviction, yet he showed all the qualities of a revolutionary leader; finally, he was a man who was known to be worshipped by two lovely women to whom he gave the romantic names of Stella and Vanessa, the first being possibly his wife, though he never lived with her, the second possibly his mistress, though she was said to have died of unrequited passion. There is enough to challenge the biographer, and the portrait painter; there was ample to disturb Dr. Johnson, to annoy Jeffrey, and to perplex even Sir Walter Scott. But it is the later development of the legend—the touch of sinister horror added in the 19th century that is more difficult to remove. Thackeray really began it, in that lecture first delivered with such moving eloquence from the pulpit of Dr. Bellows'

Unitarian Church on the east side of Broadway, on November 19, 1852, to a distinguished New York audience. He was outraged by Swift's attack on the human race in the last book of Gulliver, and deeply shocked:

> I think it horrible, shameful, unmanly, blasphemous; and giant and great as the Dean is, I say we should hoot him . . . It is Yahoo language; a monster gibbering shrieks, and gnashing imprecations against mankind—tearing down all shreds of modesty, past all sense of manliness and shame; filthy in word, filthy in thought, furious, raging, obscene.[1]

Then he hints darkly that there must have been some secret remorse rankling at this man's heart, some fever boiling in him that made him see the world bloodshot.

This nameless horror was further touched upon by Professor Masson, and elaborated into a remarkably picturesque theory of demoniacal possession:

> There is a demoniac—he says—of the supernatural—angels and seraphs, and white-winged airy messengers swaying men's phantasies from above; and there is a demoniac of the infra-natural—fiends and shapes of horror tugging at men's thoughts from beneath. The demoniac in Swift was of the latter kind . . . That communion with the invisible almost exclusively on the infernal side—that consciousness of chains wound round his moving frame at one end, and at the other tugged at by demons in the depths of their populous pit while no cords of love were felt sustaining him from countervailing heaven—had its origin, in part at least, in some one recollection or cause of dread. It was some one demon in that pit that tugged the chains . . .[2]

Not long ago a book of Shane Leslie's was made up of the same stuff—"We know that Swift left a mortal skull. It is difficult to believe that an immortal soul ever quitted that inverted bowl of bone."[3] And similarly, as we have already seen, charges of abnormality come from people like Aldous Huxley, D. H. Lawrence, and some of the professional psychologists.

This sort of interpretation of Swift is altogether too simple. It is the

---

[1] "English Humourists." See *Works*, ed. Saintsbury, XIII, 496.
[2] *Quarterly Review*, October 1854.
[3] Shane Leslie, *The Skull of Swift*, 1928, p. 10.

business of literary criticism to break down that simplicity, and to reveal by a closer analysis the fascinating varieties of tone and attitude
and interest to be found clearly enough in his work. Swift has suffered
by reason of the very force and intensity of his own sayings: "dying
like a rat in a hole," "fierce indignation tearing his heart"—such
phrases have been given too much attention. His friends would not
have been deceived by them. They not only knew him in his various
moods, but they did not forget the different characters he assumed,
the disguises he wore when he appeared in public. Nowadays one
or other of these is often forgotten. In Ireland he is still remembered as the Dean of St. Patrick's, as the Hibernian Patriot, as the
founder of St. Patrick's hospital for the insane; in the world he is
best known as that simple and disillusioned seaman, Lemuel Gulliver.
I should like to consider him now rather as Isaac Bickerstaff; and it
is all the better that he shared that title afterwards with the authors of
the *Tatler*, with Steele and with Addison, because in his Bickerstaffian
attacks upon pedantry and shams, he used the same weapons as they
did, and surpassed them not by the savagery, but by the gaiety and
inventiveness of his humour.

I do not forget that even as Isaac Bickerstaff Swift has been ma-
ligned for his ruthlessness in attacking John Partridge, a poor harmless quack and astrologer, and making the rest of his life a misery.
Partridge was responsible for one of the numerous popular almanacks
of the day, which provided a calendar, some useful information, some
partisan verse, and some predictions of coming events. Swift was, I
believe, annoyed particularly by Partridge's vulgar and violent outbursts against the Church party, as well as by his constant challenge
in his pedantic jargon to his brother almanack-makers that he could
beat them at the game of casting nativities:

> That it may be made plain and clear to the World, who have Principles
> they dare rely on, and who have not, I do friendly and fairly invite and
> challenge my Adversaries and, in particular, *Gadbury and Coley,* who
> value themselves as Masters of the Art, to pitch upon five or ten Nativi-
> ties, and like an Artist to tell the World in print which of them hath
> *no Hileg* who is *Giver of Life,* and who the *Ananeta,* who is the
> *Poionosos,* who the *Poiothanatos;* but above all, to tell us when they
> *will Dye,* with the Astrologic reasons thereof.[4]

4 *Prose,* II, xi.

What could be more urbane, more gentlemanly than the method Swift took to silence him, and to provide the town with a good joke. He simply accepted Partridge's challenge, printed a small pamphlet, called *Predictions for the Year 1708, by Isaac Bickerstaffe, Esq.,* among which was one to prove his own skill as an astrologer:

> My first Prediction is but a Trifle; yet I will mention it, to shew how ignorant those sottish Pretenders to Astrology are in their own Concerns: It relates to *Partrige* the Almanack-Maker; I have consulted the Star of his Nativity by my own Rules; and find he will infallibly die upon the 29th of March next, about eleven at Night, of a raging Fever: Therefore I advise him to consider of it, and settle his Affairs in Time.[5]

On the 30th of March there duly appeared a short paper, entitled *The Accomplishment of the First of Mr. Bickerstaffe's Predictions, Being an Account of the Death of Mr. Partridge, the Almanack-Maker, upon the 29th Inst. In a Letter to a Person of Honour.* It gives a convincing account of the last days of Partridge, until he expired at about five minutes after seven. This was immediately followed by a poetical Elegy, printed on a Broadside, with deep black edges, and hawked on the streets of London:

> Well, 'tis as Bickerstaff has guest,
> Tho' we all took it for a Jest:
> Patrige is Dead, nay more, he dy'd
> E'er he could prove the good Squire ly'd.[6]

I will not here pursue the story further, the replies of Partridge, the vindications and the continuations which followed for some years, and the final injustice when the Stationers Company who had the monopoly on such publications, brought an action in court to prevent Partridge from printing any more almanacks.

I wish only to show Swift in the role of Bickerstaff, the wit and the humourist, at his work of exposing and making fun of quacks and shams for the amusement of the gentlemen of the town. Even in the course of this Partridge affair Swift was not content with such poor sport as was provided by the trivial pedantries of an astrologer. *A Vindication of Isaac Bickerstaff,* which appeared the next year, though

[5] Ibid., p. 145.
[6] *Poems,* p. 98.

ostensibly prompted by Partridge's scurrilities, was really aimed at the great Dr. Bentley, who was as well known for his asperity and his vanity as for his scholarship. In his *Vindication* Mr. Bickerstaff protests against being called Fool and Villain, and impudent Fellow only for differing in a point merely speculative: scurrility and passion in a controversy among scholars is, he says, just so much of nothing to the purpose; the discovery of truth ought to be the great end in all disputes of the learned. He then proceeds in a perfect parody of Bentley, gravely to quote what foreign professors have said of his work. "The necessity of justifying myself will excuse my vanity, when I tell the reader, that I have near an hundred *honorary* letters from several parts of Europe, some as far as Muscovy, in praise of my performance. Besides several others, which, as I have been credibly informed, were opened in the Post-Office, and never sent me."[7] He then quotes the phrases of Leibnitz, Leclerc, Magliabecchi, the great Duke's famous librarian, and the famous Professor of Astronomy at Utrecht who differs only in one article, and here lays the error on the printer as indeed he ought.

Swift was occupied at this time in preparing for the printer an enlarged and annotated edition of his first considerable volume, which he had brought out in 1704, containing *A Tale of a Tub*, and *The Battle of the Books*, in which he had attempted to satirize the pedantries of the whole world of learning and religion, and in which Bentley had figured prominently. It was an amusing and paradoxical situation, in which Swift, who had received his master's degree from the University of Oxford, had come to the aid of the Christ Church wits in their famous struggle concerning the authenticity of the Epistles of Phalaris, with the heavy-armed champion from Trinity College, Cambridge; they being in the strategic position as supporters of the Ancients, urbanely upholding the traditional view against this monstrous Goliath of modern scholarship.

Swift appeared among the combatants in this struggle that had long been waged among the learned with all the gaiety of youthful confidence; and in the *Apology*, which he wrote for the book later, he well describes the position which he maintained fairly consistently towards the world of literature and learning. He was a young gentleman much in the world, who wrote to the taste of those like himself;

[7] *Prose*, II, 160.

whatever romantic notions he may once have had, he was now disillusioned, and could find there only material for satire and raillery.

He had always been interested in poetry and literature; he had
grown up under the shadow of the great reputation of his cousin
Dryden. But his desire to be a poet had been shaken by observing the
petty shams and insincerities used to build up a literary reputation.
He therefore determined to expose the tricks of the trade, all the
paraphernalia of Prefaces, Epistles, Advertisements, Introductions,
Prolegomenas, Apparatuses, To the Readers. They were, of course,
admirable at first, he says: "Our great Dryden has long carried it as
far as it would go, and with incredible Success. He has often said to
me in Confidence, that the World would have never suspected him
to be so great a Poet, if he had not assured them so frequently in his
Prefaces, that it was impossible they could either doubt or forget it."[8]

Similarly he exposed all the professional tricks of the seventeenth
century scholar, making fun of the Abstracts, Summaries, Compen-
diums, Extracts, Collections, Medullas, Excerpta quaedams, Florile-
gias and the like, which were in vogue. He ridicules the new educa-
tional methods of the moderns, who have discovered a shorter method
to become wits and scholars without the fatigue of reading or of
thinking:

> The most accomplisht Way of using Books at present, is twofold:
> Either first, to serve them as some Men do *Lords*, learn their Titles ex-
> actly, and then brag of their Acquaintance. Or Secondly, which is in-
> deed the choicer, the profounder, and politer Method, to get a thor-
> ough Insight into the *Index*, by which the whole Book is governed and
> turned, like *Fishes* by the *Tail*. For, to enter the Palace of Learning at
> the *great Gate*, requires an Expence of Time and Forms; therefore
> Men of much Haste and little Ceremony, are content to get in by the
> *Back-door*.[9]

He had also as a young man been stirred by the excitement caused
by the founding of the Royal Society, and the experiments of all kinds
which were going on to enlarge the field of knowledge. He had even
written an Ode in honour of that bogus Athenian Society, which the
enterprising bookseller John Dunton had founded. But this world too
seemed to be overrun by fantastic projectors of all sorts, with schemes

[8] Ibid., I, 81.
[9] Ibid., p. 91.

either wholly unpractical or absurd. As for the Honourable Robert Boyle with his pumps and his air-machines, they might be turned to account in the interests of his satire and some of the more offensive pages in *A Tale of a Tub* and in *Gulliver's Travels* owe something, I suspect, to Boyle's experiments on the properties of air. Boyle was unfortunately also given to theological speculation, and prolix moral-isings; and one of Bickerstaff's most effective little parodies was at the expense of Boyle's *Occasional Reflections upon Several Subjects*. I do not need to quote the "Meditation upon a Broomstock." It may serve as a salutary warning to all scholars who are too inclined to wander beyond the range of their own interests and knowledge.

Swift was to return to Boyle again when describing the experiments that went on in the Academy of Lagado in Laputa, very likely the last chapters of *Gulliver's Travels* to be written. Marjorie Nicolson and Nora Mohler pointed out, for instance, that Swift's description of "a man born blind, who had several apprentices in his own condition; their employment was to mix colors for painters, which their master taught them to distinguish by feeling and smelling," was probably due to his reading of an abridged edition of Boyle's *Works* which came out in 1725. The blind professor whom Gulliver saw had in the preceding century been a real blind man, whose case was reported to Boyle by "Dr. Finch, anatomist extraordinary to the duke of Tuscany." Finch had told Boyle of "a blind man at Maestricht, in the Low Countries, who at certain times could distinguish colors by the touch with his fingers." Boyle had some scruples about believing this and tried to explain it by suggesting "that the blind man might have distinguished the colors not by feeling, but by smelling"—another point which Swift was quick to catch. Boyle's account continues:

. . . for some of the ingredients employ'd by dyers, have different and strong scents, which a very nice nose might distinguish; and this I the rather suspected, because he required that the ribbons he was to judge of, should be offer'd him in the morning fasting; for I have observ'd in setting-dogs, that the feeding of them greatly impairs their strength.[10]

It was, of course, in this third book of *Gulliver's Travels*, in which

10 See *The Scientific Background of Swift's "Voyage to Laputa,"* *Annals of Science* ii, 323-5.

Swift may possibly have had the assistance of his friend, Dr. Arbuthnot, the Queen's physician and a good mathematician, that he turned
his attention mainly to the new science. Swift was never scornful of
any practical improvements, but he distrusted anything that would
make life less simple. And above all he distrusted theorizing. That
simple-hearted giant, the king of Brobdingnag, gave it for his opinion:
"that whoever could make two Ears of Corn, or two Blades of Grass
grow upon a Spot of Ground where only one grew before, would deserve better of Mankind, and do more essential Service to his Country than the whole Race of Politicians put together."[11] Such a one
Swift was also inclined to value much more highly than men like
Halley or Newton. Their researches had filled the Laputans with
terrors, terror before the comet that would return in thirty-one years,
and perhaps give the earth a brush with its tail; terror lest the nice
balance of the planetary system should be upset.

Owing to the office he held at the Mint, Newton had been drawn
into the fight over Wood's Copper Coinage for Ireland, and had then
aroused Swift's enmity; in revenge he minimized the importance of
his work as much as possible. He describes his discovery as simply
the latest fashion in vogue among the scientists; and makes Aristotle,
who appeared before Gulliver in Glubdubdrib, the mouthpiece of his
scepticism.

> This great Philosopher freely acknowledged his own Mistakes in Nat-
> ural Philosophy, because he proceeded in many things upon Conjec-
> ture, as all Men must do; and he found that Gassendi, who had made
> the doctrine of Epicurus as palatable as he could, and the Vortices of
> Descartes, were equally exploded. He predicted the same fate to At-
> traction, whereof the present Learned are such zealous Asserters. He
> said that new Systems of Nature were but new Fashions, which would
> vary in every Age; and even those who pretend to demonstrate them
> from mathematical Principles would flourish but a short period of
> time, and be out of Vogue when that was determined.[12]

Ten years later Swift referred to Newton again as

> an Instrument-maker, formerly living near Leicester-Fields, and after-
> wards a Workman in the Mint at the *Tower* might possibly pretend to

[11] *Prose,* IX, 135-6.
[12] Ibid., XI, 197-8.

vye with me for Fame in future times. The Man it seems was knighted for making Sun-Dials better than others of his Trade, and was thought to be a Conjurer, because he knew how to draw Lines and Circles upon a Slate, which nobody could understand.[13]

I am afraid it is necessary to admit that Swift did not realize that he was privileged to be living in the bright dawn of the scientific era; he did not realize that some of his contemporaries were leading mankind across the threshold of the modern world. Sceptical in all things, he saw in the activities of the scholars and projectors and antiquarians of his age not the laying of the foundations of the temple of learning of which we are so justly proud, but rather the continuation of that ill-directed and romantic enthusiasm for useless and fantastic speculation which had bedevilled the life of the later seventeenth century, and ruined that dignified and noble culture of the generation before the Civil War, which he regarded as the finest flower of the English tradition. He had grown up among those who were beginning to turn away exhausted from the unlimited expansiveness of those gatherers of all the heterogeneous paraphernalia of knowledge with their eager curiosity and their readiness for all kinds of projects. Even Sir Thomas Browne in the middle of the century had recognized in the Preface of his *Vulgar Errors* that there were two processes in the discovery of truth: that it was necessary to sift errors as well as to add new knowledge.

Twenty years later in *Gulliver's Travels* he satirizes again the megalomania of book-learning by pointing out with grand irony the defectiveness of the learning of the Brobdingnagians. This was

wholly applied to what may be useful in Life; to the Improvement of Agricultural and all mechanical Arts; so that among us it would be little esteemed. And as to Ideas, Entities, Abstractions, and Transcendentals, I could never drive the least Conception into their Heads . . . No law must exceed in Words the number of Letters in their Alphabet, which consists only of two and twenty . . . and to write a Comment on any Law is a capital Crime.[14]

In the fourth book of *Gulliver* Swift goes even further. In that country of purely rational beings, there is not to be found the least

13 Ibid., IV, 122-3.
14 Ibid., XI, 136.

idea of books or literature; their knowledge is all traditional. Reason is not among them a point problematical as with us, but strikes them with immediate conviction. Opinions, disputes, wranglings were unknown. They laughed at our systems of natural philosophy, not understanding that a rational creature could value himself upon the knowledge of other people's conjectures, and in things where that knowledge, if it were certain, could be of no use. And thereupon Gulliver adds: "I have often since reflected what Destruction such a Doctrine would make in the Libraries of Europe; and how many Paths to Fame would be then shut up in the Learned World."[15]

It was necessary, I think, to show Swift's attitude towards learning and research, before approaching the particular question of pedantry, which is more strictly limited to the matter of language, both in conversation and in writing. It was a matter to which Swift returned again and again, with the conviction, exaggerated perhaps, that ultimately the preservation of the whole tradition of a people depends on its language. He noticed the rapid changes of usage that were taking place, the pouring in of slang and provincialisms and technical jargon, and in common with many of his contemporaries felt that some action was necessary to protect it and preserve its simplicity and its usefulness as a common means of communication. It may seem today a rather silly view. Philologists had not yet investigated the modes of change in speech, and the natural development of language as it takes on new forms and adapts itself to new knowledge and ways of life. Swift's view of language rests on a simple analogy with what he supposed had happened to Greek and Latin, both of which he regarded as having been corrupted after having arrived at and maintained a period of golden age. This point he often says had been reached in England early in the seventeenth century, particularly in the reign of Charles I. Having achieved this perfection, it was above all else necessary to guard it against encroachments from all sides, against all the various forces of pedantry which threatened it. The pedantry of learning was only one danger; the pedantry of poets and wits, the pedantry of Grub-street, the pedantry of the court and polite society seemed to him equally dangerous.

Swift had very simple views on language, for he always maintained

[15] Ibid., p. 268.

that there was one virtue of more importance than anything else—the virtue of simplicity. For him the virtue of simplicity had not been a natural gift; he had acquired it with much effort. His own early poetry, much of which he had destroyed, was written in a grandiloquent manner; he had found the Muses' garden o'er spread with pedantic weeds; for years he gave up writing verse until he found a way of writing things in verse as true as prose.

Later when he began to live in the world, to move in what was called polite society, among the wits in town, he soon recognized other forces at work, disturbing the traditional beauty of the language. And from time to time, in letters to the *Tatler*, he amused himself in pointing them out. Before it had been running two months, if I am right in attributing this letter in the *Tatler* for June 21 to Swift, he is warning Steele that the language of the Inns of Court and the coffee houses—the latest polite slang—is completely unintelligible in the country. He had taken a set of *Tatlers* with him to the country and had lent them from house to house, but had been asked what they meant.

Fifteen months later Swift wrote a long paper again to the *Tatler*, elaborating further the same subject, giving a letter as an example of what the language was coming to, with its slang and its shortening of words and its phonetic spelling. He blames the wits and the war for introducing so many new and unnecessary terms that a man who had died forty years before, if he rose from the grave and came to London, would not understand a word of what people were talking about. Fashions so prevalent that they were even invading the pulpit:

> A noble Standard for Language! To depend upon the Caprice of every Coxcomb; who because Words are the Clothing of our Thoughts, cuts them out, and shapes them as he pleases, and changes them oftner than his Dress.

And he concludes with this appeal:

> I should be glad to see you the Instrument of introducing into our Style, that Simplicity which is the best and truest Ornament of most Things in human Life, which the politer Ages always aimed at in their Building and Dress, (*Simplex munditiis*) as Well as their Productions of Wit. It is manifest that all new affected Modes of Speech, whether

borrowed from the Court or the Theatre, are the first perishing Parts
in any Language; and, as I could prove by many Hundred Instances,
have been so in ours.[16]

Two years later, at the height of his power, Swift addressed a letter
to the Lord Treasurer Harley, with a *Proposal for Correcting, Improving and Ascertaining the English Tongue*. The proposal was to
found an academy somewhat on the French model to fix the language,
that is to say to protect it from all these disintegrating influences which
Swift was afraid of, in order to preserve it from such rapid changes as
would soon make the literature of the Elizabethans a foreign language. His general argument is not a very profound one, and the
scheme to set up a committee to ascertain what the standard language
should be and then to attempt to fix it was, as Dr. Johnson pointed
out, quite impracticable; "the decrees of such an academy every man
would have been willing, and many would have been proud to disobey, and which, being renewed by successive elections, would, in a
short time, have differed from itself."[17] Swift claimed that he had the
full support of Addison and all the men of wit and learning whom
he knew. They do not seem to have realized that their own writings
would be of much more importance in preserving the language, than
any scheme of this kind.

The letter is more interesting in those parts wherein Swift upholds
the prose of the English Bible and the liturgy as his standard of the
best English; and again points out the source of the main dangers
which he sees threatening its purity and integrity. He emphasizes
particularly the jargon that had been brought in during the period of
the Commonwealth in the controversies of the sects on religious and
political theories; and, at the other extreme, since the Restoration, the
affected phrases and new conceited words, either borrowed from the
current style of the court, or from those who, under the character of
men of wit and pleasure, pretended to give the law. Later, in *A Letter
to a Young Clergyman*, and in *Gulliver's Travels*, he was to add his
warning against the language of the new sciences. He makes fun of
the extreme view of those who wished to clarify the processes of thinking by eliminating from language all other functions except that simply of providing labels for things, by describing those Laputans who

[16] Ibid., II, 176-7.
[17] *Lives of the Poets*, ed. G. B. Hill, III, 16.

wished to do away with symbols altogether, and therefore carried about with them in sacks all the things that they wished to talk about:

> I have often beheld two of those Sages almost sinking under the Weight of their Packs, like Pedlars among us; who when they met in the Streets would lay down their Loads, open their Sacks, and hold Conversation for an Hour together; then put up their Implements, help each other to resume their Burthens, and take their Leave.[18]

But I am mistaken if Swift's most valuable contribution to this whole problem was not his thorough and relentless attack upon technical jargon, and the unnecessary use of hard words. The project of the Lagadans, that I have just referred to, was only defeated by the rebellion of the women, the illiterate, and the vulgar. And when he had been living among the Laputans on their flying island, he complained that he had grown heartily weary of those people, who were so abstracted and involved in speculations, that he had never met such disagreeable companions. "I conversed," he says, "only with Women, Tradesmen, Flappers, and Court Pages, during two Months of my Abode there; by which at last I rendered myself extremely contemptible; yet these were the only People from whom I could ever receive a reasonable Answer."[19]

Abstractions, obscurity, and the unnecessary use of "what is called by the better sort of vulgar, fine language"—that is the sort of pedantry Swift most heartily disliked. His remarks in the *Letter to a Young Clergyman* have sometimes been represented as a sort of childish attempt to dispense altogether with a technical or learned vocabulary. This, of course, is untrue; Swift was writing here on that language fit for the pulpit, when addressing any ordinary mixed congregation:

> I know not how it comes to pass, that Professors in most Arts and Sciences are generally the worst qualified to explain their Meanings to those who are not of their Tribe: A common Farmer shall make you understand in three Words, *that his Foot is out of Joint, or his Collarbone broken,* wherein a *Surgeon,* after a hundred terms of art, if you are not a Scholar, shall leave you to seek. It is frequently the same case in Law, Physick, and even many of the meaner Arts . . . And I defy the greatest Divine to produce any Law either of God or Man which

[18] *Prose*, XI, 185-6.
[19] Ibid., p. 173.

obliges me to comprehend the meaning of *Omniscience, Omnipresence, Ubiquity, Attribute, Beatifick Vision,* with a thousand others so frequent in Pulpits, any more than that of *Excentrick, Idiosyncracy, Entity,* and the like.[20]

Dr. Johnson picked up this remark and retorts with violence in a paper (*Idler,* No. 70) on the subject of Hard Words, defending the use of terms of art or technical language:

This could only have been said by such an exact observer of life, in gratification of malignity, or in ostentation of acuteness . . . They that content themselves with general ideas may rest in general terms; but those, whose studies or employments force them upon closer inspection, must have names for particular parts, and words by which they may express various modes of combination, such as none but themselves have occasion to consider.

A lexicographer may be excused for impatience in a controversy of this kind; and no one could be so foolish as to regret that Johnson's own magnificent usage was entirely uninfluenced by Swift's preference for simplicity. I do not think, however, that it is unfair to point out that the imitators of Johnson's abstract and ponderous manner in leading articles and learned reviews have often produced a kind of writing which gives point and renewed value to Swift's satire. And in an age when we are in danger of becoming entirely unintelligible one to another, it is not without value that for those who use the English tongue there is a powerful tradition on the side of simplicity, which owes not a little to that Bickerstaffian spirit ready with its weapons of irony and ridicule at any moment to make terrible play with any of our indulgences in confused speculations, or the abstracttions of pedantic aridities.

Both by the power of his satire and the perfection of his own art as a writer, Swift did much to drive out of the English tradition, even out of the learned world, the worst kind of pedantry, that monstrous pride in the glories of pedantry, which tends to separate learning from all human considerations, and to soar off into lunar or interstellar absurdities. He did much to preserve a tradition, which still makes it possible for us to have known classical scholars who can write like

[20] Ibid., IX, 66.

A. E. Housman, philosophers like Santayana, and historians like Carl Becker.

But Swift's concern with language was not limited to the language that is used in the pulpit, or in the printed book, or on formal occasions. He concerned himself even more deeply and persistently with the problem of language as it is used in the art of ordinary conversation. "There is no Point wherein I have so much labour'd"—he says in his seventieth year,—writing as Simon Wagstaff, now that the name of Isaac Bickerstaff which he had given away, could no longer be used—"as that of improving and polishing all Parts of Conversation between Persons of Quality, whether they meet by Accident or Invitation, at Meals, Tea, or Visits, Mornings, Noons or Evenings."[21] The volume was not published until 1738, when Swift was seventy-one, although most of it had been finished six years before. He had described it in a letter to Gay, of August 28, 1731, as a great work undertaken for the public good, "to reduce the whole politeness, wit, humour, and style of England into a short system for the use of all persons of quality, and particularly the maids of honour." And again to Pope, June 12, 1732, "I have a thing in prose, begun above twenty-eight years ago, and almost finished. It will make a four shilling volume, and is such a perfection of folly that you shall never hear of it till it is printed, and then you shall be left to guess."[22]

Later, in the preface, Swift says that he had kept it by him for several years more to test it; but he had found it so complete that not above nine valuable sentences had been added in that time. It contains at least "a thousand shining questions, anwers, repartee, replies and rejoinders fitted to adorn every kind of discourse"; and all these bright passages of wit have been in use for at least a hundred years, and may therefore be accepted as "genuine, sterling and authentic."[23] Oaths and cant words and slang have been omitted, because they are a sort of annual, and would make the book immediately out of date. Nevertheless current spelling is sometimes adopted and abbreviations and phonetic forms, which make the book of considerable value to the historian of the spoken language. I need illustrate only one fashion-

[21] Ibid., IV, 99.
[22] Corr., IV, 258, 309.
[23] Prose, IV, 101, 103.

able word which Swift gives a prominent place in his introduction—
In sickly payday. A footnote gives the very needful explanation:

> This word is spelt by Latinists, *Encyclopaedia;* but the judicious author
> wisely prefers the polite Reading before the Pedantick.[24]

The Dialogues themselves are not gay reading. The irony is so complete and pitiless. Swift is more merciless in his attack on the pedantry
of polite society than on any of the follies of the learned world. In
his *Hints towards an Essay on Conversation*, written probably in 1709
and perhaps the first form of this work, he says: "I was prompted to
write my thoughts upon this subject by mere indignation, to reflect
that so useful and innocent a pleasure, so fitted for every period and
condition of life, and so much in all men's power, should be so much
neglected and abused." And the particular manner of his attack is
clearly indicated by this statement further on:

> Raillery is the finest Part of Conversation; but, as it is our usual Custom
> to counterfeit and adulterate whatever is too dear for us, so we have
> done with this, and turned it all into what is generally called Repartee,
> or being smart; just as when an expensive Fashion cometh up, those
> who are not able to reach it, content themselves with some paltry
> Imitation.[25]

The Ladies at Their Tea

Lady Smart: Well, Ladies; now let us have a Cup of Discourse to
ourselves.

Lady Answ[erall]: What do you think of your Friend, *Sir John
Spendall?*

Lady Smart: Why, Madam, 'tis happy for him, that his Father was
born before him.

Miss Notable: They say, he makes a very ill Husband to my Lady.

Lady Answ.: Well, but he must be allow'd to be the fondest Father
in the World.

Lady Smart: Ay, Madam, that's true; for they say, the Devil is kind
to his own.

Miss Notable: I am told, my Lady manages him to Admiration.

Lady Smart: That I believe; for she's as cunning as a dead Pig; but
not half so honest.

Lady Answ.: They say, she's quite a Stranger to all his Gallantries.

[24] Ibid., p. 120.
[25] Ibid., pp. 88, 91.

Lady Smart: Not at all; but, you know, there's none so blind as they that won't see.

Miss Notable: Oh, Madam, I am told, she watches him as a Cat would watch a Mouse.

Lady Answ.: Well, if she ben't foully bely'd, she pays him in his own Coyn.[26]

This then is the refinement of cultivated society; this box of trinkets of which a surprisingly large number is still in use, and the rest only a little odd in their shape and their glitter. Irony cannot go further. It was not necessary for Swift to set down ought in malice. It was enough simply to sit by and write down the words of Lady Smart, Lady Answerall and Miss Notable for a record against them.

It is fitting to remember that through the same years Swift kept a record of another kind, and had written down with satisfaction and delight the bon mots of Stella; who, he declared, in an afternoon or evening's conversation never failed of delivering the best thing that was said in the company:

> She never had the least absence of mind in conversation, nor given to interruption, or appeared eager to put in her word by waiting impatiently until another had done. She spoke in a most agreeable voice, in the plainest words, never hesitating, except out of modesty before new faces, where she was somewhat reserved; nor, among her nearest friends, ever spoke much at a time. She was but little versed in the common topics of female chat; scandal, censure, and detraction, never came out of her mouth: Yet, among a few friends, in private conversation, she made little ceremony in discovering her contempt of a coxcomb, and describing all his follies to the life; but the follies of her own sex she was rather inclined to extenuate or to pity.[27]

Like Congreve and Meredith, Swift held that the best safeguard against pedantry and the best encouragement to real politeness and the flourishing of true wit and humour was a society in which persons of the best understanding and of both sexes met together freely to cultivate the art of conversation, "that faculty which is held the great distinction between men and brutes which might be the greatest, the most lasting, and the most innocent as well as useful pleasure of life."

[26] Ibid., p. 193.
[27] Ibid., V, 230.

THE CONCISENESS OF SWIFT

Lord Orrery was, I think, the first to draw attention to one of the most obvious marks of Swift's style: "If we consider his prose works, we shall find a certain masterly conciseness in their style, that has never been equalled by any other writer." In reply to a critic who had said that to judge from the rest of his argument he must really have meant to say correctness, not conciseness, he wrote in one of the interleaved copies of his *Remarks*, now in the Harvard library:

> I am afraid that in this Instance I am vulnerable. *Correctness* would be a better word, in this place, although the conciseness of Swift's Style is very remarkable. . . . I may boldly answer, that *Swift* is in many places as easy and delicate as *Addison*, as grave and majestic as *Tillotson*, but neither *Tillotson* nor *Addison* are in any part of their works as concise as *Swift*.

If, as I suppose, no one would dispute this, it might be useful to extend this comparison further in order to discover whether there is anyone among Swift's friends or contemporaries who is as concise as he is. Certainly not Arbuthnot or Gay, or even Pope, when he writes in prose, though Swift himself remarks upon the conciseness of Pope's verse, and envies him for it:

> When he can in one Couplet fix
> More sense than I can do in six.[1]

[1] *Poems*, p. 555.

Certainly not Bolingbroke or Pulteney, though he complains that they drove him out of date by the vigour of their political writings. Certainly not any of his circle of Irish friends, though they tried to imitate him and sometimes succeeded in passing off their imitations as his work. Is it possible then that this quality is so remarkable in all his work that it may be recognized and used as evidence of his hand?

In attempting to separate Swift's authentic work from the large mass of doubtful material that has at one time or another been attributed to him, it is dangerous to make any conjectures which depend on internal evidence of style alone. But when we have reason to suspect an attribution, because it was never acknowledged by Swift or reprinted in any edition in his lifetime, or because doubt has been expressed by his friends or earliest editors, it may be well to examine such a work carefully and try to decide whether he could have written it or not. We may possibly find something that would be enough to turn the scale.

I doubt whether it would ever be safe to assume that we could isolate a certain quality of biting humour or of irony, and say, this must be Swift's. For we know that many papers were printed by the booksellers as his on such grounds, and contemptuously rejected by him. And I doubt also whether we can find any particular mannerisms or tricks of phrase in his work so individual that they would give him away. His style is never mannered, and it is well to remember that even Stella and his friends in Dublin were never quite sure about his contributions to the *Tatler* and the *Examiner,* or even his separate political tracts written in London during the Queen's reign. Swift delighted to mislead them; but then, and much more emphatically later on, he seemed to expect that his friends ought to be able to recognize clearly that there were certain things which he could not have written, certain limits which they should know he could never be guilty of crossing. And likewise he would expect his editors and critics today to be sure that even in his most careless moments or in his lightest and most trivial mood he could never have written such sloppy, slovenly stuff as some of the papers still included among his works, or those paragraphs in *Gulliver's Travels* which were inserted in the earliest editions "contrary to the Author's manner and style and intention."

Others among his friends and enemies could write political satires

with biting power; others could use the weapons of raillery and irony
with success; others could be humorous and sceptical in their formal
sermons or their essays and letters; and others could use plain simple
language, and avoid technical jargon and learned terms. But in all
these different forms of writing, and even in his most hurried as well
as in his most deliberate work, I shall try to show that Swift is a master of conciseness, unequalled and unmistakable by reason of that
quality alone, which gives a flavour as of salt to all his work, and preserves it from certain levels of dullness, banality, or mere impoverish-
ment of style liable to appear in the writings of all his contemporaries.

I use the term "conciseness" not quite as Ben Jonson used it to
describe the style "which expresseth not enough, but leaves somewhat to be understood," though that is perhaps the reason why we
feel in Swift a strength and force lacking in other plain writers. He
leaves somewhat to be understood. But I use the term rather as Dryden used it, when he spoke of "the conciseness of Demosthenes,"
quoting the remark of Speroni, the Italian wit, that Tully wished to
achieve the copiousness of Homer, and Virgil the conciseness of
Demosthenes.[2] It will be remembered that Swift compares the art of
Demosthenes and Cicero in his *Letter to a Young Clergyman*, recom-
mending the former, with whom most divines were less conversant, as
the more excellent orator. And he draws attention to the chief purpose
of their oratory, "to drive some one particular Point, according as the
Oratory on either Side prevailed." Swift's experience as a political
journalist had formed his style and made it rigorously functional, because he had learned in that school similarly to be concerned "to drive
some one particular point" for the immediate purpose of supporting or
opposing some definite course of action. He never deviated from this
particular purpose, never allowed himself to hesitate, to make qualifications or concessions.

After *A Tale of a Tub* was put behind him, he rarely permitted
himself to indulge his humour or his literary skill in parody or raillery
or any of the tricks of his trade for his amusement only. His irresponsible play was almost entirely limited to verse and the various bagatelles
in which the little group of Dublin friends engaged for sport. In his
satires and sermons and political tracts he was careful never to spoil
the immediate effect he wanted by any display of "learning or oratory

[2] *Essays of Dryden*, ed. Ker, 1900, i, 256.

or politeness." He speaks from his own experience when he says so confidently in 1720:

> When a Man's Thoughts are clear, the properest Words will generally offer themselves first; and his own Judgment will direct him in what Order to place them, so as they may be best understood.

Then he adds a sentence which is a complete revelation of himself, an artist and a master of his craft, recognizing the quality of perfect work, but valuing it only as it performs a useful function:

> In short, that Simplicity, without which no human Performance can arrive to any great Perfection, is no where more eminently useful than in this.[3]

Though Addison with his ease and delicacy also attains a perfection of simplicity, his writing can be differentiated from Swift's, because he is never quite so concise, never quite so rigorously and exclusively concerned with making his point. This may be clearly seen if we compare a passage from one of Addison's Saturday papers, written for the *Tatler*, 17 December 1709, with Swift's use of the same theme in the *Intelligencer*, No. 9. Addison writes in a mood almost of reminiscence, as he tries to convey to us the opportunities for pleasure and profit through a proper commerce with men and books:

> I must confess, there is nothing that more pleases me, in all that I read in Books, or see among Mankind, than such Passages as represent humane Nature in its proper Dignity. As Man is a Creature made up of different Extremes, he has something in him very great and very mean: A skilful Artist may draw an excellent Picture of him in either of these Views. The finest Authors of Antiquity have taken him on the more advantagious Side. They cultivate the natural Grandeur of the Soul, raise in her a generous Ambition, feed her with Hopes of Immortality and Perfection, and do all they can to widen the Partition between the Virtuous and the Vicious, by making the Difference betwixt them as great as between Gods and Brutes. In short, it is impossible to read a Page in *Plato*, *Tully*, and a Thousand other ancient Moralists, without being a greater and a better Man for it.

Swift makes of it a weapon to attack the wealthy and the noble for neglecting their sons' education.

[3] *Letter to a Young Clergyman. Prose*, XII, 52-3, 68.

The Books read at *Schools* and *Colleges,* are full of Incitements to
Virtue and Discouragements from Vice, drawn from the wisest Reasons,
the strongest Motives, and the most influencing Examples. Thus,
young Minds are filled early with an Inclination to Good, and an Ab-
horrence of Evil, both which encrease in them, according to the Advances they make in Literature. . . .

The present Scope I would aim at is to prove, that some Proportion
of human Knowledge appears requisite to those, who, by their Birth or
Fortune, are called to the making of Laws, and in a subordinate Way
to the Execution of them; and that such Knowledge is not to be obtained without a Miracle under the frequent, corrupt and sottish Methods, of educating those, who are born to Wealth or Titles. . . .[4]

Swift is rarely content to make an observation, much less to speculate or indulge in "an amusement of agreeable words," which he always suspects are intended to put false colours upon things and make
the worse reason appear to be the better. He writes either to prove
or to disprove; to urge some action, or oppose it.

We may follow Orrery a step farther and examine his comparison
between the style of Swift and Tillotson. They both mistrusted theological speculation and regarded it as a snare rather than an aid to
religion. Tillotson gravely rebukes the "speculative Christian" who
finds the knowledge of religion a good ornament of conversation:

and because he doth not intend to practise it, he passeth over those
things which are plain and easie to be understood, and applies himself
chiefly to the Consideration of those things which are more abstruse,
and will afford matter of Controversie and subtle Dispute, as the Doctrine of the *Trinity, Predestination, Freewill* and the like.

Swift, however, spurns the whole thing with an almost brutal gesture,
using the harshest figure of compulsion by process of law:

I defy the greatest Divine to produce any Law either of God or Man
which obliges me to comprehend the meaning of *Omniscience, Omnipresence, Ubiquity, Attribute, Beatifick Vision,* &c.[5]

But the most excellent example of Swift's conciseness, in the larger
sense of its effect not upon the phrase or the sentence but upon the
construction and shape of the whole piece, is his sermon "On Doing

[4] *Prose,* IX, 69.
[5] Ibid., p. 66.

Good," which I shall compare with Tillotson's sermon on the same subject and the same text, preached at Christ Church on Easter Tuesday, 14 April 1691. The text—"As we have therefore opportunity, let us do good unto all men"—is rather an obvious one for a "spital sermon"; and Tillotson uses his sermon to introduce a direct appeal for the chief hospitals in the city. It is clearly a sermon with a specific purpose. Nevertheless, it is arranged according to a conventional pattern in which the subject of Doing Good is discussed under five heads —the nature of the Duty, the extent of it, the measure of it, unwearied perseverance in it, and encouragement to it. Each of those is further divided into several sections until the main theme has been drawn out into all its various ramifications, leading up to a final solution to persuade his hearers to the practice of it. It remains a sermon for general edification, with the particular charitable appeal added.

Swift's sermon on the text is, as he termed it himself, a pamphlet against Wood's halfpence. He admits in the course of his sermon that it may perhaps be thought by some that this way of discussing is not so proper from the pulpit. Nevertheless he preaches only good sound ethical doctrine—the importance of the public good, which is a perfectly reasonable interpretation of the text, "let us do good unto all men."

> Beside this love we owe to every man in his particular capacity under the title of our neighbour, there is yet a duty of a more large, extensive nature, incumbent on us; which is, our love to our neighbour in his public capacity, as he is a member of that great body, the commonwealth, under the same government with ourselves; and this is usually called love of the public. . . .
>
> Therefore, I shall think my time not ill spent, if I can persuade most or all of you who hear me, to shew the love you have for your country, by endeavouring, in your several stations, to do all the public good you are able.[6]

The whole of the sermon is then pointed with great directness at Wood's project. It is short, clear, concise in its whole argument, and no one could at any moment have been mistaken about Swift's intention and the immediate effect he hoped it would have upon his audience. He tells them plainly that it was the consideration of their great danger which led him to discourse on this subject and to exhort them

[6] Ibid., pp. 233-4.

to prefer the public interest before that of one destructive impostor, and a few of his adherents. He admits further that his sermon was intended also to stir up others of the clergy to exhort their congregations to show their love for their country on this important occasion. And in a final superb gesture, with the impunity of the Dean who knows no higher authority, ecclesiastical or lay, within the walls of his own cathedral, he permits himself a momentary glance over the head of the mechanic Wood and his miserable project, challenging and defying the power of his real enemy, the Whig government, with the briefest flash of irony—"And this, I am sure, cannot be called meddling in affairs of state." Nothing is quite so concise as the conciseness of irony; the meaning is tight-closed, until the reader stays to pick it up and open it. We are left with the question: When should a Dean, when should anyone, meddle with affairs of state? His irony embraces the answer of Demosthenes: "When all our national interests are imperilled; when the issue lies between the people and their adversaries. Then such is the part of a chivalrous and patriotic citizen."

There is the same method and the same irony in the sermon, a diatribe against faction and party spirit, which was preached on 1 December 1717, with the title, *On Brotherly Love*. It is almost a parody of the conventional sermon in which the subject is carefully divided into three heads: first, the causes of this lack of brotherly love; second, the effects of it; and third, persuasions to continue in it. But the real theme is stated in a preliminary sentence which sums up the whole course of the ecclesiastical history of the Christian Church:

> The last Legacy of *Christ* was Peace and mutual Love; but then he foretold that he came to send a Sword upon the Earth: The primitive Christians accepted the Legacy, and their Successors, down to the present Age, have been largely fulfilling his Prophecy.[7]

When that theme is fully exhausted, Swift again reminds us of his text only to confess that he had treated it in a manner much more suited to the present times than to the nature of the subject in general; but again he cannot resist the temptation to make use of an ironical excuse for his conduct by quoting the epistle to the Thessalonians: "Touching brotherly love ye need not that I write unto you, for ye

[7] Ibid., p. 171.

yourselves are taught of God to love one another."[8] Considering the
noisy disputes of the time and the whole course of Church history
alike, he is of the opinion that God alone can teach men to love one
another!

The more closely we analyse the few sermons that remain, the more
difficult it is to understand why it has been customary to dismiss them
casually with a reference to some phrase of Swift in which he dis-
parages his own powers as a preacher. They are the work of a man
who refused even in the pulpit to waste words, who despised unction
and distrusted the eloquent appeal to the passions, but who performed
the duties of his office with sincerity, using even in his sermons the
full force of all his gifts, his intelligence, his humour, his mastery of
language, and his hatred of hypocrisy and injustice.

Burke knew better, and his praise is unmeasured when he says that
Swift's "sermon upon Doing Good . . . contains perhaps the best
motives to patriotism that were ever delivered within so small a com-
pass." But the sermons were not all political pamphlets; and I am not
sure that the utmost perfection of form—in unity and simplicity and
conciseness—is not rather to be found in the sermon on the Trinity,
and the fullest play of his art to be seen when he preached against
sleeping in church, "with Design, if possible, to disturb some Part in
this Audience of half an Hour's sleep, for the Convenience and
Exercise whereof this Place, at this Season of the Day, is very much
celebrated."[9]

Though as far as I know no manuscript exists of any of these sermons except the manuscript of the sermon on Brotherly Love which
is in Trinity College, Dublin, and though none of them were printed
until after Swift's death, I submit that those I have referred to are not
less certainly recognizable as his handiwork than they would be if we
could read them in his own autograph. Can we also, on the other
hand, now safely attempt to analyse another sermon, to which the
following note was attached when it was first printed?

The Manuscript Title Page of the following Sermon being lost, and no
Memorandums written upon it, as there were upon the others, when
and where it was preached, made the Editor doubtful whether he

[8] Ibid., p. 179.
[9] Ibid., p. 210.

should print it as the DEAN's, or not. But its being found amongst the
same Papers; and the Hand, although written somewhat better, bearing
a great Similitude to the DEAN's, made him willing to lay it before the
Publick, that they might judge whether the Stile and Manner also do
not render it still more probable to be his.[10]

Orrery seems to put it aside as obviously not Swift's work, and the
only claim to be made for it is that Sheridan, when he reprinted it in
his edition, states that the manuscript was in the hand of Stella.

But I am here concerned to examine it on the evidence of the style,
the quality of the writing, and the plan of it, as an experiment on a
doubtful piece to see whether it is possible to find negative proof on
which we might risk the statement that Swift could not have written it.

The framework is the conventional one that Swift often uses—first
an introduction, explaining the text, then a division of the subject
into three main heads, each considered separately again in a series of
paragraphs with a final exhortation and prayer, the common form of
hundreds of volumes of sermons.

Before examining the statement of the particular topic to be treated,
it is well to remember the precision and vigour which Swift uses at
this point in other sermons, e.g.

It is upon this Subject of Brotherly Love, that I intend to discourse at
present, and the Method I shall observe shall be as follows:[11]

or,

This Day being set apart to acknowledge our Belief in the Eternal
TRINITY, I thought it might be proper to employ my present Discourse
entirely upon that Subject; and, I hope, to handle it in such a Manner,
that the most ignorant among you, may return home better informed of
your Duty in this great Point, than probably you are at present.[12]

In these he uses a directness, and force, and plainness to make sure
that even the sleepiest of his hearers might know at the beginning
exactly what instruction he intends to give them. There is no such
conciseness in the overweighted wordiness of this sentence:

[10] Ibid., p. 103.
[11] Ibid., p. 172.
[12] Ibid., p. 159.

Therefore, to bring down the Words of my Text to our present Occasion, I shall endeavour, in a further Prosecution of them, to evince the great Necessity of a nice and curious Inspection into the several Recesses of the Heart, that being the surest and the shortest Method that a wicked Man can take to reform himself:

or in the formless meandering of the rest of the paragraph, with its worn imagery:

For let us but stop the Fountain, and the Streams will spend and waste themselves away in a very little Time; but if we go about, like Children, to raise a Bank, and to stop the Current, not taking Notice all the while of the Spring which continually feedeth it, when the next Flood of a Temptation riseth and breaketh in upon it, then we shall find that we have begun at the wrong End of our Duty, and that we are very little more the better for it, than if we had sat still, and made no Advances at all.[13]

No wonder that the next sentence is introduced by the phrase "But, in order to a clearer explanation of the point," a phrase which Swift would never have allowed himself to pen without immediately recognizing the need to rewrite the previous statement. There are innumerable passages of this sort throughout, which lack all force and clarity, and there is not one single sentence that I can find which bears the certain marks of Swift's shaping.

If we are to take any account of the possibility that the sermon was preserved and attributed to Swift because it was in the handwriting of Stella, there is the obvious explanation that Stella might well have been generous enough to copy out a sermon of his own for the Rev. Thomas Sheridan, who may have needed the help of his friends to ensure that he had something written out in time for him to perform his duties in the pulpit. But in the absence of any manuscript signed by Swift himself or any definite statement that he wrote it, I submit that the internal evidence of style alone is enough to justify the statement that Swift was incapable of writing so badly as this.

It is true that in the eighteenth century some of Swift's critics objected that his style was not always impeccably correct and disapproved of his trifling; and in the nineteenth century the style of some of his political journalism was even described as "sometimes loose and

[13] Ibid., p. 351.

slovenly"; but his critics have not always been careful to set aside papers which were wrongly attributed to him, in spite of his care to make clear to his friends the real authorship of the John Bull papers, the point at which he was no longer responsible for the *Examiner*, and the exact division of labour between Sheridan and himself in the *Intelligencer* papers, which were reprinted in London in 1730 as by the author of *A Tale of a Tub*.

I should not wish to claim that Swift is at his best in the *Intelligencer*, but his characteristic quality is nevertheless clearly recognizable here, especially if we compare No. 15, which is a reprint of his *Short View of the State of Ireland* with Nos. 6 and 17, in which Sheridan writes with considerable vigour on the same topic. They both alike resented the blindness of those who refused to see the misery and poverty of Ireland and spoke of it as a rich country. Sheridan speaks of his "Indignation against those vile Betrayers and Insulters of it, who insinuate themselves into Favour, by saying, it is a rich Nation; and [his] *sincere Passion* for the Natives, who are sunk to the lowest Degree of Misery and Poverty." It might be almost enough to note how different this is in its tone from the words of Swift:

> I have been using all Endeavours to subdue my Indignation; to which indeed I am not provoked by any personal Interest, being not the Owner of one Spot of Ground in the whole *Island* . . .[14]

but I am concerned rather to show again the "conciseness" of Swift in his enumeration of the deficiencies of the people of Ireland and the powerful directness of his reply, compared with the detailed evidence which Sheridan reports from the actual sights and occurrences that had stirred him to rage and compassion on his last journey through the country.

The picture Sheridan gives is a complete one: first, the evidences of trade:

> I met nine Cars loaden with old musty, shriveled Hides; one Car-Load of Butter; four Jockeys driving eight Horses, all out of Case; one Cow and Calf driven by a Man and his Wife; six tattered Families flitting to be shipped off to the *West-Indies*; a Colony of a hundred and fifty Beggars. . . .

[14] Ibid., XII, 5.

second, the appearance of travellers on the road:

> Travellers enough, but seven in ten wanting Shirts and Cravats; nine
> in ten going bare Foot, and carrying their Brogues and Stockings in
> their Hands; one Woman in twenty having a Pillion, the rest riding
> bare Back'd: Above two hundred Horse-Men, with four Pair of Boots
> amongst them all; Seventeen Saddles of Leather (the rest being made
> of Straw) and most of their Garrons only shod before. . . .

third, the condition of the houses on the farms and in the towns:

> his whole Furniture consisted of two Blocks for Stools, a Bench on
> each Side the Fire-Place made of Turf, six Trenchers, one Bowl, a Pot,
> six Horn Spoons, three Noggins, three Blankets, one of which served
> the Man and Maid Servant; the other the Master of the Family, his
> Wife and five Children; a small Churn, a wooden Candlestick, a
> broken Stick for a Pair of Tongs.[15]

When he considers the ruined churches of Drogheda he is led to
contrast the spirit of Ireland with the spirit of the Athenians who resolved to leave their ruined temples as monuments to posterity for a
witness against the barbarians, and when he views the desolation
around Dundalk he is led to quote the philosophical reflections of
Cicero on the ruins of Greece. And in his second paper he elaborates
an ironical proof of the prosperity of Ireland by reference to wealthy
absentee landlords, its attractiveness to the robbers who come from
England, and to the idle beggars at home, and the great numbers of
its inhabitants who are able to take the long voyage to America.
Sheridan's papers are entirely concerned with his own observations
and somewhat literary-philosophical reflections. Their tendency is
unmistakable, but their aim is not wholly clear. He has only conveyed
to us his feelings, a mixture of rage and compassion which leave us
helpless in face of the situation.

There is no doubt about the purpose of Swift's *Short View of the
State of Ireland.* He wishes to prove the stupidity and dishonesty of
all those who cannot see that in spite of great natural advantages Ireland has been utterly ruined by the way in which it has been governed "against every law of Nature and Reason," "a condition I must
not call by its true uncontroverted Name." Like Sheridan he describes
ironically the riches of the country, but he sharpens his irony by

[15] *Intelligencer,* no. 6, 1729, pp. 46, 53-55.

associating this fair picture with the visiting commissioners from England.

> Let [them] ride round the Kingdom, and observe the Face of Nature, or the Faces of the Natives; the Improvement of the Land; . . . the commodious Farmers-Houses and Barns; . . . the comfortable Dyet, and Dress, and Dwellings of the People; . . . the Roads crowded with Carriers laden with rich Manufactures; . . .
> With what Envy and Admiration would these Gentlemen return from so delightful a Progress? What glorious Reports would they make when they went back to *England?*[16]

And when he turns with too heavy a heart from this irony to the actual situation, and sums up shortly and bitterly the general desolation, the English standards of the English visitor are used again the other way round to redouble the attack.

> . . . the Families of Farmers who pay great Rents, living in Filth and Nastiness upon *Butter-milk* and *Potatoes,* without a Shoe or Stocking to their Feet, or a House so convenient as an *English* Hogsty to receive them: These indeed may be comfortable Sights to an *English* Spectator, who comes for a short Time, only *to learn* the *Language,* and returns back to his own Countrey, whither he finds all our Wealth transmitted.

And once more the visitors from England are drawn unfavourably into the argument:

> I think it a little unhospitable, and others may call it a subtil Piece of Malice, that because there may be a Dozen Families in this Town able to entertain their *English* Friends in a generous Manner at their Tables, their Guests, upon their Return to *England,* shall report that we wallow in Riches and Luxury.[17]

Sheridan speaks of his indignation against the betrayers and insulters of his country and his sincere passion for the natives; but Swift's compassion and indignation are fused together into one deadly purpose, which turns every sentence into a blow against the tyranny which had enslaved the people of Ireland.

Either of necessity or choice Swift published nearly all his work

[16] *Prose*, XII, 8.
[17] Ibid., pp. 10-11, 12.

anonymously, and he was perfectly ready to allow Pope to look after
the publication of the volumes of *Miscellanies* in 1727-32, containing
—without any separate ascription—their work and some of Arbuthnot's. But when he finally decided to allow Faulkner to prepare a
collected edition of his works to be printed in Dublin, though in the
early volumes his name still did not appear on the title-page, he
showed some desire to have nothing included in the volumes which
he supervised that was not entirely his own. It seems evident that the
text was set up from the volumes of the *Miscellanies* printed in London, as it contains corrections made by Swift in a copy from his own
library, now in the possession of Lord Rothschild.

It is rather curious, therefore, that *A Letter of Advice to a Young
Poet,* which had been published in Dublin in 1721 and reprinted in
London over Swift's name, was omitted both in the *Miscellanies* and
also in the *Collected Works.* Neither was it included even later in
any of the volumes added to Faulkner's edition. Mr. John Hayward
was, I believe, the first editor to call attention to this in his Nonesuch
edition of Swift's *Selected Writings;* but even he does not express any
doubt as to the authenticity of the *Letter.* Although it is a witty piece
of writing and seems better than we could expect from an imitation,
I can find no satisfactory reason to explain why Swift did not reprint
it, if it was his work. I must regard it therefore as doubtful. If then,
with this doubt in our minds, we examine it carefully and compare it
with *A Letter to a Young Clergyman* and *A Letter to a Very Young
Lady* we notice that it lacks this very quality of directness and conciseness which we are considering. It is full of literary references,
witty sallies, and humorous tricks; and it ends with a proposal for the
encouragement of poetry in Dublin so loose and slovenly in style that
I cannot think Swift in any way responsible for these final pages. I
will give only this sample:

> I would now offer some poor Thoughts of mine for the Encourage-
> ment of *Poetry* in this Kingdom, if I could hope they would be agree-
> able. I have had many an aking Heart for the ill plight of that noble
> Profession here, and it has been my late and early Study how to bring
> it into better Circumstances. And surely, considering what *Monstrous*
> Wrrs in the Poetick way, do almost daily start up and surprize us in
> this Town; what *prodigious* Genius's we have here (of which I cou'd
> give Instances without number;) and withal of what great benefit it

might be to our Trade to encourage that Science here, . . . I say, these things consider'd, I am humbly of Opinion, it wou'd be worth the Care of our Governours to cherish Gentlemen of the *Quill*, and give them all proper Encouragements here. And since I am upon the Subject, I shall speak my Mind very *freely*, and if I added *sawcily*, it is no more than my Birthright as a *Briton*.[18]

We know now from Swift's letters to Charles Ford that he took particular interest in Faulkner's third volume, which was to contain *Gulliver's Travels*. He admits that he had been annoyed by the changes introduced in the original edition, owing to the fears of the printer, not so much because of the things omitted as because of certain passages which were added in a style so slovenly that he was unwilling to have them remain in a volume which would be known as his work. Here then are samples of writing which Swift himself felt should be recognizable as something he could never have done. Here are passages which have been printed in some later editions of *Gulliver*, which the critics ought to have suspected from internal evidence of style alone. He had written, for instance, with little attempt to disguise the real object of his attack:

> I told him, that in the Kingdom of *Tribnia*, by the Natives called *Langden*, where I had long sojourned, the Bulk of the People consisted wholly of Discoverers, Witnesses, Informers, Accusers, Prosecutors, Evidences, Swearers; etc.[19]

This is pointed and definite and unhesitating. He continues to charge the politicians in that kingdom with arranging plots to answer their private advantage and describes the methods of dealing with those who are to be accused. In the first edition, to remove the sting, it is all made hypothetical and carefully packed in soft layers of verbiage:

> I told him, that should I happen to live in a Kingdom where Plots and Conspiracies were either in vogue from the turbulency of the meaner People, or could be turned to the use and service of the higher Rank of them, I first would take care to cherish and encourage the breed of Discoverers, Witnesses, etc.

Once given the clue, it is certainly not difficult to detect the padding:

[18] Ibid., IX, 340-41.
[19] Ibid., XI, 191.

Men thus qualified and thus empowered might make a most excellent use and advantage of Plots. . . .

This might be done by first agreeing and settling among themselves.
. . .

They should be allowed to put what Interpretation they pleased upon them, giving them a Sense not only which has no relation at all to them, but even what is quite contrary to their true Intent and real Meaning; thus for Instance, they may, if they so fancy, interpret a *Sieve* etc.[20]

For Swift rarely follows that loose fashion of coupling his verbs and nouns like this—qualified and empowered, use and advantage, agreeing and settling—and is incapable of such clumsiness as "not only which has no . . . but even what."

But the chief changes were made in the Fourth Book, to cushion the blows which Swift had dealt against the profession of the Law and against a First or Chief Minister of State. I do not think we could find anywhere a better proof of the conciseness of Swift than in the fifth and sixth chapters of the Fourth Book of *Gulliver,* if we read what he wrote as printed in Faulkner's edition:

I said there was a Society of Men among us, bred up from their Youth in the Art of proving by Words multiplied for the Purpose, that *White* is *Black,* and *Black* is *White,* according as they are paid. To this Society all the rest of the People are Slaves.[21]

That is surely Brobdingnagian in style—clear, masculine, and smooth; without multiplying unnecessary words or using various expressions. The attack is direct and unqualified, and therefore dangerous. Again Swift was justified in expecting his critics to recognize that the substituted passage which appears in the early London editions could not have come from his pen, for it is cautious and qualified, and therefore out of key with the context; and its meaning is completely clouded by the multiplication of unnecessary words.

I said that those who made profession of this Science were exceedingly multiplied, being almost equal to the Caterpillars in Number; that they were of diverse Degrees, Distinctions, and Denominations. The Numerousness of those that dedicated themselves to this Profession

20 Ibid., p. 311.
21 Ibid., pp. 248-9.

were such that the fair and justifiable Advantage and Income of the Profession was not sufficient for the decent and handsome Maintenance of Multitudes of those who followed it. Hence it came to pass that it was found needful to supply that by Artifice and Cunning, which could not be procured by just and honest Methods: The better to bring which about, very many Men among us were bred up from their Youth in the Art of proving by Words multiplied for the Purpose that *White* is *Black,* and *Black* is *White,* according as they are paid. The Greatness of these Mens Assurance and the Boldness of their Pretensions gained upon the Opinion of the Vulgar, whom in a Manner they made Slaves of, and got into their Hands much the largest Share of the Practice of their Profession.[22]

The attack in the sixth chapter on the First or Chief Minister of State was not tampered with, but instead the danger was removed by introducing it with an extraordinary piece of patchwork intended to prevent the reader from a malicious interpretation at the expense of any recent British statesman. Again the style is so entirely unlike Swift and the change in tone so sudden that a careful reader could not fail to be suspicious of some tampering with the text. Had Swift been concerned to avoid any possible reference to Harley and Queen Anne, he would not have trusted to such a preposterous sentence of clumsy compliment; nor would he have ruined the whole effect of his satire by assuring his master that he was referring only to former times in Britain and to other courts in Europe now:

> where Princes grew indolent and careless of their own Affairs through a constant Love and Pursuit of Pleasure, they made use of such an Administrator, as I had mentioned, under the Title of *first* or *chief Minister of State,* the Description of which, as far as it may be collected not only from their Actions, but from the Letters, Memoirs, and Writings published by themselves, the Truth of which has not yet been disputed, may be allowed to be as follows: . . .[23]

So long as this kind of writing was reprinted over and over again as part of the Swift canon, and included in the text of his greatest and best-known work, and so long as other papers which we now know were certainly not his and a great many very doubtful pieces, like the sermon I have examined, have been included in every fresh

[22] Ibid., pp. 315-16.
[23] Ibid., p. 318.

edition of his collected works, it is difficult to set precise limits to possible variations of quality in his work, and to be sure that there is a point where we can boldly say: Thus far he might go, but no farther, from the essentials of good prose, which he himself set down so clearly.

Whether he wrote as Drapier, Bickerstaff, or Gulliver, or as the Dean of St. Patrick's, there were, I believe, certain standards which we may always apply, certain qualities which we can always recognize; for they are the marks of the mind and of the art of Jonathan Swift. And the particular quality of his prose that we have been considering as something both distinctive and remarkable—its conciseness—is also an essential mark of his mind and his art. That explains his greatness and his intensity; it explains also what were the things he could not do. In order to be plain and simple it is necessary to clear the mind of speculation and compromise, and to avoid in art the distortions of height and depth and the deception of colour.

He held that all knowledge is intended for use, not for idle curiosity or the pleasure of speculation. In matters of belief there must be boundaries between the spheres of faith and reason, and limits set to prevent disorder from the revolutionary forces of scepticism and critical inquiry. In matters of ethics he was content with a simple form of dualism, which defines the borders of right and wrong and when applied to political and social matters divides everything into a system of parties—Whigs and Tories, Ancients and Moderns, conformists and nonconformists, the forces of enlightenment and the forces of dullness—and finally into a world of friends and enemies. In matters of political and ecclesiastical history he makes astonishing simplifications which provide a series of political parallels endlessly recurring, and of constant validity for all mankind. It is evidently a pattern simplified for common use which sometimes surprises us almost into a belief that it must be true, when it enables him to pack into a concise statement such a telling political generalization as this:

> in the course of many Ages they have been troubled with the same Disease, to which the whole Race of Mankind is subject; the Nobility often contending for Power, the People for Liberty, and the King for absolute Dominion.[24]

[24] Ibid., p. 138.

Like most of his contemporaries he approved of the activities of the
scientists in so far as their work could be of practical use in agricul-
ture and manufactures and navigation and medicine. But he feared
the quackery and conceit of these investigators and logically was
driven to make his attack on all kinds of technical jargon, as the very
symbol of that kind of speculation which was in danger of separating
its activities from all connexion with the common needs of man, and
becoming, as law and theology and medicine had already done, a
separate guild whose activities had long been of questionable value
to the public, whom they had each in their own way made their
ignorant slaves.

And finally, the art of the writer is likewise for use, not for his own
pleasure, nor for the pleasure of his readers. It is functional. Therefore the method will vary whether it is for edification in sermons, for
moral or political instruction in essays and pamphlets, or whether it
is intended to sting and vex the world into a greater concern for political justice or the decencies and proprieties of social life. But it will
always be short, clear, and concise, and directed to the immediate
purpose. And there is a further requirement: if it is to be effective, it
must never be dull. The task of the satirist is attack, and the weapons
in his hands must be sharp and keen. His strokes must be brilliant
and rapid. He must overcome his antagonist by cunning and surprise.
He must lure him on by raillery and irony, and confound him by the
brilliant flashing of wit. But above all he must preserve all his strength
and force, avoiding unnecessary flourishes. His vision must be clear
and his glance unwavering until the bout is over and his opponent is
overcome. There is no place here for heroic boasting or laughter, for
the wildness of anger and rage, for primitive outbursts of hatred and
lust. He cannot cry to the gods to help him or rouse the spirits from
the vasty deep. He cannot lift his eyes to the hills for help or wait
for the right configuration of the stars to give him confidence. He
has nothing but his own skill and his own knowledge of the weakness
of his adversaries. His art is confined within very human boundaries,
within the limits of his own age and social order and of the common
idiom of his time.

But if he succeeds in attaining that "Simplicity without which no
human Performance can arrive to any great Perfection,"[25] he may not

[25] Ibid., IX, 68.

only be eminently useful to his own age but also by reason of that perfect simplicity may continue to be eminently useful at other times and in other places, wherever men may still be concerned to probe into the causes and cure of those same diseases which are common to the whole race of mankind. Although it is often said that *Gulliver's Travels* is such a good story that for more than two hundred years it has delighted children and ceased to hurt their parents, the truth is that, if we may judge by the comments of some of his critics who have been rash enough to read it all, Swift is, in fact, still successful in what he set himself to do: he is still able to vex the conscience of his readers. And there are not many who have written in English who are envied so much as he is today for that quality in him which is most distinctive and remarkable—that conciseness which gave such concentrated force and perfect clarity to his style.

SOME FREE THOUGHTS
OF A TORY DEAN

"Politicks, as the Word is commonly understood,
are nothing but Corruptions; and consequently
of no use to a good King, or a good Ministry:
For which Reason, Courts are so over-run with Politicks."
Thoughts on Various Subjects.[1]

It amused Jonathan Swift to be shown in a New England newspaper, not long after the appearance of "Gulliver's Travels," the name of a real person, Jonathan Gulliver, who was a member of the Massachusetts legislature then living in Boston; and, at about the same time, to get an account "from the assizes of one Lemuel Gulliver who had a cause there and lost it on his ill reputation of being a liar." Pope shrewdly remarked that the fame of that traveller must have travelled very quickly to have folks christened already by the name of the supposed author; and suggested that if he were already old enough to be in Parliament he must be an Anabaptist, christened at full age. But whatever may have been the fame of Gulliver in New England, we know that in other parts of the country the book had found admirers, and was known to be the work of the Tory Dean of St. Patrick's, Dublin; for in May, 1729, the Dean had received the present of "a gammon, the product of the wilds of America" from an unnamed Quaker admirer in Philadelphia, who wrote that he had been often agreeably amused by his tale, and wished him to know that his wit and good parts were in esteem in distant places.[2]

As we should expect, it is mainly as the creator of Gulliver that Swift has continued to be known in America. Nevertheless, there were other aspects of his work which aroused considerable interest in some quarters. As a result of the great popularity of Gulliver, a Lon-

[1] *Prose*, IV, 246-7.
[2] *Corr.*, IV, 17, 18, 29, 74.

don bookseller reprinted, at the end of 1729, a volume of Swift's dangerous political writings in which, five years before, he had challenged the English government in the matter of its political and economic treatment of Ireland, and had endeavored to teach the people of Ireland to use the method of "boycott" to protect themselves against the importation of goods manufactured in England; and had also succeeded in preventing the introduction of a debased copper coinage for which a certain English hardwareman, William Wood, was reported to have paid a very large bribe to the King's mistress. The account of this revolutionary campaign against the power of a government which, as Swift said, looked down upon the Kingdom of Ireland "as if it had been one of their colonies of outcasts in America" must have been exciting reading for those who were eager for the independence of the American colonies; and some of Swift's arguments were to prove useful later on to the young Republicans, who adopted the same tone and made the same appeal to reason and the rights of man, as found, for instance, in this slogan of William Molyneux which Swift had made the very foundation of his case:

That Ireland should be bound by Acts of Parliament made in England is against Reason and the Common Rights of Mankind.[3]

The more dangerous passages in his "Letter to the Whole People of Ireland" would have found ready understanding from his American readers, when he speaks with indignation of the phrase "a *Depending Kingdom*" and the intolerable suggestion that "the People of *Ireland* is in some State of Slavery or Dependance different from those of England." He declares that such a notion of dependence has no "Ground of *Law, Reason* or *Common Sense*"; and he is led on by the logic of his argument to that bold declaration, which sounded so treasonable that it provoked a Proclamation against him for writing "such seditious and scandalous paragraphs":

I declare, next under God, I *depend* only on the King my Sovereign, and on the Laws of my own Country; And I am so far from *depending* upon the People of *England*, that if they should ever *rebel* against my Sovereign (which God forbid) I would be ready at the first Command

[3] *The Case of Ireland's Being Bound by Acts of Parliament in England, Stated,* 1720, p. 127.

from his Majesty to take Arms against them, as some of *my* Countrymen did against *theirs at Preston.*[4]

In defending himself against this charge of sedition he had no
difficulty in showing that his political principles were taken from
very respectable liberal writers, and that he had been taught by
Englishmen to talk of "Liberty as a Blessing, to which the whole
Race of Mankind hath an original Title, whereof nothing but unlawful Force can divest them"; and he had thought that it was univer-
sally agreed that "Freedom consists in a People being governed by
Laws made with their own Consent, and Slavery in the Contrary." It
was only when they crossed the Irish Sea or the Atlantic that such
words tended to become inflammatory, rebellious stuff, especially as
they might be used to incite men to revolt against oppression. The
Anabaptist in New England and even perhaps the Quaker in Philadelphia would not have been altogether unmoved by such an argument as this:

> The Scripture tells us, that *Oppression makes a wise Man mad;* there-
> fore, consequently speaking, the Reason why some Men are not *mad,*
> is because they are not *wise:* However, it were to be wished that *Opres-
> sion* would, in time, teach a little *Wisdom* to *Fools.*[5]

But the younger revolutionaries seem to have found even better
stuff for their liking in Swift's satirical verses, "On Poetry: A Rapsody," which had been published in London and Dublin in 1733, for
here he had allowed himself to include in his satire the Crown as
well as the Ministers. Printed copies were so hard to come by in
America that students in the universities were making manuscript
copies to circulate among their friends. In the Johnson Family Papers
at Yale there is a letter from William Livingston, who later became
governor of New Jersey, to Noah Wells, then at Yale, which is dated
May 27th, 1742, where he comments with great satisfaction on Swift's
satire upon the King and the Prince of Wales, and encloses a manuscript copy of the poem. "It is so rare a book," he says, "that but two
of them ever came to this province, being in great measure prevented
by Walpole against whom the plan of the poem is levelled, mine also
being in manuscript." The poem is written in a style and manner

4 *Prose,* X, 62.
5 Ibid., IX, 18.

which would appeal directly to the undergraduate. As one experienced in the world Swift begins by offering advice to the young aspiring poet:

> Lay now aside all Thoughts of Fame,
> To spring more profitable Game.
> From Party-Merit seek Support;
> The vilest Verse thrives best at Court.
> A Pamphlet in Sir *Rob*'s Defence
> Will never fail to bring in Pence;
> Nor be concern'd about the Sale,
> He pays his Workmen on the Nail.[6]

He goes on to paint a scathing picture of the literary world, with all its jealousies, its railing, and its criticism; its descending degrees of badness all the way from "Elephants to Mites in Cheese," down to the worst of all, who

> prostitute the Muse's Name,
> By flatt'ring (Kings) whom Heaven design'd
> The Plagues and Scourges of Mankind.
> Bred up in Ignorance and Sloth,
> And ev'ry Vice that nurses both.[7]

And then, very gravely, but with irony which was never missed by any of his American readers, he describes the blessings of the British nation, with such a constellation as the King, his consort, and his family, and his minister of state, and claims that here it is impossible to err on the side of flattery.

> . . . what the World refus'd to Lewis,
> Apply'd to (George) exactly true is:
> Exactly true! Invidious Poet!
> 'Tis fifty thousand Times below it.[8]

The scorner of kings and courts and the denouncer of governments who tyrannized over peoples subject to them had an audience in the American colonies such as he has probably never had in the American Republic. But it should not be forgotten that this same contemptuous

[6] *Poems*, p. 646.
[7] Ibid., pp. 654-5.
[8] Ibid., p. 657.

satirist was also a Tory and a Churchman and a Dean, who, twenty years earlier, had played an important part in political life as the chief government propagandist during the last years of Queen Anne's reign. Then he had deigned to appear at court and to dine with ministers of state; and he had even asked for the appointment of historiographer, so that he might write the official account of the Queen's reign and leave for posterity a record of her glory and her greatness. And though he was never appointed to this office, he nevertheless set himself the task of writing the history of that part of her reign when he had been at the centre of things and had had opportunity to observe what was being done.

He had then been on the side of authority and had shown little tolerance towards the opponents of the Queen and her ministers. He was then using all his powers to support the reasonable but inglorious policy of putting an end to the long war in which the Duke of Marlborough and the allied forces under his command had won a series of great triumphs against France, which had done much to restore the balance of power in Europe. He had pointed out that the successes of the campaign had only led to the continuance of a struggle which was piling up enormous burdens of debt on the country, and benefiting nobody except the General and his friends and the bankers who were financing the public loans. It is rather curious to read just now some of Swift's arguments, so rash in their simplicity, so cool in their daring appeal to the sensible dictates of self-interest. In arguing for peace he never for a moment allows his own moral dislike of war to appear. He strips his words of every shred of sentiment; he puts down his case with the detachment of a balance-sheet:

> The Motives that may engage a wise Prince or State in a War, I take to be one or more of these: Either to check the overgrown Power of some ambitious Neighbour; to recover what hath been unjustly taken from Them; to revenge some Injury They have received; (which all Political Casuists allow); to assist some Ally in a just Quarrel; or lastly, to defend Themselves when They are invaded.[9]

With the obvious exception of the last case, where everything is at stake, he argues that no country can afford to get involved beyond a certain limit:

[9] *Prose*, VI, 7.

. . . never proceeding so far as to exhaust the Strength and Substance of their Country by Anticipations and Loans, which, in a few Years, must put them in a worse Condition than any they could reasonably apprehend from those Evils, for the preventing of which they first entered into the War: Because this would be to run into real infallible Ruin, only in hopes to remove what might perhaps but appear so by a probable Speculation.[10]

And in this kind of war, the next thing to be considered is when it is prudent to make overtures of peace:

Which I take to be, either when the Enemy is ready to yield the Point originally contended for, or when that Point is found impossible to be ever obtained; or when contending any longer, though with Probability of gaining that Point at last, would put such a Prince and his People in a worse Condition than the present Loss of it.[11]

He is not unaware of the argument that the expense of a struggle which is undertaken in the hope of establishing peace and safety in the world for the benefit of posterity may well be shared by them; but he reminds us of the crazy pattern of history and the possibility that in the future they might be on the other side.

'Tis easy to entail Debts on succeeding Ages, and to hope they will be able and willing to pay them; but how to insure Peace for any Term of Years, is difficult enough to apprehend. Will Human Nature ever cease to have the same Passions? . . .

It will, no doubt, be a mighty Comfort to our Grandchildren, when they see a few Rags hang up in *Westminster-Hall*, which cost an hundred Millions, whereof they are paying the Arrears, and boasting, as Beggars do, that their Grandfathers were Rich and Great.[12]

With such quiet arguments, broken with occasional flashes of satire, Swift maintains the reasonableness of his own attitude and the absurdity of any other; but he knew that this alone was not enough. In all his political propaganda he recognized the necessity for attack, to rout his opponents and destroy them. If he is in the right, they must be wrong; and they must be shown to be utterly wrong. He does not spare them, whoever they are: Dutch Allies, who have long shared

10 Ibid.
11 Ibid., p. 8.
12 Ibid., pp. 55-6.

the fortunes of a glorious war; the great General himself and all his supporters; Scottish lords and Irish senators, Whig Dukes and commoners; bankers and traders, Dissenters and free-thinkers.

In this campaign to put an end to the European war, all his sympathies as a moralist, a Churchman, and an old-fashioned Tory were with the cause he was defending; and all the groups he most heartily disliked were his opponents. He had not much in common with the Dutch and the other Protestant allies in Europe, and seemed to enjoy the task of exposing all their infringements of every article in the treaties and agreements that had been made with them. He had convinced himself that the family of the Duke of Marlborough had made themselves troublesome to the Queen, and were eaten up with ambition for money and power. And, though he doubted the wisdom of depriving the Duke of all his appointments and the justice of some of the charges brought against him in the heat of party zeal, he was himself ruthless and implacable in the detestation he expresses for his greed and avarice. In "The Conduct of the Allies" he did not hesitate to place the blame for the gross impositions which we had suffered from our allies upon the General himself:

> I know no other way so probable, or indeed so charitable to account for it, as by that unmeasurable Love of Wealth, which his best Friends allow to be his predominant Passion. However I shall waive any thing that is Personal upon this Subject. I shall say nothing of those great Presents made by several Princes, which the Soldiers used to call Winter-Foraging, and said it was better than that of the Summer; of Two and an half *per Cent.* substracted out of all the Subsidies we pay in those Parts, which amounts to no inconsiderable Sum; and lastly, of the grand Perquisites in a long successful War, which are so amicably adjusted between Him and the States.[13]

And this was followed by a pleasant little satire in verse, called "The Fable of Midas," who turned everything he touched to gold:

> Whene'er he chanc'd his Hands to lay,
> On Magazines of *Corn* or *Hay*,
> *Gold* ready Coin'd appear'd, instead
> Of paultry *Provender* and *Bread*:[14]

. . . .

[13] Ibid., pp. 41-2.
[14] *Poems*, p. 156.

With similar violence he turns upon the main supporters of the Whig party and declares that they had continued the war far beyond the time when it could have been satisfactorily settled, and were still working to prolong it, because of the profits they were making out of it.

> With these Measures fell in all that Sett of People, who are called the *Monied Men;* such as had raised vast Sums by Trading with Stocks and Funds, and Lending upon great Interest and Præmiums; whose perpetual Harvest is War, and whose beneficial way of Traffick must very much decline by a Peace.[15]

It is hardly surprising that the victims of Swift's attacks denounced him as an irresponsible opportunist, ready to make use of any weapons and to shift his ground for his own advantage at a particular moment, just as he happened to be engaged on the side of the government or in opposition. Some of his later critics also have condemned him for changing sides, none more bitterly than Jeffrey in the Edinburgh Review for September, 1816, where he is dealing with Sir Walter Scott's edition of Swift, and the too favourable account Scott gives of his character. It is clear that what disturbed Jeffrey most was Swift's political behaviour, which he condemns in these terms:

> He makes his approaches to Harley in a manner which we should really imagine no *rat* of the present day could have confidence enough to imitate.
> We think there are not many of those who have served a regular apprenticeship to corruption and jobbing, who could go through their base task with more coolness and hardihood than this pious neophyte.

But the fact is that Swift remained a loyal Churchman and moderate Tory throughout his life, and opposed to Walpole and the Whigs alike when they were in opposition under Queen Anne and in power under the Hanoverians. But he was too independent, too clear-sighted, too humane, and too liberal to be quite at ease in any political or ecclesiastical party. He was a moralist and had a humorous, satirical bent, with little inclination for any enthusiasm or sentiment, either in religion or in politics. But he claimed that he had always striven for justice and human freedom:

[15] *Prose,* VI, 41.

Fair LIBERTY was all his Cry;
For her he stood prepar'd to die;
For her he boldly stood alone;
For her he oft expos'd his own.
Two Kingdoms, just as Faction led,
Had set a Price upon his Head;
But not a Traytor cou'd be found,
To sell him for Six Hundred Pound.[16]

II

This, however, does not give us much clue to his real opinions on politics, and we cannot be content with such poetical memorials, even though from his own pen. We are tempted to look again for some indication of what he really thought about politics and politicians, after the experience that he had had at the centre of affairs from his forty-third to his forty-seventh year, when he was at the height of his powers. And just at that moment, in the spring of 1714, two months before the death of the Queen, when he had given up all hope of reconciling his friends, Oxford and Bolingbroke, and had gone off into the country to await events, he sat down to write what he called "Some Free Thoughts on the Present State of Affairs." Here, in the first few pages, before entering on a discussion of current problems, he indulges in some interesting generalizations on politics and affords a glimpse of his mind, already detached, a little aloof, no longer engaged, but with all the exciting memories of the preceding four years fresh upon him. He writes, of course, in a mood of disillusionment, frustrated by his inability to make the leaders of the government see the precariousness of their position and take the simple and quite straightforward action demanded by the circumstances. But he may well have felt that in such a mood he might hope to discover the secret of politics and the gifts required of politicians, and therefore have determined to try and set down his thoughts freely. He finds, however, that all his observations and experiences have served only to confirm his simple belief that politics is "nothing but Common Sense" and not a matter of refined and subtle statecraft. He appeals to history to support his view and is able to show that princes and ministers who were famous for their mysterious skill in government

[16] *Poems*, pp. 566-7.

or had the reputation of being "Men of deep Intrigue" usually ended in disgrace or dishonor, and left behind them a train of factions and discontents which disturbed the happiness and ease of their peoples. Therefore he concludes that not subtlety and statecraft, but general ability and character are the qualities necessary to make a statesman.

> I know no Station in Life where great abilities and Virtues of all Kinds are so highly necessary and where the Want of any is so quickly or universally felt. A great Minister hath no Virtue for which the Publick may not be the better, nor any Defect by which the Publick is not certainly a Sufferer.[17]

He emphasizes the importance of virtue because, as a moralist, he firmly believed that there was the possibility of an ordered society. "The Bulk of Mankind would easily be governed by Reason if it were left to their Choice." The best way to a good end is "the most plain, short, easy, safe and lawful Way."[18] He will not allow that any special gifts "of the lower Politicks" are required even in the management of parties under any tolerable administration. Even in dealing with the complicated pattern of international relationships constantly shifting with every change in the balance of power, which would seem to demand the skill of the most expert diplomatists, he still refuses to admit that any special talents are demanded "besides Method and Skill in the common Forms of Business," though he realizes the need for thorough knowledge and for much wisdom. In the particular problem of negotiating treaties he had made himself an expert by studying all the official documents and correspondence connected with the Treaty of Utrecht, in preparation for his history of the negotiations. He probably knew more about what had been going on than any other person who had not been one of the official representatives; and, as he looked back over all the various episodes, he found himself still in complete agreement with the observation he had often heard "that plain good Sense and a firm Adherence to the Point have proved more effectual than all those Arts which I remember a great foreign Minister used in contempt to call the *Spirit of Negotiating*."[19]

Without the faith of a Burke in the organic growth of the life of a

---

[17] *Prose*, VIII, 80, 206.
[18] Ibid., VI, 77.
[19] Ibid., p. 78.

people, and certainly without any sense of economic determinism, Swift was nevertheless always conscious of certain movements in the affairs of nations and peoples, which were entirely independent of the guidance of their rulers, however skilful they felt themselves to be in controlling events. In his own experience he could remember so many events "which in reality were either the mere effects of negligence, weakness, humour, passion or pride, or at least, but the natural course of things left to themselves."[20] In fact, a good many politicians were only quacks, who had claimed to cure their patients of malignant diseases "whereas, in truth, nine parts in ten of those who recovered, owed their lives to the strength of nature and a good constitution." There is in this point of view a curious mixture of scepticism, rooted in a distrust of human nature and motives, and a belief in good sense and the possibility that a simple reasonable way may be found to any good end. This is not so paradoxical as it sounds, for it implies a willingness to trust to "Nature's simple plan," which might work reasonably enough, if it were not for the interference of cunning politicians with their skill in the lower politics, or of ambitious generals whose victories do nothing but increase their appetite for glory and wealth, or of the money-changers whose only fear is lest their tables be overthrown.

It may seem to be rather a naïve and innocent point of view for such an experienced and hard-boiled politician as Swift. Nevertheless he continued to maintain it; and when, twelve years later, he published the full story of his travels in the world, he took occasion to repeat exactly these same views on politics in a passage where his passionate sincerity is shown by the very force of his irony. In the second of his adventures, where he found himself in the Utopia of Brobdingnag among those simple-hearted, innocent giants who taught him so much, he was encouraged by the king to report on the affairs and on the past history of his own country, and attempted to use this opportunity to impress his majesty with the glories of Western civilization. After listening on several occasions to Gulliver's panegyrics, the king's horror and astonishment grew until finally

> taking me into his Hands and stroaking me gently, he delivered himself in these Words, which I shall never forget, nor the Manner he spoke them in. My little friend *Grildrig;* you have made a most ad-

mirable panegyric upon your Country. You have clearly proved that Ignorance, Idleness, and Vice are the proper Ingredients for qualifying a Legislator. That Laws are best explained, interpreted, and applied by those whose Interest and Abilities lie in perverting, confounding, and eluding them. I observe among you some Lines of an Institution, which in its Original might have been tolerable; but these half erased, and the rest wholly blurred and blotted by Corruptions.[21]

Gulliver confessed that he was so shocked and puzzled by this that he would like to have omitted all account of it from his story, if it had not been for his extreme love of truth. He tried to defend himself by protesting that he had done his best "to hide the Frailties and Deformities of his Political Mother, and place her Virtues and Beauties in the most advantageous Light."[22] Nor was he content to leave the matter there. He decided that he would yet vindicate himself by placing at the disposal of his majesty all his superior political skill and knowledge of the ways of civilized nations and their methods of gaining power and extending their influence over the world. He therefore took an opportunity of revealing to the King of the Brobdingnagians the invention of gunpowder. But once again he found that he had made a mistake and had only brought upon his head another surprising outburst:

> He was amazed how so impotent and groveling an Insect as I (these were his Expressions) could entertain such inhuman Ideas, and in so familiar a Manner as to appear wholly unmoved at all the Scenes of Blood and Destruction, which I had painted as the common Effects of those destructive Machines . . . he would rather lose Half his Kingdom than be privy to such a Secret; which he commanded me, as I valued my Life, never to mention any more.[23]

Gulliver was at a loss to explain such narrow principles and short views. He had the utmost admiration for his majesty, his wisdom and his talents for government and his many virtues, and was worried at discovering such a defect in him, as to be hindered by *nice unnecessary scruples* from making himself absolute master of the lives, liberties, and fortunes of his people. He could only conclude that it was

21 Ibid., XI, 132.
22 Ibid., p. 133.
23 Ibid., pp. 134-5.

due to the general state of ignorance of the Brobdingnagians, who had not "reduced *Politicks* into a *Science,* as the more acute Wits of *Europe* have done."

> For, I remember very well, in a Discourse one Day with the King; when I happened to say, there were several thousand Books among us written upon the *Art of Government;* it gave him (directly contrary to my Intention) a very mean Opinion of our Understandings. He professed both to abominate and despise all *Mystery, Refinement,* and *Intrigue,* either in a Prince or a Minister. He could not tell what I meant by *Secrets of State,* where an Enemy or some Rival Nation were not in the Case. He confined the Knowledge of governing within very *narrow Bounds;* to common Sense and Reason, to Justice and Lenity, to the Speedy Determination of Civil and criminal Causes; with some other obvious Topicks which are not worth considering.[24]

[24] Ibid., pp. 135-6.

ALECTO'S WHIP

Swift claimed to write so simply that even an Irish footman could understand him. Nevertheless he found it necessary to point out to readers of *A Tale of a Tub* where he had used parody and irony; and readers of *Gulliver's Travels* continue to disagree about its intention and meaning, in spite of all the analysis of the form and structure, and all the anatomy of the satire and examination of the rhetorical devices employed. Our understanding of Swift's meaning and intention must still depend on our conception of the kind of person he was, after we have become thoroughly acquainted with everything that he wrote. For he left a surprising amount of diaries and letters and verse which offer a glimpse of him undisguised. Here I would like only to consider some of his verse which seems to me to reveal a side of his nature not always remembered in recent criticism of *Gulliver's Travels*.

Even in his earliest Ode, where we see him impatiently and awkwardly trying to wrap the voluminous folds of his singing robes around him, as he joins the tuneful choir who were offering their congratulations to William III upon his successes in 1690, instead of allowing himself to be caught up by "the spirit of exalted poetry" which his subject demands, he begins with scorn and contempt to express his real feelings about pomp and splendour:

> What can the Poet's humble Bays
>
> .   .   .   .   .   .
>
> Add to the Victor's Happiness?
> What do the Scepter, Crown and Ball,

> Rattles for Infant Royalty to play withal,
>> But serve t'adorn the Baby-dress
>> Of one poor Coronation-day,
>>> To make the Pageant gay:
>> A three Hours Scene of empty Pride,
>> And then the Toys are thrown aside.[1]

In the first of his printed poems, the *Ode to the Athenian Society*, where he surprises us by revealing for a moment a youthful enthusiasm for transcendent merit, this very ardour turns to contempt for the world's silliness, as he disdainfully surveys it from a distance:

> *These Days!* where ev'n th'Extravagance of Poetry
>> Is at a loss for Figures to express
>> Men's Folly, Whimsyes, and Inconstancy,
>> And by a faint Description make them less.[2]

In that most revealing of his early poems, addressed to Congreve in 1693, his compliments and praise soon turn to satire on the follies of the time, and he gives us fair warning of the force of hatred, that is already devouring him:

> *My hate, whose lash just heaven has long decreed*
> *Shall on a day make sin and folly bleed;*[3]

When much later, in the height of his political activities during the last years of Queen Anne's reign, he used his skill as a writer of verse to attack his opponents, he often needed in that dangerous game to disguise his hand, to parody old prophecies, carefully printed in black letter, or to imitate Ovid's Fables, with a moral suitable for the times. But whatever the device he uses, he never allows it to weaken the force of his hate, or—as here in the *Fable of Midas*—to lessen the relentlessness with which he exposes Marlborough as a monster of avarice. He begins at first in a tone of almost gentle raillery:

> This Tale inclines the gentle Reader,
> To think upon a certain *Leader*,
> To whom from *Midas* down, descends
> That Virtue in the Fingers ends:

[1] *Poems*, p. 6.
[2] Ibid., p. 21.
[3] Ibid., p. 47.

> What else by *Perquisites* are meant,
> By *Pensions, Bribes* and *three per Cent?*
> By *Places* and *Commissions* sold
> And turning *Dung* itself to *Gold?*[4]

then by the use of terms like "defiles" and "fouls" introduces a tone
of moral repugnance:

> But *Gold* defiles with frequent Touch,
> There's nothing *fouls* the Hands so much:
> And Scholars give it for the Cause,
> Of *British Midas* dirty Paws . . .

This is repeated mercilessly in the final couplet:

> And *Midas* now neglected stands,
> With *Asses Ears,* and *dirty Hands.*[5]

We cannot understand Swift, or measure aright the purpose of his
satire unless we take such things into account. He was not content
to attack his opponents only in the heat of the conflict, to denigrate
their character when it may have seemed necessary to justify the policy
of the Ministry in getting rid of them. He was concerned to bring his
adversaries before the bar of posterity, that all evil-doers might know
that their crimes would be revealed for the instruction of future ages.
Why else did he trouble to write an elegy on Marlborough after he
was dead? He can no longer hurt him, but in this way he can somehow assume the role of Alecto and borrow her whip of scorpions,
steeped in Gorgonian venom—and take vengeance on those who have
escaped the punishment they deserved.

> Well, since he's gone, no matter how,
> The last loud trump must wake him now:
> And trust me, as the noise grows stronger,
> He'd wish to sleep a little longer.[6]

There is a brutal callousness in the voice, ringing with contempt:

> This world he cumber'd long enough;
> He burnt his candle to the snuff;

[4] Ibid., p. 157.
[5] Ibid., p. 158.
[6] Ibid., p. 296.

> And that's the reason, some folks think,
> He left behind *so great a stink*.[7]

There is no word of extenuation, no mercy, no pity. We are not allowed for a moment to remember the late famous General, the brilliant strategist, the oft-repeated successes of his splendid campaigns,
the great reputation that made his name envied and feared and mar-
velled at in all the courts of Europe. Instead we hear only the voice
of the moralist who had always hated war and despised military glory,
and the harsher tones of one who often thinks of himself as the scourge
of the gods. He is very fond of the word "lash" already used in those
lines to Congreve. It occurs more than once in *An Epistle to a Lady,
Who desired the Author to make Verses on Her, in the Heroick Style,*
1733:

> Still to lash, and lashing Smile,
> Ill befits a lofty Stile.[8]

And though he boasts that all the madness of the world but makes him
merry, yet within a few lines he has worked himself into a passion, and
is clamouring to apply Alecto's whip to the villains' posteriors, "till
they wriggle, howl and skip."[9] The *Verses on the Life and Character
of Dr. Swift* end with this couplet:

> Then, since you *dread* no further *Lashes,*
> You freely may *forgive his Ashes*.[10]

And in the *Verses on his own Death,* he cheerfully contradicts himself
in these couplets:

> His Vein, ironically grave
> Expos'd the Fool and lash'd the Knave:[11]

> Yet, Malice never was his Aim;
> He lash'd the Vice, but spar'd the Name.[12]

He may even try to persuade us that he can write *A Rapsody* about
Kings and Parliaments and Ministers without anger or hatred, using

[7] Ibid.
[8] Ibid., p. 634.
[9] Ibid., p. 635.
[10] Ibid., p. 550.
[11] Ibid., p. 565.
[12] Ibid., p. 571.

only the more civilised weapons of irony and raillery, and enjoying
the fun of offering his unsophisticated victim compliments he might
be tempted to find acceptable:

> What Justice in rewarding Merit?
> What Magnanimity of Spirit?
> What Lineaments divine we trace
> Thro' all the features of his Face . . .[13]

But this playfulness could not really satisfy him, and privately he
indulged in such invective as no printer would have dared to include
in the poem. The symbols are borrowed from a poem he had written
the year before, called *The Beast's Confession to the Priest*. After
Prometheus had formed mankind—a mingled mass of good and bad—
he then turns to the business of creating suitable rulers for them:

> Then from a Clay of Mixture base
> He shap'd a King to rule the Race
> Endow'd with Gifts from every Brute
> That best the regal Nature suit,
> Thus think on Kings, the Name denotes
> Hogs, Asses, Wolves, Baboons, & Goats
> To represent in Figure just
> Sloth, Folly, Rapine, Mischeif, Lust
> O! were they all but Nebuchadnazzars
> What Herds of Kings would turn to Grazers.[14]

These are the sort of verses Swift wrote in the wisdom of his age,
when he was over sixty and had no more to fear or to hope from
courts and ministers. He constantly reminds himself that it is in vain
to storm and rage; it only stupefies the brain. Better be content with
laughter mingled with scorn. But there are some subjects—like the
Bench of Bishops—which seem to rouse him to such fury that he cannot help calling down vengeance from the skies upon them:

> As antient *Judas by Transgression fell,*
> And *burst asunder* e'er he went to Hell;
> So, could we see a Set of new *Iscariots,*
> Come headlong tumbling from their mitred Chariots,
> Each modern Judas perish like the first;

13 Ibid., p. 655.
14 Ibid., p. 659.

> Drop from the Tree with all his Bowels burst;
> Who could forbear, that view'd each guilty Face,
> To cry; *Lo, Judas, gone to his own Place:*
> *His Habitation let all Men forsake,*
> *And let his Bishoprick another take.*[15]

Swift had been ready to admit that perhaps there had been too much
satire in his vein, but he had pleaded that it had always been designed
with a moral view—

> To cure the Vices of Mankind.

As a moralist he was concerned rather to heal than to hurt; and even
as a judge he would have us believe that he has heard the case without bias or passion, before proceeding to award those punishments the
law demands. But he had never suffered fools gladly, nor had he
grown kindlier and more tolerant with age. And when at last, even
in Dublin, his authority was flouted, and his warnings unheeded,
when he could no longer provide protection for his friends the print-
ers, nor save them from being flung into a plague-stricken gaol, he
turned to the only resource left, and in his sixty-ninth year, attacked
directly and by name his enemies in the Irish Parliament, pouring
upon them invective as powerful as he ever wrote. There is irony only
in the title—*A Character, Panegyric, and Description of the Legion
Club*—and a deceptive calm only in the opening lines:

> As I strole the City, oft I
> Spy a Building large and lofty,
> Not a Bow-shot from the College,
> Half the Globe from Sense and Knowledge.[16]

He does not stay to describe the building where at that time the Irish
Parliament met, but proceeds briskly to his business:

> Tell us, what this Pile contains?
> Many a Head that holds no Brains.
> These Demoniacs let me dub
> With the Name of *Legion Club*.

That is enough to set his imagination to work; the thought of this

[15] Ibid., p. 806.
[16] Ibid., p. 829.

legion of devils leading him on to a lovely vision of their final destruction:

> Could I from the Building's Top
> Hear the rattling Thunder drop,
> While the Devil upon the Roof,
> If the Devil be Thunder Proof,
> Should with Poker fiery-red
> Crack the Stones and melt the Lead:
> Drive them down on every Scull,
> While the Den of Thieves is full,
> Quite destroy that Harpies Nest,
> How might then our Isle be blest?[17]

But a better idea occurs to him. It is after all a good solid building that will stand. Let it remain to house Swift's hospital for lunatics and fools; there they are already within its walls. He then proceeds to draw our attention to some of their lunatic activities with more scathing contempt than the worst critics of Washington or Westminster have ever indulged in:

> Let them, when they once get in
> Sell the Nation for a Pin;
> While they sit a picking Straws
> Let them rave of making Laws;
> While they never hold their Tongue,
> Let them dabble in their Dung;
> Let them form a grand Committee,
> How to plague and starve the City; etc.[18]

In the next section of the poem the tone is changed, and Swift uses one of his favourite devices, parody, calling the Muse to his assistance to conduct him as he approaches the gate of hell, and like Virgil in the sixth book of the Aeneid praying the gods to help him unfold the secrets buried in the darkness of the earth:

> All ye Gods who rule the Soul . . .
> Let me be allowed to tell
> What I heard in yonder Hell.[19]

[17] Ibid., p. 830.
[18] Ibid., p. 831.
[19] Ibid., p. 832.

As an example of the force and conciseness that Swift sometimes manages to get into his verse, the lines that follow may be compared with Dryden's translation of Virgil:

> Just in the Gate and in the Jaws of Hell,
> Revengeful Cares and sullen Sorrows dwell;
> And pale Diseases, and Repining Age,
> Want, Fear and Famine's unresisted rage;
> . . . and Strife, that shakes
> Her hissing Tresses, and unfolds her Snakes.[20]

And this is Swift:

> Near the Door, an Entrance gapes,
> Crouded round with antic Shapes;
> *Poverty* and *Grief* and *Care*,
> Causeless *Joy*, and true *Despair*;
> *Discord*, periwigged with Snakes,
> See, the dreadful Strides she takes.

For a moment he seems to have forgotten his anger and the horrors that await him, and is clearly amusing himself at his favourite game of transposing the heroic style into plain terms, so that the horrible figure of discord seems to be masquerading in a periwig of snakes. Yet somehow he manages to keep the two scenes focused together, the entrance to the underworld and the porch on the Dublin street leading into the Chamber:

> By this odious crew beset,
> I began to rage and fret
> And resolv'd to break their Pates,
> 'Ere we enter'd at the Gates;
> Had not *Clio* in the Nick,
> Whisper'd me, let down your Stick;[21]

Now he has to get rid of the gentle Muse before concentrating on the real stuff of the poem. Though disguised she is in terror, and, overcome with the noise and the smell, she abandons him:

> In a Fright she crept away,
> Bravely I resolved to stay.

[20] Book VI, ll. 384-93.
[21] *Poems*, pp. 832-3.

> When I saw the Keeper frown,
> Tipping him with Half a Crown;
> Now, said I, we are alone,
> Name your Heroes one, by one.[22]

Then he can launch forth unhindered on his abuse of the worst of them there, who are duly named with their crimes and the crimes of their ancestors. First there are Swift's two most violent opponents, Richard Tighe and Sergeant Richard Bettesworth, already the victim of several lampoons:

> Keeper, shew me where to fix
> On the Puppy Pair of *Dicks*;
> By their lanthorn Jaws and Leathern,
> You might swear they both are Brethren:
> *Dick Fitz-Baker, Dick* the Player,
> Old Acquaintance, are you there?
> Dear Companions hug and kiss,
> Toast *old Glorious* in your Piss.
> Tye them Keeper in a Tether,
> Let them stare and stink together;
> Both are apt to be unruly,
> Lash them daily, lash them duly,
> Though 'tis hopeless to reclaim them,
> Scorpion Rods perhaps may tame them.[23]

After this we are given samples of squires and lords and swaggerers from the garrison, and we are assured that he could produce hundreds more; but he grows weary of the task and feels that it is too much for the mere satirist in verse. It is not enough just to describe them; they need to be painted, just as they are, to preserve their hideous features as a record for posterity. If only he were acquainted with that pleasant rogue, Hogarth, they might work together on "this odious Group of Fools":

> Draw the Beasts as I describe 'em,
> Form their Features, while I gibe 'em;
> Draw them like, for I assure you
> You will need no *Car'catura*;

22 Ibid., p. 834.
23 Ibid., p. 835.

> Draw them so that we may trace
> All the Soul in every Face.[24]

In this poem he was content to leave the bishops alone; but in the following year, when the Bill was passed for lowering the gold coin in Ireland, he was not satisfied to show his displeasure by muffling the peal and hanging out a black flag at St. Patrick's but, in almost the last verses he ever wrote, he took his revenge on the man he held responsible, Hugh Boulter, Archbishop of Armagh and Primate of all Ireland. Whether or not Swift was responsible for the ballad about him, to be sung in the streets, there can be no doubt that he wrote those dangerous verses which describe the encounter between the Dean and the Archbishop when they met at the Lord Mayor's dinner:

> At *Dublin's* high feast sat Primate and Dean,
> Both dress'd like divines, with band and face clean.
> Quoth *Hugh* of *Armagh,* 'The mob is grown bold.'
> 'Ay, ay,' quoth the Dean, 'the cause is old gold.'
> 'No, no,' quoth the Primate, 'if causes we sift,
> 'This mischief arises from witty Dean *Swift.*'
> The smart-one replied, 'There's no wit in the case;
> 'And nothing of that ever troubled your Grace.
>
>   .   .   .   .   .   .
>
> 'The Irish dear Joys have enough common sense,
> 'To treat gold reduc'd like *Wood's* copper pence.
> 'It's a pity a Prelate should die without law;
> 'But if I say the word—take care of *Armagh!*"[25]

It was difficult for Swift to reconcile his position as Drapier, Hibernian Patriot, and the hero of the people who lived in the Liberty of St. Patrick's and banded themselves together to protect him against the threats of Sergeant Bettesworth, with the Christian virtue of humility, or even with the clerical duty of obedience to his superiors in the Church. Or perhaps it was simply impossible for the wit not to allow himself a little fun at the expense of the dignity of the Archbishop and the government he represented.

For, though Swift was a very loyal Anglican and a great Dean, he shows himself in these verses where he borrows Alecto's whip and

[24] Ibid., p. 839.
[25] Ibid., p. 843.

wields it with such undisguised satisfaction as a satirist who belongs
ultimately to a wider world and an older tradition, in which he takes
his place, as Pope saw, by the side of Rabelais and Cervantes and their
great Roman predecessors, who fashioned the weapons of satire and
used them for the liberation of the human spirit. That is how Pope
thought of him when he dedicated to him the Dunciad; and he well
knew that it was the kind of compliment which would give the most
satisfaction to Swift. If he had felt that it might be necessary to qual-
ify this tribute, it would not have been because Swift was less free or
uninhibited than they, or more limited in the range of his satire; it
would have been because Swift had persuaded Pope when he wrote
to him about *Gulliver's Travels* that he "would rather be employ'd as
an Avenging Angel of wrath, to break (his) Vial of Indignation over
the heads of the wretched creatures of this World,"[26] and because he
often gives the impression that he is a little too fond of Alecto's whip,
a little too ready to take over the business of punishment as well as
judgement and to enjoy his power and his triumph as he lashes his
victims until they howl and wriggle and skip. It would be because,
as he himself summed up the case:

> the Dean
> Had too much Satyr in his Vein;
> And seem'd determin'd not to starve it,
> Because no Age could more deserve it.[27]

[26] *Pope's Corr.*, I. Sherburn, ii, 332.
[27] *Poems*, p. 571.

THE AUGUSTAN ART OF
CONVERSATION

It was in 1700, at the very turn of the century which was to produce such literature in England as to recall the splendours of Augustan Rome, that Congreve wrote his last comedy—*The Way of the World,* where he seems to have best succeeded in giving us a glimpse of the fashionable society of his day and allowing us to overhear dialogue as brilliant as has ever been spoken in English. In dedicating his play to the Earl of Montagu, who had twice been English Ambassador Extraordinary to Louis XIV, Congreve ascribes any superior merit it may have "to the honour of your Lordship's admitting me into your conversation, and that of a society where everybody else was so well worthy of you, in your retirement last summer from the Town." And he recalls the advantages possessed by Terence, who enjoyed the freedom of conversation with Scipio and Laelius, two of the greatest and most polite men of his age, and adds: "Indeed, the privilege of such a conversation is the only certain means of attaining to the perfection of dialogue." You will notice that Congreve uses the word "conversation" here to convey something larger than its current meaning today. He has in mind not merely the advantages of sharing the pleasant, witty or valuable discourse at my lord's dining table, or afterwards at tea with the ladies, but the benefits he obtained from the whole human relationship he enjoyed as a member of their society; he uses the word almost as it is used in King James' Bible, to translate St. Paul's phrase—"our conversation is in Heaven," which became in the revised version "citizenship." But the other-worldliness of that Pauline conception of a citizenship in heaven is changed among the Augustans of eighteenth century England into something thoroughly mundane—or rather urbane; instead of the City of God, they are content to inhabit the City of Man: to make it beautiful and well-ordered so that at least those who have the freedom of that society, ladies and gentlemen of intelligence and wit and wealth and elegance, may enjoy to the full all the privileges of human intercourse and bring to perfection in it the highest art of conversation.

Congreve himself was perhaps the perfect embodiment of this Augustan ideal. For him life was not literature but conversation. After 1700 he ceased to write poetry and plays, though he still remained at the centre of literary society in London during Queen Anne's reign. He belonged both to the Kit-Kat Club and to the Scriblerus Club, being free of both political parties; and he was one of the few people who managed to remain on good terms with Lady Mary Wortley Montagu, who said of him: "I never knew anybody that had so much wit as Congreve." And later, when Congreve was an old man, Voltaire, on his first visit to England, came to pay his respects to him as the greatest dramatist living in London, and was shocked at what seemed to him an affectation, in that he disclaimed the character of a poet and said that he wished to be "visited on no other Foot than that of a Gentleman who led a life of Plainness and Simplicity." Whereupon, according to the version which appeared in Voltaire's *Letters concerning the English Nation,* published in London in 1733, Voltaire "answer'd, that had he been so unfortunate as to be a mere Gentleman, I should never have come to see him."[1]

This has often been interpreted as a kind of snobbishness, or at least a sort of old-fashioned unwillingness to be regarded as a professional writer. But I would suggest that it may equally well be regarded as an urbane preference for what the Augustans accepted as the higher art, the art of conversation, the expression of the most urbane form of human intercourse among men and women in a free society.

This conception of conversation was not new; it had been often put forward by M. Saint-Évremond, that Epicurean Frenchman, who had settled so happily in England under Charles II, and remained until his death in 1703, having enjoyed, as he said, the best of both

[1] P. 189.

worlds, among "les Français qui pensent et les Anglais qui parlent."
In a pleasant essay, *Of Study and Conversation*, as published in the
English edition of his *Works* in 1700, he emphasizes the horrors of
solitariness and the delights of society:

> The State of a Solitary Person, is a State of Violence . . . What
> distinction is there between Death and Retirement, between Solitude
> and the Grave? To live then as Man, 'tis necessary to converse with
> Men; 'tis fit Conversation should be the most agreeable Pleasure of
> Life . . .[2]

You may be surprised if I suggest that this view of conversation as
the highest of the arts in a civilized society was equally emphasized
by one who is generally regarded as the most uncompromising critic
of that Augustan world. But it is true I believe that Swift, like Congreve, had formed his ideal of conversation not after the fashion of
courts or clubs or coffee-houses or taverns, but after the older fashion
of the great country houses which had sheltered so much in the English tradition of grace and beauty and learning during the seventeenth
century. For he had spent the last years of the century in the household of Sir William Temple, at Moor Park, and there he had learned
to accept those standards of conversation which he was consistently
to uphold in all kinds of company. For, if conversation was indeed to
be "the Bond of Society"—as Saint-Évremond had called it—by which
"the Mind communicates its Thoughts and the Heart expresses its
Inclinations," it could not consist of chatter or commonplaces; it could
have nothing to do with mere fluency of speech, which as Swift
pointed out, was rather an indication of emptiness of mind:

> The common Fluency of Speech in many Men and most Women is
> owing to a Scarcity of Matter, and Scarcity of Words; for whoever is
> Master of Language, and hath a Mind full of Ideas, will be apt in
> speaking to hesitate upon the Choice of both; Whereas common Speak-
> ers have only one Set of Words to cloath them in; and these are always
> ready at the Mouth. So People come faster out of a Church when it is
> almost empty than when a Crowd is at the Door.[3]

The treatise *On Polite Conversation* was one of the last things Swift
saw through the press, when he was over seventy. It was printed in

[2] I, 311-12.
[3] *Prose*, IV, 244.

Dublin in 1738, and an English edition was published in London at the same time. But it was a work which had been in preparation over a period of more than thirty years; and during that time, he must have noticed the appearance in England in new translations of many of the Renaissance books of manners, like Della Casa's *Galateo*, which was reprinted in 1703 with the title, *Galateo of Manners, or, Instructions to a young Gentleman how to behave himself in Conversation*, and Guazzo's *Art of Conversation*. But the most popular handbook, also used as a French conversation book with the French and English text side by side, was *The Art of Pleasing in Conversation* by Pierre Ortique, Sieur de Vaumorière, which was finally revised, corrected, and enlarged by Mr. Ozell in 1736, for which notable work he is mentioned in the Introduction to Swift's *Polite Conversation*.

In this work there is thus a sort of double parody, the Dialogues themselves parodying actual conversations; and the introductory treatise parodying these courtesy books. In this "perfection of folly," as he called it, he promises to deal with the subject finally and establish permanently the whole art of conversation in England, by providing wit and humour for all occasions and all companies. He guarantees that it can never become outmoded because every single example has been already fixed by traditional usage for at least a hundred years. Thus the book has something of the fascination of Ray's collection of Proverbs; for it gathers up all the stale jokes, quips, and sayings, which do in fact have a perennial existence in every language, because of their association with the commonest acts of daily life as we meet at meals, or for various social occasions. It will be enough to give the simplest example:

Lord *Sparkish*. Miss, shall I fill you another Dish of Tea?
Miss. Indeed, my Lord, I have drank enough.
Ld. Sp. Come, it will do you more Good than a Month's fasting. Here, take it.
Miss. No, I thank your Lordship, enough's as good as a Feast.
Ld. Sp. Well, but if you always say no, you'll never be married.[4]

Swift has drawn it so near the worst reality in his desire to travesty the utter stupidities that can take the place of reasonable human intercourse. His purpose was also political—to expose the banality of

[4] Ibid., p. 136.

the tasteless, moneyed society of the Whig Hanoverian era. This is, he explains, "the genteel and ingenious conversation according to the most polite mode and method, now used at Court, and in the best companies in England." And he presses the irony further as he waxes eloquent in describing the glories of his own dear country, which has outdone all the nations of Europe in advancing the art of polite conversation to the greatest height it is capable of reaching. He has himself only some slight smattering in the French; but he has read all the popular writers and reigning wits, who have received praises from the Court, and has always been careful to enforce loyalty and do honour to his Majesty. He will provide perfect models for every occasion, far better than these Frenchmen or Italians—a collection so full and complete that he can guarantee that all the genius and politeness of England is summed up in it. Indeed, he has taken such pains to insure that nothing has been lost that he might well expect at a proper juncture to receive the public thanks of both Houses of Parliament:

> I may venture to affirm, without the least Violation of Modesty, that there is no Man now alive, who hath by many Degrees, so just Pretensions as myself, to the highest Encouragement from the Crown, the Parliament, and the Ministry, towards bringing this Work to its due Perfection. I have been assured, that several great Heroes of Antiquity were worshipped as Gods, upon the Merit of having civilized a fierce and barbarous People. It is manifest I could have no other Intentions . . .[5]

In these ironical Dialogues it is to be noticed that Swift is not less severe upon the ladies of the company than their lords or the wits about town. And we may remember that he had always been much concerned with their proper education, to fit them for their place in mixed society. Like Congreve, his ideal was the conversation of a company of intelligent and well-mannered men and women. They both belonged to the modern world and had no thought of restoring a Roman society in which women would have no part. Congreve has no hesitation about endowing Millamant his heroine with as much— if not more—of his wit than Mirabell; and when, before she accepts him, she insists on drawing up articles to preserve her freedom in

[5] Ibid., p. 119.

marriage, she is not only given a chance to delight us with her spirit and her wit, but she is being allowed also to reveal to us the possibilities of a relationship between men and women which had never been possible either in the ancient or the mediaeval world. The comedy of human life in the Enlightenment was to be something quite new. Listen, for example, to the demands of the new woman! After she has laid down very detailed rules for his conduct as a lover and a husband, Mirabell asks:

> Have you any more Conditions to offer? Hitherto your Demands are pretty reasonable.
> *Millamant.* Trifles!—As Liberty to pay and receive Visits to and from whom I please; to write and receive Letters, without Interrogatories or wry Faces on your part; to wear what I please; and choose Conversation with regard only to my own Taste; to have no Obligation upon me to converse with Wits that I don't like, because they are your Acquaintance; or to be intimate with Fools, because they may be your Relations. Come to Dinner when I please; dine in my Dressing-Room when I'm out of Humour, without giving a Reason. To have my Closet inviolate; to be sole Empress of my Tea-Table, which you must never presume to approach without first taking leave. And lastly, wherever I am, you shall always knock at the Door before you come in. These Articles subscribed, if I continue to endure you a little longer, I may by degrees dwindle into a Wife.

This is of course all very reasonable, but we are not surprised that even the enlightened Mirabell should reply:

> Your Bill of Fare is something advanc'd in this latter Account.—Well, have I liberty to offer conditions—that when you are dwindled into a Wife, I may not be beyond measure enlarg'd into a Husband.[6]

And the main condition that he proceeds to lay down is that her acquaintance should be general; he is afraid only of "some sworn confidant of your own sex" and of the cronies at her tea-table. He also recommends the advantages of a mixed society.

But, you may say, it is all very well to go on talking about the possibilities of the art of conversation in these companies of enlightened men and women, and quote the dialogue that could be heard on the London stage, but did the art come to any flowering in life at this period? The conditions were there—the wealth, the elegance, the

[6] *The Way of the World*, IV, v, 67-91.

pleasant admirably furnished great houses in town and country, the terraces and gardens; but what can we know of this art, which by its very nature can take no permanent form? It consists of speech and gesture, and grows and comes to perfection in a certain atmosphere created by the living presence of men and women; it can be made and enjoyed only by the participants. It cannot by its very nature be preserved. Even the talk at the Mermaid's Tavern, or at White's Coffeehouse, though we know it took place and can imagine what it may have been from our knowledge of those who were there, had no existence beyond the moment, or at most, beyond the memories of those who heard it. And even if we have some records of table-talk—like Luther's or Selden's or Ben Jonson's—there is little left of the full flavour if we do not know the moment and the company. We get glimpses sometimes in Swift's *Journal to Stella* of what went on at an evening dinner of the Brothers Club, we may even be told who was there and given some interchange of remarks between them; but we cannot conjure up the faces or hear the sound of the voices. There is among the Swift MSS in the Morgan Library the record of a conversation at Dublin Castle, at which Swift and some of his friends, Sir Andrew Fountaine, Tom Ashe, the Bishop of Clogher, and Dr. Molyneux, were entertaining the Lord Lieutenant of Ireland. It is called a *Dialogue in the Castilian Language,* but alas, though there is some attempt at imitation of the different manner of speaking, the conversation is mainly a string of puns or riddles. When Tom Ashe becomes insufferable with his interruptions, the Doctor remarks:

> Mr. Ash if I had an Engine to shut your Mouth I should value it more than that we make use of to stretch the Mouths of our Patients.
> Sir A. F. The Dr. says that I suppose by way of OS-tentation.
>
> . . . . . .
>
> Dill. Pray, my Lord, what Town in England is that, where the People may afford to keep the best Fires, and the Lord is best able to putt them out.
> Mr. F. Tis Newcastle I suppose, because there are the most Coals, and the D. of Newcastle is very rich, and rich Folks can do any thing, and so they can put out Fires.
> Dill. No, tis Cole-chester, and the Lord is Ld. Rivers.[7]

[7] *Prose*, IV, 257-8.

I once ventured to suggest that possibly some relics of Augustan conversation may have been preserved in the collection of *Thoughts on Various Subjects,* which Pope included in the first two volumes of the *Miscellanies,* published in 1727. For the editors promise to include things in which they have casually had any share, particularly those which they wrote in conjunction with Dr. Arbuthnot and Gay. But I had overlooked Pope's account as reported in Spence's *Anecdotes:*

> When Swift and I were once in the country for some time together, I happened one day to be saying, 'that if a man was to take notice of the reflections that came into his mind on a sudden as he was walking in the fields, or sauntering in his study, there might be several of them perhaps as good as his most deliberate thoughts.'—On this hint we both agreed to write down all the volunteer reflections that should come thus into our heads, all the time we staid there. We did so; and this is what afterwards furnished out the maxims published in our miscellanies. Those at the end of one volume are mine; and those in the other Dr. Swift's.[8]

Nevertheless they added further some which they attributed to their friends, Arbuthnot, Henley, etc. And these were presumably remarks made to Swift and Pope in the course of conversation. I have sometimes fancied that it is possible to distinguish between those that were the fruit of meditation—stray thoughts that drift into the mind—and those that were struck out in a contest of wit. A short aphorism: "How inconsistent is man with himself" or "No wise man ever wished to be younger"[9] sound to me like the product of meditation. But if we consider this remark of Dr. Arbuthnot: "We may see the small value God has for riches, by the People he gives them to!"[10] it seems to me to have the quality of a witty stroke, nicely played before a company of friends who could appreciate it. For, to quote another of the remarks:

> Wit in Conversation is only a readiness of Thought and a Facility of Expression, or (in the midwife's Phrase) a quick Conception and an easy Delivery.[11]

[8] *Anecdotes,* 1820, p. 158.
[9] *Miscellanies,* 1727, I, 403, 399.
[10] Ibid., II, 355.
[11] Ibid., p. 350.

In conversation among congenial company the mind is excited and
the tongue is loosened, as one retort provokes another. The pace becomes faster and the wit more pointed. Sometimes we may possibly
detect in the more elaborate of these *Thoughts* ideas compressed together which may well have been contributed by different members
of the company.

But if conversation was the favourite art of the Augustans you will
challenge me to give better samples than this. Where might we expect to find it recorded? There are many books of Memoirs, and there
are Spence's *Anecdotes;* but he is too much concerned with the sayings of Pope, or the comments of others about Pope and his work to
give us real conversational pieces. We find there a retort like Swift's
reply to Lord Bolingbroke, when he was trying to persuade Swift to
dine with him: "I'll send you my bill of fare," said Lord B. "Send
me your bill of company," said Swift.[12] Sometimes there is a rather
more sustained example:

> Ambrose Philips was a neat dresser, and very vain. In a conversation
> between him, Congreve, Swift and others, the discourse ran a good
> while on Julius Caesar. After many things had been said to the pur-
> pose, Ambrose asked what sort of person they supposed Julius Caesar
> was? He was answered, that from medals etc. it appeared that he was a
> small man, and thin-faced.—'Now, for my part,' said Ambrose, 'I should
> take him to have been of a lean make, pale complexion, extremely
> neat in his dress; and five feet seven inches high;' an exact description
> of Philips himself. Swift, who understood good breeding perfectly well,
> and would not interrupt anybody while speaking, let him go on, and
> when he had quite done, said: 'And I, Mr. Philips, should take him to
> have been a plump man, just five feet five inches high; not very neatly
> dressed, in a black gown with pudding-sleeves.'[13]

I have naturally been particularly interested in all the available records of Swift's conversation, and I thought that perhaps I should find
some good samples in Mrs. Pilkington's *Memoirs.* She does in fact
retail quite a number, in her engaging fashion; and she boasts that
she had a very remarkable memory. But she is inclined to be so concerned about her own reputation that most of the conversations she
relates tend to be of a similar pattern, showing the Dean in his most

[12] *Anecdotes*, p. 355.
[13] Ibid., pp. 375-6.

playful humour, and generally leading up to some sort of back-handed compliment to herself. It soon becomes obvious that we must not expect to find much of the Augustan spirit in Mrs. Pilkington.

Everywhere we find evidence of the general belief that conversation was one of the important arts of civilized society. In his *Familiar Letters* Richardson gives rules for agreeable conversation, and explains very solemnly that everyone must be given an opportunity to display his capacity on the subject he believes himself most able to handle with advantage. It is all the more strange that we find only in these few odd places any attempt to set down a record of this chief glory of the age. But perhaps this had to wait for another generation who had been themselves brought up by the Augustans. For it was done almost at the last moment, before a new age came to overthrow the ideals of the Enlightenment. It was left for a young Scot, born in 1740, to devise a method to preserve in all its fulness the conversation of Samuel Johnson, a professional man of letters, who yet, like Congreve and like Swift, was not content to live for literature alone. He had written for profit and for his own satisfaction; but his life had gone as much into conversation as into books. And indeed—such was James Boswell's great achievement—many of Johnson's warmest admirers in later generations have known and liked him better in his talk than in his formal writings: and Boswell's book is the embodiment of the spirit of the age triumphing in the art of conversation.

Boswell knew quite well what he was doing; and he knew that no one had ever done such a thing before.

> What I consider—he says—the peculiar value of the following work, is, the quantity it contains of Johnson's conversation; which is universally acknowledged to have been eminently instructive and entertaining . . .
> Had his other friends been as diligent and ardent as I was, he might have been almost entirely preserved. As it is, I will venture to say that he will be seen in this work more completely than any man who has ever yet lived.[14]

Boswell's success is partly due to the fact that he could not bear to waste any of the material he had collected—"even the idle talk of a good man ought to be regarded"; he was unwilling that "anything however slight, should perish" and therefore felt justified in "preserv-

[14] *Life of Johnson*, 1934, I, 30, 31.

ing rather too many of Johnson's sayings, than too few; especially as from the diversity of dispositions it cannot be known beforehand, whether what may seem trifling to some, and perhaps to the collector himself, may not be most agreeable to many."

Thus we have, not a collection of chosen sayings, of important critical opinions, or even moral axioms, but a reliable record of whole conversations, in which a number of persons took part, and in which we can sit quietly and overhear the conversation, as words are bandied back and forth, and Johnson is lured on to retort, judiciously or wildly or gaily, according to the mood of the moment.

There is a good deal of discussion about the subject of conversation, and it is evident that Johnson's conception and practice was in many ways different from that of the Augustans. For them it meant agreeable pleasant discourse in a company where everyone was at his ease. Johnson, it is true, once remarked to Boswell that "That is the happiest conversation where there is no competition, no vanity, but a calm quiet interchange of sentiments."[15] That was all very well between the two of them, but in larger companies Johnson was tempted to consider conversation a contest. Once when he was feeling ill, at the mention of Burke, he remarked: "That fellow calls forth all my powers. Were I to see Burke now, it would kill me."[16] And when Boswell put the question to him directly: "But, Sir, may there not be very good conversation without a contest for superiority?" his reply was: "No animated conversation, Sir, for it cannot be but that one or other will come off superior."

On another occasion Boswell remarks:

> Though his usual phrase for conversation was *Talk*, yet he made a distinction; for when he once told me that he dined the day before at a friend's house with a 'very pretty company'; and I asked him if there was good conversation, he answered, No Sir, we had *talk* enough, but no *conversation*; there was nothing *discussed*.[17]

It is evident that Johnson had grown up accepting the Augustan conception of the art, but as he grew older and was more inclined to indulge in discussion, all his comments show that he comes to think of conversation as an opportunity to excel in "sallies of raillery

15 Ibid., II, 359.
16 Ibid., p. 450.
17 Ibid., IV, 186.

or sentences of observation"; or at least as an excuse for remarks "either pointed or solid, wise or merry." Once he described the ingredients of conversation:

> There must, in the first place, be knowledge, there must be materials;— in the second place, there must be a command of words; in the third place, there must be imagination, to place things in such views as they are not commonly seen in;—and in the fourth place, there must be presence of mind, and a resolution not to be overcome by failures; this last is an essential requisite; for want of it many people do not excel in conversation.[18]

And here is a beautiful example of the excellence of Boswell's method, even at the very moment when he gives himself away. One can imagine him writing down the four points with satisfaction—here is a definition to be remembered. But then Johnson adds a merry quip: "Now *I* want it: I throw up the game upon losing a trick." This transition, this sudden change of tone, seems too much for Boswell, who remarks solemnly: "I wondered to hear him talk thus of himself, and said: 'I don't know, Sir, how this may be; but I am sure you beat other people's cards out of their hands.'" There was no response, so Boswell explains: "I doubt whether he heard this remark." And then, recreating the scene so vividly for us, he goes on:

> While he went on talking triumphantly, I was fixed in admiration and said to Mrs. Thrale, 'O, for short-hand, to take this down!' 'You'll carry it all in your head (said she) a long head is as good as short-hand.'[19]

Boswell did succeed in getting a great deal recorded, and we owe it to him that we can overhear the talk of a whole group of Johnson's friends, and his comments on them and their conversation. And I suspect that Johnson's analysis of the ingredients, which he thought essential, was the result of observing the talk of Burke. For on one occasion when they were discussing him, Johnson remarked on his "great variety of knowledge, store of imagery, and copiousness of language"—which were three of the four ingredients; and the fourth, the "resolution not to be overcome" he always allowed to Burke to the fullest degree. But when Robertson said: "He has wit too"; Johnson replied: "No, Sir; he never succeeds there. 'Tis low, 'tis conceit. I used

[18] Ibid., p. 166.
[19] Ibid., p. 166.

to say, Burke never once made a good joke." He had other deficiences
too; he was not a good listener. "But he does not talk from a desire
of distinction, but because his mind is full. . . . He is the only man
whose common conversation corresponds with the general fame he
has in the world."[20]

Charles Fox, on the other hand, the vehement orator of the House
of Commons, seems from all that has been said of him to have better
preserved the Augustan mode of conversation. In London, in mixed
society he conversed little, but at his own home in the country with
his intimate friends, Rogers says, he would talk on for ever, with all
the openness and simplicity of a child. It is amusing to see how Johnson, who had experienced this reserve himself, explains it.

> Fox never talks in private company; not from any determination not
> to talk, but because he has not the first motion. A man who is used to
> the applause of the House of Commons, has no wish for that of a
> private company. A man accustomed to throw for a thousand pounds, if
> set down to throw for sixpence, would not be at pains to count the
> dice.[21]

Johnson, however, was generally ready to talk for applause or victory,
and could sometimes use the power of his voice and the brutality of
his words in a manner which would not have been approved by the
Augustans. He has been taken to task for this in a very charming
essay by one who might be described himself as the most Augustan
of all the English writers of this century in the delicacy of his wit
and the pointedness of his satire. You will find this essay, entitled
"A Young Clergyman" in one of the later volumes of Max Beerbohm,
And even Now. He recalls the scene as Boswell set it down. It was
at the Thrale's on Tuesday, April 7, 1778, before dinner. Boswell had
been asked by Sir John Pringle to find out what Johnson thought
were the best English sermons for style, so he began to examine him
on the subject, throwing out such names as Atterbury and Tillotson,
and going on to the elegant preachers of his own day, and then putting the question:

> What I want to know is, what sermons afford the best specimen of
> English pulpit eloquence.

[20] Ibid., pp. 19-20.
[21] Ibid., p. 167.

Johnson. We have no sermons addressed to the passions that are good for anything; if you mean that kind of eloquence.

A Clergyman (whose name I do not recollect). Were not Dodd's sermons addressed to the passions?

Johnson. They were nothing, Sir, be they addressed to what they may.

"No one should be able to read this without receiving a shock. I know not," says Beerbohm,

> which is the more startling—the début of the unfortunate clergyman, or the instantaneousness of his end. Why hadn't Boswell told us there was a clergyman present? Well, we may be sure that so careful and acute an artist had some good reason. And I suppose the clergyman was left to take us unawares because just so did he take the company . . . He sat forgotten, overlooked; so that his self-assertion startled every one just as on Boswell's page it startles us.[22]

But even then how can we account for Johnson's ferocity? Beerbohm points out that he was in excellent humour, and a good dinner was in prospect. He had befriended Dodd, and it had always been agreed that Dodd was very emotional. Perhaps it was the way the clergyman spoke. Knowing Johnson to be deaf, he let his high thin voice soar too high, in a kind of scream. Johnson was startled and let out a loud roar.

I have referred to this scene and given you this interpretation of it to show how far Johnson in his dictatorial mood has moved from the more restrained and correct tones of an earlier society. But we must be on our guard against Boswell's liking for dramatic effects, and remember that sometimes it was due to his planning that the conversations took place at all. He himself notes that he had come to know Johnson and Wilkes about the same time:

> Two men more different could perhaps not be selected out of all mankind. They had even attacked one another with some asperity in their writings; yet I lived in habits of friendship with both; I could fully relish the excellence of each; . . . I conceived an irresistible wish, if possible, to bring Dr. Johnson and Mr. Wilkes together. How to manage it was a nice and difficult matter.[23]

It was, however, not too difficult for Boswell. And he duly managed it and had the satisfaction of recording their subsequent conversations.

22 Max Beerbohm, *And Even Now*, 1921, pp. 234-5.
23 *Johnson*, III, 64, 65.

It is thus partly due to Boswell that we are likely to remember particularly those conversations which call out Johnson's argumentative powers and which encouraged him in his love of a contest.

But we have other records of Johnson in other company. We may perhaps remember him first as he sat among the members of the Club, with Sir Joshua Reynolds and Goldsmith and Garrick and Burke at their dinners; but Johnson was no more content with the company of men alone than were Congreve and Swift. And in the diaries of Mrs. Thrale and Fanny Burney there are records of a very different kind of behaviour and a very different sort of conversation in those mixed parties, which may seem to preserve more of an earlier mode. But here too we may detect a difference, for there emerges in his conversation with the ladies of his acquaintance a new note, a tenderness, a touch of sentiment and a playfulness which is rarely found in his predecessors. He is often at his best, in his highest good humour when in the company of Mrs. Thrale and Fanny Burney, and their records reveal the richness of his humanity and sometimes an unexpected gaiety of spirit. He liked to be teased by them and to pay them pretty compliments, and he boasted that he had known all the wits among the ladies of his time from Mrs. Montagu to Bet Flint.

'Bet Flint!' cried Mrs. Thrale, 'pray who is she?'
'Oh, a fine character, madam! She was habitually a slut and a drunkard, and occasionally a thief and a harlot.'
'And, for heaven's sake, how came you to know her?'
'Why madam, she figured in the literary world too! . . . [She] brought me her verses to correct; but I gave her half-a-crown, and she liked it as well. Bet had a fine spirit; she advertised for a husband, but she had no success, for she told me no man aspired to her! Then she hired very handsome lodgings and a footboy; and she got a harpsichord, but Bet could not play; however she put herself in fine attitudes and drummed.'[24]

But there were some occasions when Mrs. Thrale seemed to think his humour had left him; and his wide sympathy and charity led him to reprove her lack of imagination or perhaps her hardness of heart. She just notes these curious notions as "the fæculancies of his low Birth" which she believes never fails to leave its stigma indelibly in every human creature; and she remarks that "no Flattery was so welcome

[24] *Dairy and Letters of Madame D'Arblay*, 1842, I, 64-5.

to him, as that which told him he had the Mind or Manners of a
Gentleman, which he always said was the most complete and most
difficult to obtain."

This is of course the essence of Augustan gentility; in his exaggerated respect for it Mrs. Thrale evidently detected a taint in him
which showed that his conversation did not wholly belong to that
world, just as the manner of his expression of sympathy for the poor
and the hungry reveals that he belongs to a generation where the
narrow bounds of Augustan society were being broken down. And
indeed, before the end of the century, the standards and ideals of this
society were being sharply challenged from two different sides.

The more obvious reaction is shown very simply in a poem published in Edinburgh 1795, *An Epistle in Verse occasioned by the
death of James Boswell Esq. of Auchinleck*, by the Rev. Samuel
Martin, who laments that Boswell should have chosen such a man of
prejudice and whim for his esteem

> Whom hospitality could not assuage,
> Fierce and confirm'd in anti-Scotian rage;
> Whom bigotry would not permit to share
> The boon, to hear a Robertson or Blair.

And then he turns to warn his readers against this social life and questions how far this sort of conversation serves the real purposes of
human life.

> The knot of friends, the club, the social hour
> What thought, what time, what business they devour!
> The better purpose break, the better scheme
> Defeat, and substitute an idle dream.
> The stream of wit and talk, and repartee,
> Outrun calm reason and philosophy;
> Good sense o'er-run, and, as it bounds along,
> Covers and drowns a sense of right and wrong.

But during Johnson's life time there were already indications that
the spirit of man could no longer be contained within the forms and
conventions of social life, nor be wholly satisfied to accept as its greatest glory the wit and elegance and ease of Augustan society. Even a
Horace Walpole, who had been born to the freedom of that society,
and had tasted all the sweets of it, grew early weary of it. When he

was only twenty-five, we find him writing to a friend from his father's great house at Houghton, complaining eloquently of the burden of society:

> I am so far from growing used to mankind by living amongst them, that my natural ferocity and wildness does but every day grow worse. They tire me, they fatigue me; I don't know what to do with them; I don't know what to say to them; I fling open the windows, and fancy I want air; and when I get by myself, I undress myself, and seem to have had people in my pockets, in my plaits, and on my shoulders! I indeed find this fatigue worse in the country than in town, because one can avoid it there and has more resources; but it is there too. I fear 'tis growing old; but I literally seem to have murdered a man whose name was Ennui, for his ghost is ever before me. They say there is no English word for *ennui*; I think you may translate it most literally by what is called 'entertaining people', and 'doing the honours'; . . . Oh! 'tis dreadful![25]

And he turns away to real delights, and describes the loveliness of the latest picture, a Dominichin, which his father has just acquired and hung in the gallery at Houghton.

Nearly twenty years later, sitting alone in the same house, left empty and desolate after the death of his father, he writes to his friend George Montagu (of the same family as Ralph, the first Duke of Montagu, to whom Congreve had dedicated his *Way of the World*, and from whose conversation he professed to have learnt so much) and complains that he had been drawn away from his pleasant retirement at Strawberry Hill to adventure on a new vocation of election-eering and had been forced to endure hours of conversation, *the thing upon earth I most hate*. He was no longer willing to accept that beautiful well-ordered society of the City of Man, where "Conversation was the most agreeable Pleasure of Life, and where solitude seemed no better than the grave."

He admits that conversation has improved—"To do the folks justice, they are sensible and reasonable, and civilised." Nevertheless he turns his back upon them, and gaily proclaims a newer fashion:

> Well! how comfortable it will be tomorrow, to see my perroquet, to play at loo, and *not to be obliged to talk seriously*.[26]

[25] *Selected Letters*, ed. W. S. Lewis, 1926, I, 29-30.
[26] *Horace Walpole's Correspondence*, ed. W. S. Lewis, 1941, IX, 350.

THE AUGUSTAN CONCEPTION
OF HISTORY

Ernest Cassirer has maintained in *The Philosophy of the Enlightenment* that "the common opinion that the eighteenth century was an 'unhistorical' century, is not and cannot be historically justified." For, he continues "it was the eighteenth century which raised the central philosophical problem in this field of knowledge. It inquires concerning the 'conditions of the possibility' of history, just as it inquires concerning the conditions of the possibility of natural science." And he goes on to point out that all great historical works of the eighteenth century in France and in England were written under the influence of Voltaire's philosophical achievement, in formulating "an original and independent conception, a new methodological plan, for which he paves the way in his *Essay on Manners.*"[1] But though in France the beginnings of this movement can be traced back into the seventeenth century—at least to the work of Bayle, who planned his *Critical Dictionary* in 1690—yet in England, in spite of the work of the antiquaries and the writers of memoirs, Hume could say in 1753 "that there is no post of honour in the English Parnassus more vacant than that of history." This remark is justified by Godfrey Davies in an essay on Hume,[2] which begins by quoting a number of examples of the contemptuous comments made on English historians by Augustan critics and satirists. And it would not be difficult to add to the number.

Nevertheless I hope to show that these very remarks of the critics

[1] *The Philosophy of the Enlightenment*, 1951, pp. 197, 200.
[2] *Elizabethan and Jacobean Studies*, presented to F. P. Wilson, 1959, pp. 231-34.

and satirists indicate a real concern with the matter of writing history, and that we may find plenty of other material in the works of the Augustans to reveal to us their conception of its character and purpose. And I should claim that their constant preoccupation with the function of history, their study of classical and French and Italian historians, their ability to appeal to an audience˙ who would understand their references to persons and events in classical history as parallels to guide their judgments in current political controversies— all this contributed more than is generally realized to the achievement of the great historians of the second half of the century.

Hume was not the first to notice the empty place in the English Parnassus. From early in the seventeenth century the unworthiness and deficiencies of English history had been commented on, by Bacon, Hayward, and Raleigh,[3] and the standards by which such criticisms were made had remained pretty well the same from the sixteenth to the eighteenth century. What men looked for was the kind of history they were familiar with in their reading of Greek and Latin authors; they were waiting for an English Plutarch or Thucydides, a Livy or a Tacitus. Under the Tudors and the Stuarts however it was still dangerous to write history, as men like Hayward and Raleigh were well aware: "who-so-ever in writing a moderne Historie, shall follow truth too neare the heeles, it may haply strike out his teeth." But after the Revolution of 1688, and after the removal of restrictions on the press, it must have seemed that the time was ripe for an English historian to appear. Yet we still find Sir William Temple, in 1695, lamenting "that so ancient and noble a Nation as ours . . . so adorned by excellent Writers in other Kinds, should not yet have produced one good or approved general History of England."[4]

To encourage some worthy spirit to undertake this task Temple published in that year An Introduction to the History of England, which breaks off abruptly at the end of the first Norman reign. Eight years later, after he had finished editing Temple's Miscellanies, Swift set to work to continue the history; but he soon abandoned it for more exciting tasks, as he explains in a letter to the Count de Gyllenborg, dated November 2, 1719:

[3] See D. Nichol Smith, Characters of the Seventeenth Century, 1918. pp. xi-xv.
[4] An Introduction to the History of England, 1695. Preface, A2.

It is now about sixteen years since I first entertained the design of writing a History of England, from the beginning of William Rufus to the end of Queen Elizabeth; such a History, I mean, as appears to be most wanted by foreigners, and gentlemen of our own country; not a voluminous work, nor properly an abridgment, but an exact relation of the most important affairs and events, without any regard to the rest. . . .

I was diverted from pursuing this History, partly by the extreme difficulty, but chiefly by the indignation I conceived at the proceedings of a faction, which then prevailed. . . . I publish them now . . . for an encouragement to those who have more youth, and leisure, and good temper than I, towards pursuing the work as far as it was intended by me, or as much further as they please.[5]

When Temple speaks of the nation not having produced an approved account of its history, and when Swift speaks his intention to supply what "appears to be most wanted by foreigners, and gentlemen of our own country," it is evident that their conception of history is somewhat narrow and traditional. It is very different from that of Bayle, who demands that the historian should be

like Melchizedech, without father, without mother, and without genealogy. If he is asked; "Whence art thou?" he must reply: "I am neither a Frenchman nor a German, neither an Englishman nor a Spaniard, etc.; I am a citizen of the world; I am not in the service of the Emperor, nor in that of the King of France, but only in the service of Truth. She is my queen; to her alone have I sworn the oath of obedience."[6]

Swift, as we know, would have had no compunction about accepting the office of Historiographer Royal, in which he would have implicitly sworn an oath of obedience to Queen Anne. His attitude at that time is abundantly clear from the words he used in presenting to the Lord Treasurer his *Proposal for correcting, improving and ascertaining the English Tongue*:

[it] would very much contribute to the Glory of her Majesty's reign; which ought to be recorded in Words more durable than Brass, and

[5] *Prose*, V, 11-12.
[6] Quoted by Cassirer, p. 209.

such as our Posterity may read a thousand Years hence, with Pleasure as well as Admiration.[7]

Indeed the main argument for his project is that the memories of princes and their chief ministers can only be preserved "by the pens of able and faithful historians"; and yet, even if one appeared with a genius for history, equal to the best of the ancients, what likelihood would there be of his taking up the task, when he considered that in an age or two he would hardly be understood without an interpreter.

Even those who can find no evidence in Swift's work that he had any genius for history must admit that he was very much preoccupied with the subject, had carefully studied both classical and modern historians, and had made great efforts to leave behind a record of the last years of the Queen's reign. And when he had finished that task, he claims that he "had no other bias than my own opinion of persons and affairs" and that he had been under no obligation to the Crown or any of the Ministers. In the opening paragraph of his *History* he states what he believes the function of the historian to be.

> Although in an Age like ours I can expect very few impartial Readers; yet I shall strictly follow Truth, or what reasonably appeared to me to be such, after the most impartial Inquiries I could make, and the best Opportunityes of being informed by those who were the principal Actors or Advisers. Neither shall I mingle Panegyrick or Satire with an History intended to inform Posterity, as well as to instruct those of the present Age, who may be Ignorant or Misled: Since Facts truly related are the best Applauses, or most lasting Reproaches.[8]

Here is the appeal to truth, in so far as it may be revealed to the individual judgment; and the declaration of a double purpose so characteristic of the Augustan Age—to bring the light of reason to those who sit in darkness, and to leave a record for the enlightenment of posterity.

The conception of history as a study of the utmost importance for all those who might be in any way concerned with public affairs, and as a literary art of which many noble examples had been left by the Greeks and the Romans, was firmly established in England before the close of the sixteenth century. It was Sir Henry Savile who had written in 1591, in the preface to his translation of Tacitus, that

[7] *Prose,* IV, 17.
[8] Ibid., VII, 1-2.

"there is no learning so proper for the direction of the life of man as Historie."[9] And from his time there had been established in England as well as in France and Italy a tradition of historical studies. The Camden Readership in Ancient History, for instance, was founded in Oxford in 1622, and the first incumbent, Degory Whear, published his lectures, *De Ratione et Methodo legendi Historias dissertatio,* in 1623. These were enlarged and reached a fifth edition in 1684, and after that there were three further editions in an English translation, with the title *The Method and Order of Reading History,* before the end of the century.

In a work which appeared in 1695, the theory and practice of the ancients, and particularly the Latin historians, the natural mentors of the Augustans, were described by the French Jesuit Pierre Le-Moine under the title *Of the Art Both of Writing and Judging of History, with Reflections upon Ancient as well as Modern Historians, Shewing through what Defects there are so few Good, and that it is impossible there should be any so much as Tolerable.* Here we may find conveniently brought together many of the classical common-places which were the foundation of the Augustan conception of history; and we may perhaps detect in some of the expressions introduced into the English translation their transformation into the very manner and accent of the Augustans: "History, according to Cicero, is the Director of Manners, and the Mistress of Life . . ."; or, "History is a kind of Civil Philosophy, and her proper Office is to instruct the *present* by the *past.*" But it has also another function, according to Tacitus, "of shewing the Rod to Tyrants, and advertising them of the Punishment she prepares. . . . Their future Fame keeps them more in awe than their Conscience."[10] From this it follows that the historian must be capable of judgment. He need not be a minister of state or a great commander, but he must be a "man of wit," with proper standards of truth and virtue.

If we examine some of the statements in which this duty of judging is discussed, we shall find that the distinction between the historian and the wit or satirist, who exercises his judgment in commenting on the contemporary scene, tends to become blurred. Such a

[9] Quoted by D. Nichol Smith (p. xx), who also drew my attention to the lectures of Degory Whear.
[10] Pierre LeMoine, *Of the Art of History* (Eng. trans.), 1695. pp. 28, 32.

passage as this, for example, would surely have been accepted by Pope and Swift as indicating their function as critics of society and justifying their satirical portraits of their enemies:

> Judgment follows the Narration of things . . . and this, though the least in *Mass,* ought not to be the least in *Wit.* 'Tis here the knowledge of Good and Evil must be unfolded; the Politick and Moral have their Place; that Virtue is crown'd and Vice punished; that the Historian (hardly otherwise more than a *Tale-teller*) becomes a *Statesman* and a *Soldier;* makes himself *Judge* of *Princes* and their Ministers; and Arbitrator of their good and evil Actions: 'Tis here he gives Instructions and Counsels, Degrees of Honour and Infamy, establishes a School for the time to come, and a Tribunal for the past.[11]

And again, they would certainly have approved the claim, alike for the historian and the satirist, that it is his duty

> to be as free in declaring the Vices as Virtues of great Persons: He is Judge, and Judgment reaches the Bad as well as the Good: His Function is a publick Witness, and 'tis the part of a Witness to conceal nothing. And in fine, 'Tis the publick Interest, that great Men and Princes to whom the *Laws* are but *Cobwebs,* should have some Bridle to stop them. And to a People that take *Religion* for a *Fantasm,* and *Hell* for a *Bugbear* to frighten Children, we cannot propose any thing stronger, than the *Eternal Infamy* is prepared for them in *History.*[12]

In this sense Swift could claim that he was fulfilling the most important duty of a historian in what are generally regarded as his Tory tracts for the times. For in his role as Examiner he assumes this very function as a public witness against those political leaders, whose crimes were exempt from any other punishment:

> whereby those whom neither Religion, nor natural Virtue, nor fear of Punishment, were able to keep within the Bounds of their Duty, might be with-held by the Shame of having their Crimes exposed to open View in the strongest Colours, and themselves rendered odious to Mankind.[13]

And so it is quite natural in prosecuting his case for him to carry his appeal further, and to summon his victim not merely to appear before

11 Ibid., p. 117.
12 Ibid., p. 110.
13 *Prose,* III, 141.

a tribunal of his peers, but to convict him before the bar of history by transforming him, so that the English Duke is changed into the likeness of a Roman Emperor (as in his Letter to Crassus); or by himself assuming the mantle of Cicero and attacking the Earl of Wharton in the very terms of condemnation borrowed from the impeachment of Verres.[14] And even when he impatiently throws off his borrowed robes and confesses that the show had not been worth the pains he took over it, Swift still appeals to history when he maintains that he can find nothing to his purpose in Roman history or oratory, since "modern Corruptions are not to be paralleled by ancient Examples."

Pope expresses the other side of this—the possibility of an appeal from the judgment of one's own generation to the ultimate verdict of posterity, and the responsibility of the historian as a witness—in his letters to Atterbury: "I congratulate not you only, but Posterity, on this Noble Defence. I already see in what Lustre that Innocence is to appear to other Ages." And in his farewell letter he points out that Atterbury has now an opportunity, like Tully and Bacon and Clarendon, to achieve his greatest triumph in this latter, disgraced part of his life:

> At this time, when you are cut off from a little society and made a citizen of the world at large, you should bend your talents not to serve a Party, or a few, but all Mankind. . . . Remember it was at such a time, that the greatest lights of antiquity dazzled and blazed the most; in their retreat, in their exile, or in their death: . . . it was then that they did good, and they gave light, and that they became Guides to mankind.[15]

Pope and Swift would have been less ready to accept some of the restrictions which LeMoine wished the historian to observe, though he also refers to the example of such Latin historians as Sallust, Livy, and Tacitus, who when writing of the vices of men "seem to blush for Human Kind, and their Words as a Veil cover their Shame as much as possible." LeMoine recommends Christian writers to imitate their tact and discretion, and adds further warnings to the historian against prying into things that are better left hidden, and forgetting the distinction between what is private and what is public.

14 Ibid., pp. 83-85, 27-29.
15 Correspondence of Pope, ed. George Sherburn. 1956. II, 169-70.

> If the Church herself to whom the Son of God committed the Keys,
> assumes not the Authority of opening what is shut, and judging of hid-
> den things, much less ought it to be allowed History. Since the Perfec-
> tion of a Civil Life is the end where his Labours tend, he must expose
> nothing to the publick View that has not regard to it, must therefore
> abstain from all sorts of Scandalous Relations, as are those that serve
> but to make People lose the Respect they owe their Prelates and
> Princes, the Hierarchy, Church and publick Government; and gives
> way to Heresies, Revolts and Schisms, both in Church and State.[16]

His remarks upon the style suitable for history are borrowed from
Aristotle and Cicero, though he adds arguments of his own justifying
the grand manner because of the dignity of the subject and the audience for whom the historian writes:

> She is designed to instruct the Great; and the Governour of a Prince
> ought to be otherwise cloathed than a Petty Schoolmaster: . . . If a
> man can but crawl upon the Earth, and work in little, let him leave to
> others History . . . and satisfie himself as much as he pleases with
> writing *Chronicles* and *Legends*.

The style of the historian must be pure; there must be no mixture of
various styles. It must be clear; the words must be all intelligible and
placed in proper order. It must be concise;

> there must be no unnecessary verbiage, for "History is a Structure, she
> demands Order and Connexion."[17]

LeMoine would have condemned Burnet for his style alone, as
Swift did in his comments on the *History of his Own Time,* with its
"silly coffee-house chatter" and "pretty jumping periods." It lacked
the dignity and propriety required for the writing of history: "His
style is rough, full of improprieties, in expressions often Scotch, and
often such as are used by the meanest people."[18]

But he would have found all the dignity and splendour, all the
qualities of style he demanded—except perhaps brevity—in that great
book, which was first published in 1704 and must have found its way
into every library throughout the land as it continued to be reprinted,
Clarendon's *History of the Rebellion.* And he would also have found

16 LeMoine, p. 114.
17 Ibid., p. 202.
18 *Prose,* V, 183, 274, 287.

a structure with order and connexion, the work of a mind enriched by a wide experience of men and affairs and ready to give judgment upon them; an example of a tradition recognized by Pope when he brings together so naturally in a phrase the names of Tully and Bacon and Clarendon. The adornments of the three tall folio volumes, "printed at the Theater in Oxford," engravings of classical and mythological figures symbolizing truth and justice, fame and inspiration, and the magnificent frontispiece showing the author in his high dignity as the Lord High Chancellor of England, lend splendour to the work. There is no attempt to hide the author's place in the events he describes, his loyalty to the crown, his natural desire to vindicate the royal cause. The reader is warned in the Preface that he will meet with many passages that

> may disoblige the Posterity of even well-meaning Men in those Days; much more then of such as were crafty, cunning, and wicked enough to design the mischiefs that ensued: But he shall meet with none of Malice, nor any but such as the Author, upon his best information, took to be Impartially true. He could not be ignorant of the Rules of a good Historian (which, Cicero says, *are such foundations, that they are known to every body*) That he should not dare to speak any Falsehood; and should dare to speak any Truth. . . . and we hope that the representing the Truth . . . will be received rather as an Instruction to the present Age, than a Reproach upon the last.[19]

In the opening sentence of his story the author likewise proclaims in Ciceronian periods his intention and his purpose:

> That Posterity may not be Deceived by the prosperous Wickedness of those times of which I write, into an Opinion that nothing less than a general Combination, and universal Apostacy in the whole Nation from their Religion and Allegiance, could, in so short a Time, have produced such a total and prodigious Alteration, and Confusion over the whole Kingdom; And, that the Memory of those, who, out of Duty and Conscience, have opposed that Torrent, which did overwhelm them, may not lose the recompense due to their Virtue, but, having undergone the injuries and reproaches of This, may find a vindication in a better age.[20]

Above all else, he wishes to contribute somewhat to the blessed end of binding up the wounds left by those divisions "to make the future

---

[19] Edward Hyde, Earl of Clarendon, *History of the Rebellion.* 1704. I, iii.
[20] Ibid., p. 3.

Peace not less pleasant and durable." And therefore he promises to
preserve himself "from the least sharpness that may proceed from
private provocation, and in the whole, observe the rules that a man
should, who deserves to be believed."

He does not claim the impartiality of the judge, much less the im-
personality of the scientific historian. He is the vindicator of a cause,
the pleader for the defence. His appeal is to the judgment of posterity.
But he does claim to give a fair account; and he quotes largely from
documents and speeches, so that the chief characters of the drama
may condemn or justify themselves out of their own mouths. He could
have reminded us that he did not begin to write his history until his
own public career had ended in failure and exile, when he must have
felt some resentment against the royal master he had served so well
and some bitterness against those at the court who had helped to
bring about his fall. But his misfortunes seem rather to have led him
to idealize the memories of youth, especially those twelve years of
Charles I's reign, before the Long Parliament, when

> this Kingdom . . . enjoy'd the greatest Calm, and the fullest measure
> of Felicity, that any People in any Age, for so long time together, have
> been bless'd with; to the wonder, and envy of all the other parts of
> Christendom. . . .
>
> In a word, many Wise men thought it a Time, wherein those two
> Adjuncts, which Nerva was Deified for uniting, *Imperium* & *Libertas*,
> were as well reconciled, as is possible.[21]

Swift was also to describe this period as "the highest period of Politeness in England," but he could not accept it as a time of political
liberty. He underlines "Libertas" and writes in the margin "Nego."
Later in 1733, when writing *The Presbyterian's Plea of Merit*, he
remembers this passage and explains why he did not agree that there
was no thought until 1640 of making any alteration in religion or
government:

> I have found, by often rumaging for old Books in *Little Britain* and
> *Duck-Lane*, a great Number of Pamphlets printed from the Year 1630
> to 1640, full of as bold and impious railing Expressions against the law-
> ful Power of the Crown, and the Order of Bishops, as ever were uttered

[21] Ibid., pp. 58, 60.

during the Rebellion, or the whole subsequent Tyranny of that Fanatic Anarchy.[22]

But the real glory of that felicity did not consist for Clarendon in the balancing of any adjuncts such as sovereign rule and freedom, rather in the full flowering of a rich and noble humanity. It is perhaps not too much to say that in this he saw the full tragedy of the Rebellion, that it had destroyed this felicity. He wrote his history to leave for posterity a record of the values that had been lost, and perhaps in the hope of showing the way in which they might be recovered.

It can hardly have been without deliberate intention that he placed in the centre of his great work a portrait of Lord Falkland as the symbol of that moment of felicity at this high point of English life and culture, the ideal of what the statesman, courtier, soldier, and scholar should be, whose loss early in the conflict is its tragic climax, when that fair spirit which could alone have triumphed over the angry passions of the opposing forces was destroyed. For he does not hesitate to interrupt his narrative, and to draw our attention with all the eloquence at his command, as he approaches the performance of what he regards as the highest duties of a historian:

> If the celebrating the memory of eminent and extraordinary Persons, and transmitting their great Virtues, for the imitation of Posterity, be one of the principal ends and duties of History, it will not be thought impertinent, in this place, to remember a loss which no time will suffer to be forgotten, and no success or good fortune could repair.

And then he devotes himself to the task of describing the unparalleled goodness and virtue of Falkland:

> A Person of such prodigious Parts of Learning and Knowledge, of that inimitable sweetness and delight in Conversation, of so flowing and obliging a humanity and goodness to Mankind, and of that primitive simplicity and integrity of Life, that if there were no other brand upon this odious and accursed Civil War, than that single loss, it must be most infamous, and execrable to all Posterity.[23]

I find it satisfying to observe that one of his most sceptical Augustan readers falls completely under his spell, and cannot read through these

---

[22] *Prose*, V, 296; XII, 264.
[23] Clarendon, II, 270.

pages without deep emotion; for when he comes to the last sentence, Swift pencils in the margin these words: "It moves grief to the highest Excess."

It must be admitted that Swift is equally approving when in his rather old-fashioned manner Clarendon on another occasion describes the miserable end of the ungodly John Pym, "who died with great Torment and Agony of a disease unusual, and therefore the more spoken of, *Morbus pediculosus,* as was reported"; for he adds this comment: "I wish all his clan had dyed of the same disease."[24] We are still not very far from Fuller's *Holy and Profane State,* with the virtuous characters followed by studies of their opposites; and that this remained a popular taste well into the eighteenth century is evident from the publication of a curious popularization of Clarendon's History by Ned Ward in 1713, in three volumes, entitled *The History of the Grand Rebellion etc. together with the Impartial Characters of the most Famous and Infamous Persons, for and against the Monarchy. Digested into Verse. Illustrated with about a Hundred Heads, of the Worthy Royalists and other Principal Actors; drawn from the Original Paintings of Vandike, An. More, Dobson, Cor. Johnson, and other eminent Painters; and Engrav'd by the best modern Artists etc.* He explains that he had first begun to collect the portraits as illustrations for those who had purchased Clarendon's *History,*

> that the World might behold a lively Representation of those dead Worthies, whose Images ought, for their Love and Loyalty to their King and Country, to remain imprinted, for ever, in the Minds of Posterity; also, that the Curious might be acquainted with the rigid Countenances of the mouldering Incendiaries of those bleeding Times, and observe what a Sympathy or Analogy there seems to be between their Looks and Actions.[25]

Then he decided that it would be more useful if a "Chain of the History" done in verse were added, to give a very brief résumé of Clarendon's very copious observations. The character of the verse is not unfairly represented by the lines referring to the above account of the death of John Pym:

> Still rushing on till Heav'n stop'd his speed,
> And with a loathsome Evil struck him dead,

[24] Ibid., 353.
[25] Ward, *History of the Grand Rebellion.* 1713. I, ii-iii.

> That e're he perish'd, as he lay and mourn'd,
> His Sins, his Flesh was into Vermin turn'd,
> That his best Friends could neither bear the smell
> Or sight of such an odious Spectacle.

Here is history in its most naïve form, turned to moral tales of good and bad men, with a little tag at the end of each portrait so that its significance cannot be overlooked:

> Therefore if Men who ruffle humane peace,
> Would call to mind such Instances as these,
> They'd stop their wicked course, no further run,
> But tremble and repent the Ills they've done.[26]

But history had always been regarded also as the source of valuable political experience; the sermons and the political pamphlets of the seventeenth century had drawn on the minutest details of Old Testament history to show how God had dealt with his people, and to draw suitable conclusions for the present times. And the Augustans were but following the same method in finding parallels in the histories of Greece and Rome. Swift provides a good example of this in an early work published in 1701, *A Discourse of the Contests and Dissensions between the Nobles and the Commons in Athens and Rome; with the Consequences they had upon both those States.* He is concerned with the problem of the balance of power in all form of government; he gives a chapter to the dissentions in Athens between the few and the many, and another to the dissentions between the Patricians and the Plebeians in Rome, and then some examples of popular impeachments. These chapters contain only a discussion of certain abstract problems of government illustrated with suitable examples. Then he continues:

> Some Reflections upon the late publick Proceedings among us, and that Variety of Factions, in which we are still so intricately engaged, gave Occasion to this Discourse. I am not conscious that I have forced one Example, or put it into any other Light than it appeared to me, long before I had Thoughts of producing it. . . .
> I cannot possibly see, in the common Course of Things, how the same Causes can produce different Effects and Consequences among us, from what they did in *Greece* and *Rome*.[27]

[26] Ibid., p. 169.
[27] *Prose*, I, 228, 236.

The same appeal to the details of ancient history is repeated again and again in the journals and pamphlets of the period. The historians are appealed to and are used as familiarly as the poets, whose works had become known to a wide audience through the translations of Dryden and Pope. And when the poets writing in English seemed to be vying with Virgil and Horace the question was bound to be asked— why not an English Tacitus or Livy? In a letter to Pope on February 18, 1723-24, written from France, Bolingbroke has this in mind, but though it is clear enough what kind of history he is looking for, he is quite certain that it is not yet to be found in English:

> Eloquence and History are God knows, at the lowest ebb imaginable among us. The different Stiles are not fix'd, the Bar and the Pulpit have no Standard, and our Historys are Gazettes ill digested, & worse writ. The case is far otherwise in France and in Italy. Eloquence has been extreamly cultivated in both Countrys, and I know not whether the Italians have not equall'd the Greeks and the Romans in writing History. Guicciardine seems to me superior to Thusidides on a Subject still more complicated than that of the Peloponesian war, and perhaps the vastness of the undertaking is the principal advantage which Livy has over Davila.[28]

He naturally considered the possibility of filling this role himself, and in his letter to Pope the following August he tells him that he is occupied not with writing his own memoirs—"the Subject is too slight to deserve to descend to Posterity in any other manner than by that occasional Mention which will be made in the History of our Age"—but with preparations for a larger project, of which he sends a sketch, afterwards published as a "Plan for a General History of Europe." He proposed to make the beginning of his study the great scene at the opening of the century, after a preliminary introduction which would give a summary account of the events which followed the Pyrenean Treaty, and led to the Treaty of Ryswick in 1697. From then on he felt the task would be easier:

> I think I could speak . . . with some knowledge, and with as much indifference, as Polybius does of the Negociations of his Father Lycortas, even in those points where I was myself an Actor. I will even confess to you that I should not despair of performing this part, better than the former.

[28] *Correspondence of Pope*, II, 220.

But for our present purpose the most interesting remark in his letter is his attempt to describe what he considers the most difficult task of the historian, which the ancients have never done well, and which he had found most successfully carried out by Machiavelli and Father Paul, among the moderns. For here he may be said to introduce a new dimension into the conception of the task of an historian—something different from the business of narration, comment, and judgment on men and events—the need for discovering and tracing a pattern, giving a shape to the course of affairs:

> There is nothing in my opinion so hard to execute as those Political Maps, if you will allow me such an Expression, and those Systems of hints rather than Relations of Events, which are necessary to connect and explain in them and which must be so concise and yet so full, so complicate and yet so clear. It is Natures Master-piece in the most difficult kind of Writing; . . .[29]

Bolingbroke's historical masterpiece was never written, but he used some of the materials he had prepared in his *Letters on the Study and Use of History*, the first of which was dated from Chantelou in Touraine, November 6, 1735, though not published until 1752, after his death. They are not marked by any great originality; they are not even influenced by what Voltaire had already written, nor do they indicate any recognition of the importance of his work; they may therefore be taken as representing ideas about history which had been current among the Augustans, and must serve here to provide the last piece of evidence.

Though careful to warn us against the danger of applying particular examples in particular cases, he is still content to quote such commonplaces as "history is philosophy teaching by examples how to conduct ourselves in all the situations of private and public life." He still maintains likewise that the aim of the historian must be to instruct posterity by the examples of former ages, and to reveal all the possibilities of human nature. The interest must be centred upon the deeds and the characters of men:

> Man is the subject of every history; and to know him well, we must see him and consider him, as history alone can present him to us. . . . All history that descends to a sufficient detail of human actions and char-

[29] Ibid., pp. 249-52.

acters, is useful to bring us acquainted with our species, nay with
ourselves.

And, further, the emphasis is laid on the moral instruction it affords:

> History is a collection of the journals of those who have travelled
> through the same country, and been exposed to the same accidents: and
> their good and their ill success are equally instructive.[30]

This rather naïve view of morals and history in the tradition of the
Roman moralists did not wholly satisfy the Augustans, if we may
judge by a remark of Pope's in a letter to Swift written about Bolingbroke's preoccupations just at this time:

> Lord B. . . . is so taken up still (in spite of the monitory Hint given
> in the first line of my Essay) with particular Men, that he neglects
> mankind, and is still a creature of this world, not of the Universe: This
> World, which is a name we give to Europe, to England, to Ireland, to
> London, to Dublin, to the Court, to the Castle, and so diminishing, till
> it comes to our own affairs, and our own persons.[31]

It was left for the poet to remind the historian that if he was really
concerned with the whole experience of mankind and the full story
of man's attempt to make himself at home on the face of the earth, he
must enlarge the Augustan idea of history, with its emphasis on
politics and morals, and be ready to make use of the work of those
who were patiently extending the boundaries of human knowledge,
whether as antiquaries or as natural philosophers:

> Awake, my St. John! leave all meaner things
> To low ambition, and the pride of Kings.
>
> . . . . .
>
> Together let us beat this ample field,
> Try what the open, what the covert yield;
> The latent tracts, the giddy heights explore
> Of all who blindly creep, or sightless soar;
> Eye Nature's walks, shoot Folly as it flies,
> And catch the Manners living as they rise;
> Laugh where we must, be candid where we can;
> But vindicate the ways of God to Man.[32]

[30] Bolingbroke, *Letters on the Study and Use of History.* 1752. I, 170, 172.
[31] *Correspondence of Pope,* III, 445.
[32] *Essay on Man,* I, 1-16.